TIMOTHY HUTTON

of Clifton Castle and Marske-in-Swaledale

Other books by Jane Hatcher

The Industrial Architecture of Yorkshire 1985

Richmondshire Architecture 1990

George Cuit the elder (1743-1818) 1992

Exploring England's Heritage – Yorkshire to Humberside 1994

The History of Richmond 2000

Life in Georgian Richmond, North Yorkshire, A Diary & Its Secrets
(with Bob Woodings) 2018

TIMOTHY HUTTON (1779-1863)
of Clifton Castle and Marske-in-Swaledale
The Life and Times of a North Yorkshire Gentleman

Jane Hatcher was born and educated in York. She has a BA(Hons) in Architectural Studies, and an MPhil in architectural history research. Her career in architectural history has included conservation, research, writing, editing and lecturing. She was a Fieldworker for the Re-Survey of Listed Buildings, and served as a member appointed by the Secretary of State on the Yorkshire Dales National Park Committee. For many years she has lived in Richmond, North Yorkshire.

Portrait in chalks of Timothy Hutton by John Harrison of London, originally from York and better known as a miniaturist. The portrait was drawn shortly after Timothy Hutton's death, from a photograph which had been taken of him in his lifetime. At Clifton Castle. Photo: Guy Carpenter.

TIMOTHY HUTTON (1779-1863)
of Clifton Castle and Marske-in-Swaledale

The Life and Times of
a North Yorkshire Gentleman

Jane Hatcher

JANE HATCHER

Published by C. J. Hatcher

A CIP catalogue record for this book is available from the British Library.

ISBN 978-0-9515880-1-7

Book layout and cover design by Clare Brayshaw

Prepared and printed by:

York Publishing Services Ltd
64 Hallfield Road
Layerthorpe
York YO31 7ZQ

Tel: 01904 431213

Website: www.yps-publishing.co.uk

CONTENTS

ILLUSTRATIVE MATERIAL

Frontispiece

Colour Illustrations

Black and White Illustrations

Illustrations in text

Maps

Family Pedigrees

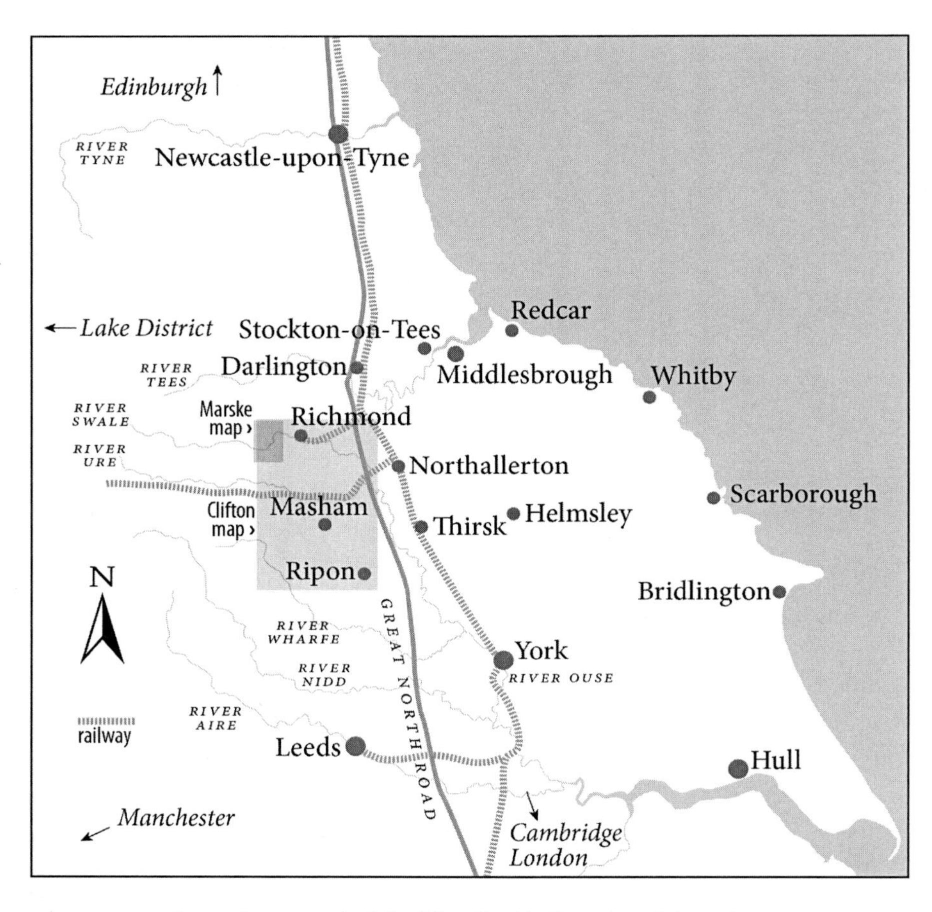

Area where most of the Timothy Hutton story takes place

FOREWORD

This is not a conventional biography, although it contains many dates and details relating to the life of Timothy Hutton (1779-1863), and to his relatives, friends and acquaintances. Instead it is a book written in terms of how this remarkable man spends his time, with whom he chooses to involve himself, and where he lives and goes. Here are his enthusiasms, his satisfactions, his aspirations and, above all, the interface between the public and private aspects of his life.

All this is possible because of the survival of his diaries and other notebooks, spanning sixty years of his lifetime. He kept at least thirty-three volumes of diaries, amounting to perhaps over a quarter of a million words. The daily entries tell us of artists, social activities, the church, the agricultural revolution, lead mining and other topics, over a period which saw immense changes, nationally and locally.

The quotations from Timothy Hutton's diaries which have precise dates are taken from transcriptions made by the historian Leslie Peter Wenham (1911-1990). He accomplished his task remarkably well, as the diaries are not always easy to read, and the spellings in them are sometimes haphazard. Where parentheses occur in round brackets, they are Timothy's; those in square brackets are the author's, such as [*sic*] where a word seems puzzling. Other sources of material used in the text are indicated as appropriate, mainly as footnotes.

Monny Curzon, a descendant of the family which inherited Clifton Castle, says his family always referred to the builder of the house as Timmy Hutton. Had this diminutive come down correctly through the generations? Early in life he sometimes used the signature 'Tim'y. Hutton', so perhaps he was indeed thus known, but later on he certainly used 'Timothy Hutton'. The author has decided to refer to him with, she hopes, affectionate respect, as Timothy.

CHRONOLOGIES

Timothy Hutton timeline

LIFE

- 1774 — Birth of brother John Hutton
- 1776 — Birth of brother James Hutton
- 1777 — Birth of brother Matthew Hutton
- 1779 — BIRTH OF TIMOTHY HUTTON, also of Elizabeth Chaytor
- 1782 — Death of father
- 1796 — Goes up to Cambridge
- 1802 — Moves into Clifton Lodge and begins work on Clifton Castle
- 1803 — Death of brother James; visits Scotland
- 1804 — MARRIAGE
- 1810 — Timothy and Elizabeth move into Clifton Castle
- 1812 — Timothy and Elizabeth visit Scotland
- 1813 — Death of brother Matthew
- 1814 — Timothy and Elizabeth visit Scotland
- 1826 — Visits Europe
- 1828 — Death of mother
- 1830 — Servants' Hall completed
- 1840 — London railway line reaches York
- 1841 — Death of brother John
- 1844 — Serves as High Sheriff of Yorkshire
- 1846 — Darlington to Richmond railway line opened
- 1848 — Has eye operation in London
- 1859 — Death of wife Elizabeth
- 1863 — DEATH OF TIMOTHY HUTTON

HISTORICAL EVENTS

- Declaration of American Independence — 1776
- End of American War of Independence — 1783
- French Revolution begins — 1789
- Execution of Louis XVI of France — 1793
- Nelson defeats Napoleon at Battle of the Nile — 1798
- Battle of Trafalgar and death of Lord Nelson — 1805
- Slave Trade abolished in British Empire — 1807
- Prince George appointed Regent; Luddite riots in North and Midlands — 1811
- Napoleon defeated at Battle of Waterloo — 1815
- Peterloo Massacre — 1819
- Death of George III — 1820
- Opening of Stockton to Darlington Railway — 1825
- Robert Peel sets up Metropolitan Police — 1829
- Death of George IV — 1830
- Reform of Parliament — 1832
- Municipal Corporations Act — 1835
- Death of William IV — 1837
- Queen Victoria marries Prince Albert; Penny Post introduced — 1840
- Great Exhibition in London — 1851
- Death of Duke of Wellington — 1852
- Start of Crimean War; Charge of the Light Brigade — 1854
- End of Crimean War — 1856
- Indian Mutiny — 1857
- Death of Prince Albert; start of American Civil War — 1861

TIMOTHY HUTTON : A Brief Biography

Timothy Hutton was born in Marske Hall, in Swaledale in North Yorkshire, on 16 October 1779, the youngest of the four sons of John and Anne Hutton. He received a good education at Richmond Grammar School. Those years were to have an immense influence on his adult life. He retained close friendships with many of his contemporaries, and particularly kept up his strong links with the town of Richmond.

Timothy went up to Christ's College, Cambridge but seems not to have graduated, apparently not wishing further to pursue an academic career. Instead he chose to follow the life of a country gentleman. He showed benevolence not only to his extended family, but also to his tenants and employees. He took a keen interest in new technology, particularly as it affected his agricultural activities, and the means of travel.

Having no expectation of inheriting the family's main seat at Marske, which was destined for his eldest brother John, and seemingly having no interest in the military careers pursued by the middle Hutton brothers James and Matthew, Timothy made his home at one of the family's minor properties, Clifton-upon-Ure. Here he threw himself wholeheartedly into a major project, building a handsome Palladian-style villa which he called Clifton Castle, furnishing it elegantly, and landscaping the grounds.

In 1804 he married Elizabeth Chaytor, who belonged to a similarly worthy North Yorkshire gentry family. They had a long and happy, though childless, marriage, pursuing shared interests and activities. The couple lived a full social life, playing an active role among a large extended family, and enjoying travel together. Their lifetimes saw the introduction of the railways, so they were latterly able more easily to attend events and meetings in London, including for Timothy's eye operation there in 1848.

Timothy was clearly an astute businessman. He was active in many profitable ventures, including banking and lead mining as well as agriculture. He generously contributed to the well-being of his community, sitting on a number of bodies, including courts and turnpike trusts, and taking an interest in numerous church restoration projects. The peak of his public service was taking his turn to serve as High Sheriff of Yorkshire for the year 1844.

Timothy was active not only in the small towns near Clifton – Masham and Bedale – but particularly in the somewhat grander echelons of the borough of Richmond, with its mayoral dinners, ancient guild of Mercers, Grocers and Haberdashers, and its lodge of freemasons. As squire also of Walburn near Richmond, he developed the nearby moorland into a grouse shooting estate.

In 1841, when Timothy's unmarried eldest brother John died, Timothy's life changed dramatically, as he now also became the owner of the family's Marske estate, his two middle brothers having already died relatively young. Thus Timothy found himself responsible for furthering the improvements to the Marske estate achieved by John, and also the charitable activities established by various members of the family.

Timothy spent his last years shuttling between Marske and Clifton, and planning for the futures of both estates when he was no more. Outliving Elizabeth by just a few years, he died at the age of eighty-four on 18 November 1863, and was buried at Downholme Church as squire of Walburn, rather than of Marske or Clifton Castle. His remarkably long and active life, spanning the second half of the Georgian period and the first half of Queen Victoria's reign, encompassed an age of great and fascinating change.

Born and bred in Swaledale, Timothy Hutton based himself in Wensleydale for most of his adult life. Later taking command also of the family seat in Marske, he thus returned to his Swaledale roots. So he might accurately be described in the same terms as the later name of the bank founded by his eldest brother John, and which he devotedly continued – 'Swaledale and Wensleydale'. However, his diaries place him in the wider context of North Yorkshire, where he was in every sense of the word, a gentleman. Hence the author's tribute to him as a gentleman of North Yorkshire.

Timothy Hutton perfectly fits a description of the landed gentry as owning modest country estates in a single county, with income mainly from agricultural sources, but having no London town house from which to participate in the social rituals of high society.[1]

1 See Cannadine, David, *Victorious Century, The United Kingdom, 1800-1906*, Allen Lane (2017), p.35.

PROLOGUE

Hutton Ancestry

The ancestors of Timothy Hutton down to his grandfather's generation

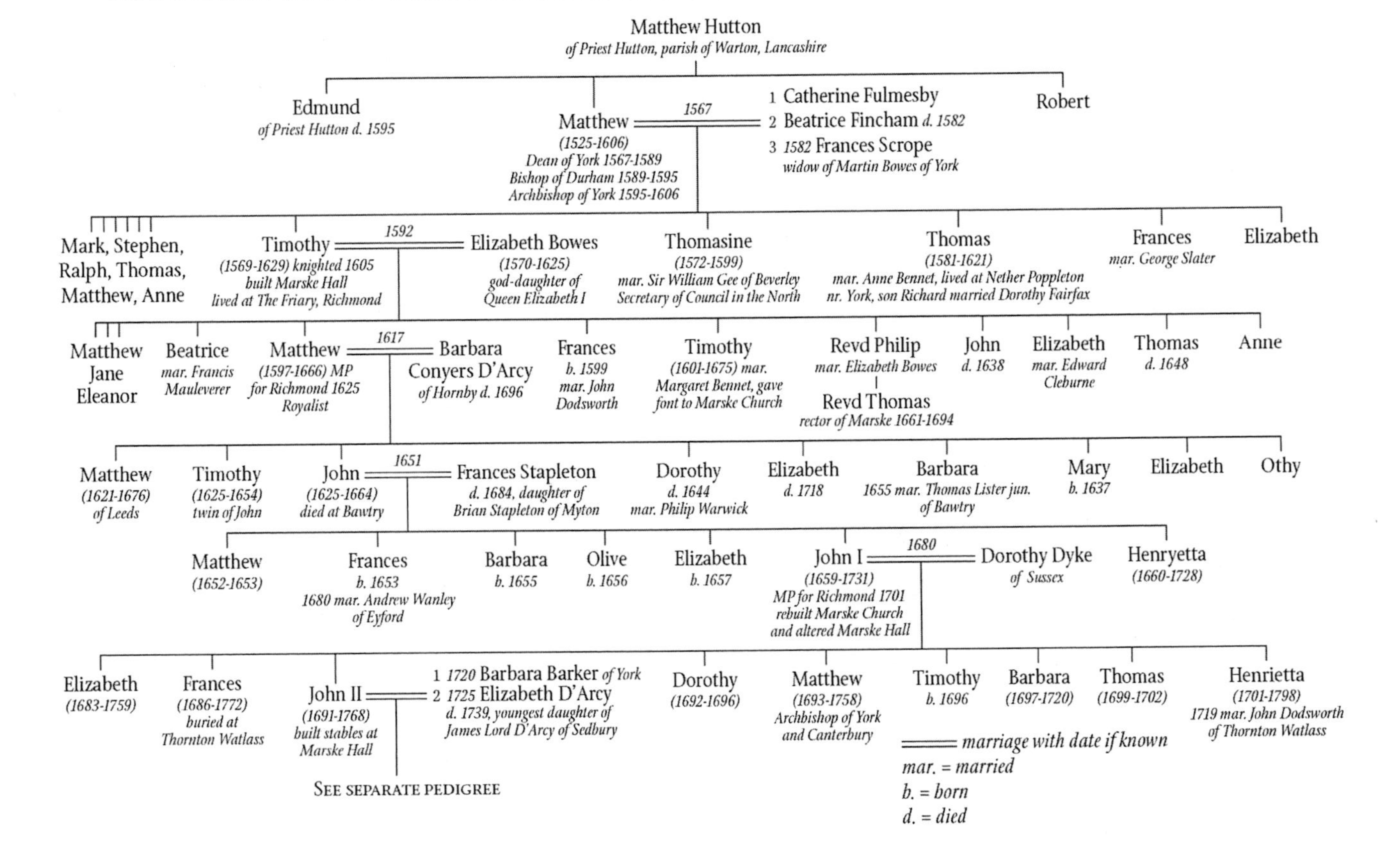

HUTTON ANCESTRY

Timothy Hutton was the descendant of a gentry family long based in North Yorkshire, a lineage producing members of great ability, some respectably holding high office, others living surprisingly unconventional lives. The Hutton family is one of only two[2] in England which had produced two archbishops. Both Hutton archbishops were called Matthew – the family used the same biblical names over and over again – an Elizabethan one of York, the second a Georgian one of York and later Canterbury.

The Hutton family hailed from the hamlet of Priest Hutton in the parish of Warton, not far from Lancaster. But after establishing a branch of the family across the Pennines in North Yorkshire, they came to play a significant part in the history of Swaledale and Richmond. This phase began in the reign of Henry VIII with Matthew Hutton, whose children were born in Priest Hutton. The eldest son, Edmund, remained in his birthplace, presumably inheriting land there, but the second son, Matthew, born about 1525, became the earlier of the family's archbishops of York.

This Matthew's outstanding career reflected that of many talented people during Queen Elizabeth I's reign, when so many new families rose to distinction. Typically of many able schoolboys from the north of England in general, and the Hutton family in particular, he went up to Cambridge – Trinity College in his case – before holding various university posts. He distinguished himself as a sound theologian and became known as an eloquent preacher.

In 1567, by now a Doctor of Divinity, he was appointed Dean of York, where he worked hard to advance the cause of Protestantism in the north of England. Here many people not only adhered to the old Catholic faith, but also supported a series of rebellions against Queen Elizabeth. His diplomacy saw him kept in his York post until after the final quelling of the Spanish Armada in 1588. In 1589 he was appointed Bishop of Durham. Not uncommonly this See predicted his translation, only six years later, to York.

The city of York was the base of the Council in the North, a body charged with preventing treason, including that by those with Catholic sympathies. Following the death in 1596 of Henry Hastings, Earl of Huntingdon, who

2 Much later there were two Archbishops Temple.

had served as the Council's Lord President, Queen Elizabeth asked Hutton to become acting Lord President, in addition to his archiepiscopacy. Already a man of about seventy, he was burdened with this dual workload until the Queen relieved him of the presidency in 1599.

He was still Archbishop of York when Queen Elizabeth died in 1603. Now over seventy, he had been excused travelling up to London to attend Parliament, but his intellectual vigour and even-handed counsel was still much valued. With the succession of James I, it was now for ways of curbing increasing Puritan influence that his advice was sought. He recommended the Privy Council to keep church liturgy as it had been in the Queen's time, in order to steer a middle path between the extremes of religious view held by either Papists or Puritans.

Matthew Hutton died at Bishopthorpe Palace near York on 16 January 1606 and was buried in York Minster, where there is a large monument to him in the south choir aisle. The monument bears a Latin epitaph, part of which can be translated as, 'You see here, reader, the effigy of his body; would you see also the image of his mind, think of Ambrose or of Augustine, for he possessed the genius and acuteness of the one, the accuracy and judgement of the other.'[3]

Matthew Hutton married three times, but produced his large number of children only with his second wife. After her death he married a rich widow, and having also amassed considerable income from his numerous appointments, he became a wealthy man, able to provide handsomely not only for his children, but also friends and distant relatives, and to endow a school and almshouse at Warton near where he had been born. Thus he provided the capital for his eldest son Timothy (1569-1629), the first Timothy of this story, to buy property in Swaledale, so beginning the family's link with the area which was to last over 360 years.

The initial purchase was at Marrick, but in 1598 a more advantageous property was acquired at Marske, and from then onwards, until the mid-twentieth century, the Huttons were the squires of Marske. Soon after acquiring that estate, the archbishop replaced the old manor house there with a new mansion, probably to a design by the leading northern architect of the day, Robert Smythson. Typical of such houses it is of squarish plan, and has a long gallery running from front to back centrally through the building.

3 Pattison, Ian R., and Murray, Hugh, *Monuments in York Minster*, Friends of York Minster, (2000), p.34.

Samuel Buck's sketch of Marske Hall, showing the late-Elizabethan house before the early-Georgian alterations. The sketch was made during the winter of 1718/19. It is clear that many fires were burning on that cold day!

Samuel Buck's Yorkshire Sketchbook, a facsimile produced by Wakefield Historical Publications in 1979.

Throwing himself with vigour into life in the area, Timothy also acquired The Friary in Richmond, the house created from the former Greyfriars site, as a base for his participation in the town's activities. He also invested in corn watermills in Richmond. In 1605 Timothy was knighted, and in 1606 served as High Sheriff of Yorkshire, as several later Huttons would also do. He was also twice elected as Alderman of Richmond, the equivalent of Mayor, in 1617 and 1629. It was during this second term as Alderman that he died, in The Friary. Doubtless his funeral was a grand civic occasion.

In 1592 Timothy had married Elizabeth, the third daughter of Sir George Bowes of Streatlam, Queen Elizabeth I's knight marshal, who had been largely responsible for quelling the Rising of the Northern Earls, that 1569 rebellion against her authority. In gratitude for this service, the Queen had become godmother to Sir George's next child, a daughter born in 1570, and therefore called Elizabeth. The Queen also presented the couple on their marriage with a beautiful silver-gilt standing cup, a treasure which remained in the Hutton family until it was sold in 1957.

On the south chancel wall of St Mary's Parish Church in Richmond is a very impressive monument to Timothy and Elizabeth. She had died before him, in 1625. The design of the monument was, like their mansion, probably based on a design by Robert Smythson. The monument provides a remarkable portrait of the family and their times, with full-size effigies of Sir Timothy and Lady Elizabeth, he dressed as a knight in armour, she in her finest gown, kneeling towards the high altar. Below them are ranked their twelve children, depicted either as smaller adults or, if they had died in infancy, as swaddled babes. Much is made of the Hutton and Bowes heraldry. There are no Christian symbols, but rather female figures representing the classical virtues of Faith, Hope and Charity, and the monument is surmounted by Fate blowing her trumpet. There are texts in Greek, Latin and English, composed by Revd John Jackson, who was appointed rector of Marske in 1623 and served as such until the Civil War of the 1640s. He was sufficiently close to the Hutton family to live in their household in Marske Hall. His texts for the monument are somewhat pedantic, but he was undoubtedly a scholar, having been Master of Richmond Grammar School between 1618 and 1620.

Thomas, one of Timothy's younger brothers, also benefited from his father's wealth, and established a branch of the Hutton family at Nether Poppleton near York. This lasted for some generations, and thus maintained for some time the family's links with the city of York.

The next squire of Marske was Timothy and Elizabeth's eldest surviving son, Matthew (1597-1666), named after his illustrious grandfather, and who in 1617 had married Barbara Conyers D'Arcy of Hornby Castle. He has been labelled an extragant spendthrift,[4] and it is certainly true that the family's wealth greatly declined in his time. To honour the bequests in his father's Will he had to dispose of family property in Marrick and Richmond, and another expenditure must have been the fine monument to his parents in Richmond church. Matthew was further financially strained by being fined as a Royalist in the Civil War.[5] However, Ferdinando, Lord Fairfax, Lord General of the North for the Parliamentarians, ordered that Matthew Hutton's estate at Marske was not to be 'plundered, pillaged, nor

4 Raine, Revd James, *Marske, A Small Contribution towards Yorkshire Topography,* (1860), [hereafter 'Raine, *Marske*'], p.60; Cliffe, J.T., *The Yorkshire Gentry from the Reformation to the Civil War,* University of London Historical Studies, Athlone Press, (1969), p.372.

5 It has been incorrectly stated that he had garrisoned Walburn Hall for the king, but the family did not own this property until the eighteenth century, and Walburn Hall was actually garrisoned against the king.

any way injured in his person, howeses [*sic*], or goodes.'[6] This was almost certainly because Ferdinando Fairfax's daughter Dorothy had married into the Poppleton branch of the Hutton family.

Thus Matthew Hutton was able to continue as owner of Marske. But, outliving all his sons, when he died in 1666 Marske was inherited by his young grandson John, the first of four John Huttons successively to become squires. John Hutton I (1659-1731), having inherited Marske so young, had an extraordinarily long period as owner. He and his wife Dorothy Dyke had a large family. Near the end of his life this John began remodelling Marske Hall, the house built by his great-grandfather. He inserted magnificent walnut panelling in the entrance hall, with high quality carved door-cases, and fireplace overmantel showing his coat-of-arms impaling that of his wife. In his Will he requested 'to be decently & very privately interred'.[7] As a result his burial place in Marske Church, which he had improved early on in his time as squire in 1683, was unmarked. Such a lack of ostentation was to characterise many later members of the Hutton family of Swaledale.

It was John Hutton I's second son, Matthew (1693-1758), who became the family's second archbishop, first of York in 1747 and briefly of Canterbury from 1757 until his death. He seems to have had little influence on the family's life in North Yorkshire.

John Hutton I's eldest son, however, John Hutton II (1691-1768), played a major role in determining the position the Hutton family was to continue in the Swaledale area. Not only was this in terms of the respect and affection in which the family was held, but also in the physical improvements carried out to its lands and properties. John Hutton II further modernised Marske Hall, replacing its original mullioned-and-transomed windows with the now-fashionable Georgian sash windows it still has today, and extending it both in plan area and also by adding an extra storey. There used to be five lead rainwater heads, dated 1735, at this new eaves level.[8]

In 1741 John Hutton II also built the handsome stable block designed by Thomas Worsley of Hovingham, a gentleman architect and fellow devotee of horses. John Hutton II owned many famous racehorses of the period, including 'Marske', 'Eclipse' and 'Silvio'. This second John Hutton had also purchased, in 1735, the manor of Clifton-upon-Ure, in the parish

6 Raine, Revd James (ed.), *The Correspondence of Dr Matthew Hutton, Archbishop of York etc.*, Surtees Society Publications, (1843), p.261.

7 Raine, *Marske*, pedigree between pp.48 and 49.

8 Taken down in 1950 to have their 3" dimension enlarged to 4" to improve rain dispersal, and stolen.

of Thornton Watlass near Masham,[9] which would eventually pass to the Timothy Hutton who is the subject of this book.

John Hutton II was squire of Marske at the time of the Jacobite Rebellion of 1745. He raised a fifty-strong company of foot against the rebellion and, with other local members of the gentry, conspicuously took Holy Communion in Marske Church on 13 October 1745 as a symbolic demonstration of allegiance to the Hanoverian monarchy.[10] The officiating minister that day was Richard Horne, then perpetual curate of Downholme, but from 1747 the rector of Marske, a living he held for well over fifty years until he died in 1803. During Horne's incumbency, John Hutton II built what was Marske Rectory, and Horne planted its garden with many named varieties of fruit trees.[11] Throughout the generations the Huttons continued to be improving landlords.

John Hutton II married twice. He had six children by his second wife Elizabeth, daughter of James, Lord D'Arcy of Navan, of Sedbury, near Scotch Corner. This was the second time that a Hutton had married a D'Arcy, and the name would be used frequently by later generations. Five of John and Elizabeth's offspring lived to adulthood, and three of them – John, Elizabeth and James – would play major parts in the story of Timothy Hutton.

The eldest son, John Hutton III (1730-82), became Timothy's father. The eldest surviving daughter, Anne (1731-81), married George Wanley Bowes of County Durham who was buried in Lincoln's Inn Chapel in 1752, though she later died at Cheltenham. The second son, Matthew (1733-82), died in Ripon on 31 December 1782 and has a monument in the cathedral there. The second daughter, Elizabeth (1734-1816), had a prominent role as Timothy Hutton's aunt. She married Henry Pulleine of Carlton Hall near Aldbrough St John, although the couple later lived at Crakehall near Bedale. Their sons Robert and James occur often in Timothy's diaries. The youngest Hutton son, James (1739-98), married Mary Hoyle of Ashgill near Middleham and they lived at Aldburgh near Masham. James, as his uncle, was very close to the young Timothy, and James and Mary's son, known as D'Arcy, was a major part of Timothy's adult life.

John Hutton II was buried in Marske Church but, unlike his father, his resting place, near the north side of the chancel arch, was marked by an inscribed ledger stone. However, this was hidden by later pews, and only

9 Bulmer, T., *History, Topography and Directory of North Yorkshire*, (1890), p.611.

10 An undated pamphlet, *The Parish of Marske*, quoting from Marske parish registers.

11 Raine, *Marske*, p.20.

discovered in 1992 when the church floor was being repaired. The ledger stone is inscribed 'Here lies interr'd the body of John Hutton of Marske in the county of York Esq'r. who departed this life the 13th day of January 1768 aged 77'.[12] He was buried on 16 January 1768. His Will, dated 19 March 1767, was proved in York.[13]

12 Letter from Sebastian Rowe, church architect, dated 27 February 1992.

13 NYCRO ZAW 93 includes a paper copy of the Will.

PART ONE: THE STORY BEGINS

Family Background

Childhood

Formative Years

THE FOUR GENERATIONS OF SQUIRES OF MARSKE CALLED JOHN HUTTON

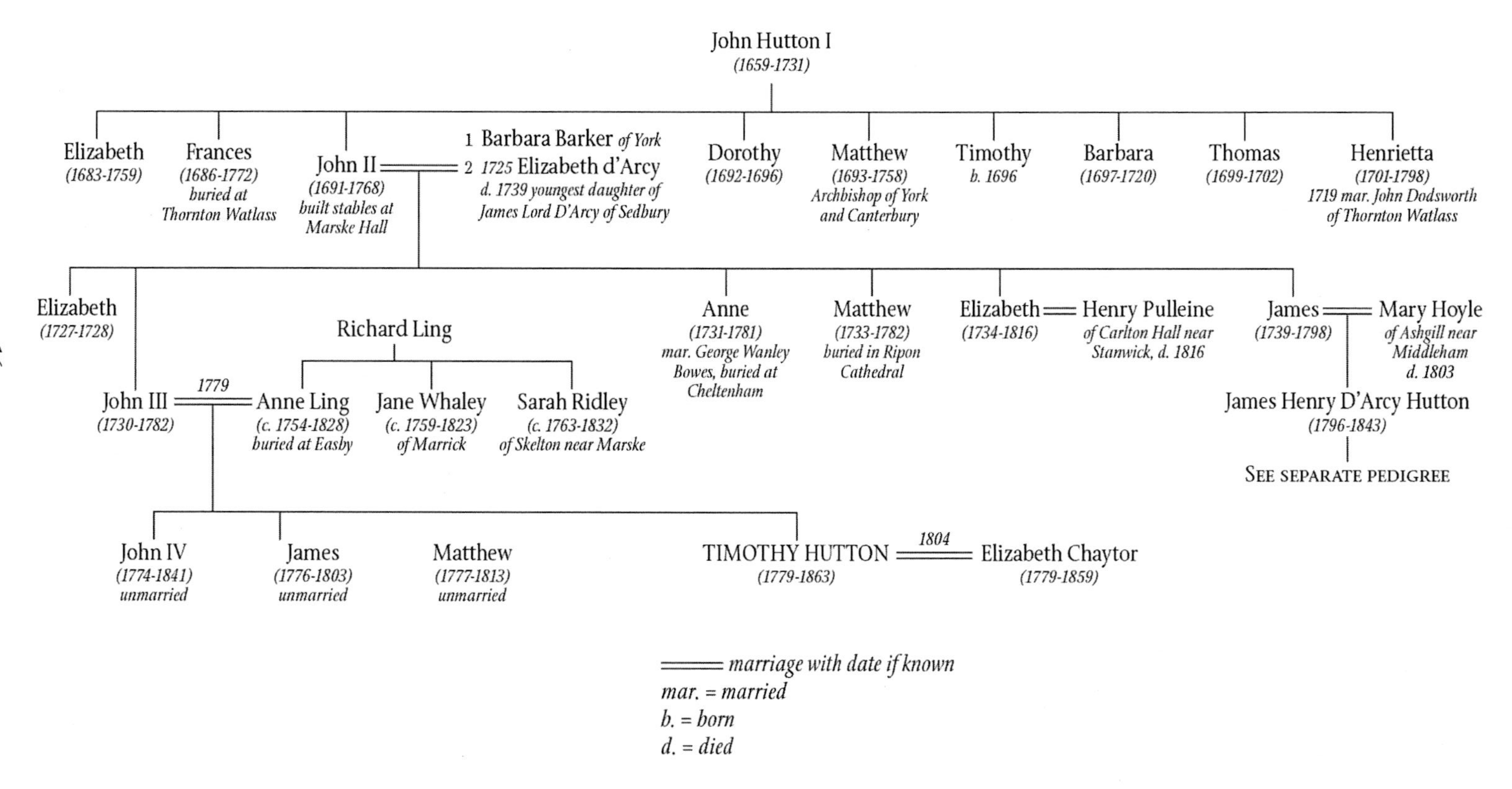

FAMILY BACKGROUND

John Hutton III (1730-82) was clearly an able boy. He began his education at Coxwold School, where he was a contemporary of Anthony Temple, who later became the Master of Richmond Grammar School from 1750 to 1795, and thereby the mentor of the next generation of Hutton boys. After Westminster School, John Hutton III went up to Christ's College, Cambridge in 1747. In his late thirties when his father died in 1768, leaving to him the serious business of running the family estate, he might have been expected to settle down, marry and produce an heir. It would seem, however, that he avoided this pattern, though John Hutton III was clearly a sociable man, mixing with other local families, including the Yorke family who had a large house on The Green in Richmond.

The owner of The Green mansion was Thomas Yorke, who spent most of his time in London, and so the Richmond house was occupied by his son, John, a popular local figure. John Yorke and his first wife Sophia had only one child, a little girl who sadly died as a toddler. Sophia died soon afterwards. John remarried, his second wife being Elizabeth Campbell, who came from a British family which for trading reasons had settled in Jamaica.

She had brought with her when she returned to England two young black boys, whom she had trained to be male attendants, it being fashionable for wealthy women in her position to be waited on by such. That fashion, however, began to fade, for two reasons. Firstly, such boys, if they survived moving to the English climate, soon grew into adolescents, and some people felt it was less than proper for well-born ladies to be in close companionship with male servants. Secondly, the Lord Chief Justice, William Mansfield, in 1772 delivered a legal judgement ruling out the keeping of 'slaves' in Britain.

To prevent the Yorkes sustaining any embarrassment, both young black men were, about 1772, handed over to the household of the bachelor John Hutton III and given the names 'York' and 'Richmond'. 'Richmond' soon entered the employment of Revd Lister Metcalfe, curate of Muker in Swaledale from 1773 to 1797, but 'York' (later called John York) remained at Marske Hall, where John Hutton III kept a large entourage of staff.

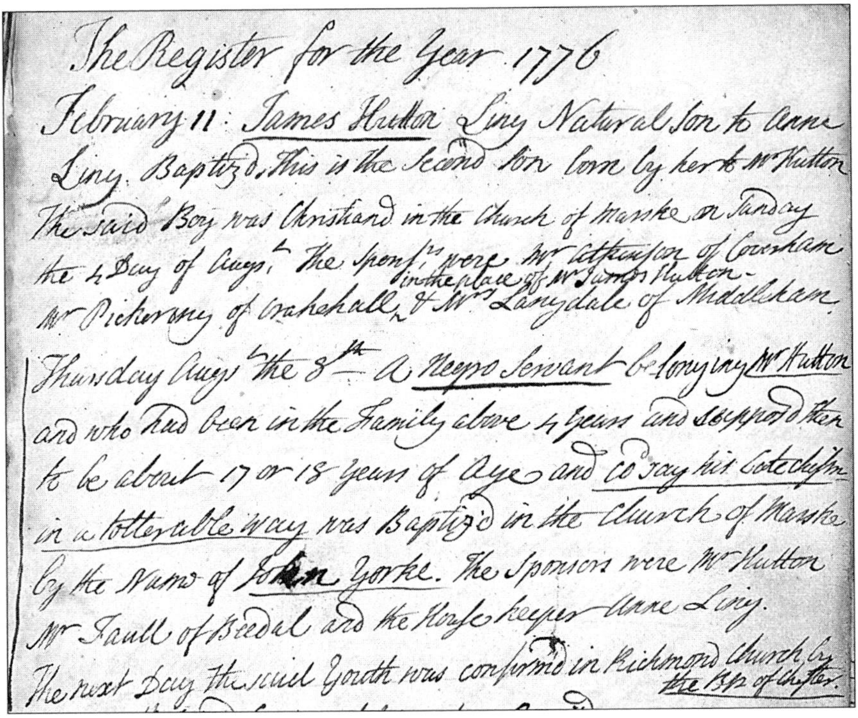
The Register for the Year 1776
February 11: James Hutton Ling Natural Son to Anne Ling. Baptiz'd. This is the Second Son born by her to Mr Hutton
The said Boy was Christian'd in the Church of Marske on Sunday the 4 Day of Augt. The Sponsors were Mr Atkinson of Cowsham in the place of Mr James Hutton - Mr Pickering of Oranhall & Mrs Langdale of Middleham.
Thursday Augt the 8th A Negro Servant belonging Mr Hutton and who had been in the Family above 4 years and supposed then to be about 17 or 18 years of Age and co'd say his Catechism in a tollerable way was Baptiz'd in the Church of Marske by the Name of John Yorke. The Sponsors were Mr Hutton Mr Faull of Beedal and the Housekeeper Anne Ling.
The next Day the said Youth was confirm'd in Richmond Church by the Bp of Chester.

Extract from the Marske parish register recording the baptism of John Hutton's black servant. On the same page is the earlier baptism of Timothy's older brother James.
Courtesy of North Yorkshire County Record Office, PR/MAK 1/3.

An entry in the Marske parish register for 8 August 1776 records his baptism:

> *A Negro Servant belonging Mr Hutton and who had been in the Family above 4 years and supposed then to be about 17 or 18 years of Age and co[ul]d say his Catechism in a tollerable way was Baptiz'd in the Church of Marske by the name of John Yorke. The sponsors were Mr. Hutton, Mr. Faull of Beedal and the Housekeeper Anne Ling. The next Day the said Youth was confirm'd in Richmond Church by the B[isho]p of Chester.*

That John York did indeed grow to manhood, and remained at Marske Hall for many years, is beyond doubt, as is the fact that he integrated well into the local community. It would seem he had a good singing voice, as he was taught to sing 'Psalmody' in the Marske Church choir.[14] He was presumably among the twelve male servants known to have been employed at Marske Hall in 1780.[15] He was still working there in 1801, when he was among the twelve household staff each left five guineas in the Will of John Hutton III's second son, James Hutton.[16] John York eventually married a local girl, and they had at least five children. Not only was he highly regarded by the Hutton family, he also became something of a local celebrity, and will be mentioned again later.

The reference in John York's baptismal record to the Marske Hall housekeeper, Anne Ling, is critical in the story of Timothy Hutton and his older brothers. Anne had come from near Appleby in Westmorland, one of the daughters of Richard Ling. At least two of her sisters also made a similar journey across the Pennines to take up senior domestic positions in Swaledale.

Anne was appointed to the household of John Hutton III at the beginning of 1774, when she was not yet twenty. Though her employer was in his mid-forties, and apparently a confirmed bachelor, before October was out she had borne him a boy, John Hutton IV (1774-1841), whom he openly acknowledged as his eldest son and heir. This was only possible because the Marske estate was not entailed as most such estates were, so it could be inherited by other than legitimate male heirs.

One wonders what John Hutton's tenants and neighbours made of this baby, born to the established squire John Hutton and his young housekeeper. Were they shocked? If so, no record of such seems to have survived. Perhaps they were pleased that the future of the Hutton inheritance at Marske was secured with the arrival of a son who could succeed to the estate.

In such circumstances it might have been expected that John Hutton would now marry his housekeeper. But no. Fifteen months later, on 24 January 1776, she bore James, who was similarly acknowledged as John Hutton's son. On the last day of December 1777 she had another baby boy, Matthew, so in just over three years she had three illegitimate little boys. The surname of all of them was at their births and baptisms, of course, Ling, even though John Hutton acknowledged them all as being his offspring. And all the children were given names – John, James and Matthew – which had occurred over and over again in successive generations of the Hutton family.

14 Annotation in the Marske parish registers.

15 Cartwright, J.J., "List of Persons in Yorkshire who Paid the Tax on Male Servants in 1780", *Yorkshire Archaeological Journal*, vol.14 (1898), pp.65-80, [hereafter "Tax on Male Servants"].

16 National Archives PRO PROB 11/1388/234.

By August 1779 Anne was heavily pregnant with her fourth child. At last she and John Hutton decided to get married, but not quietly by licence. Instead, banns were called in Marske Church by the rector Richard Horne on 15, 22 and 29 August. John and Anne were married on 31 August 1779 by John Langhorne, the curate at Grinton Church.

Witnessing the marriage were William Chaytor and Christopher Pickering,[17] both of whom would feature prominently in the story of this generation of the Hutton family. Clearly they were close friends of John Hutton, and perhaps they had put pressure on him, as he was getting older, to legalise his unusual situation. Born on 16 October 1779, the couple's fourth child was also a son, and he too was given a family name, Timothy. He is the Timothy Hutton of this book. He was different from his three older brothers in one particular way: they were technically illegitimate, he was the only legitimate Hutton of his generation.

17 These details of this marriage are taken from family records extracted from various parish registers by Timothy Hutton and listed in a notebook kept with his diaries.

CHILDHOOD

John Hutton III made his last Will on 3 February 1780, just over five months after his marriage. He may already have been concerned about his health, although he was not yet quite fifty. Was he finding life with a house full of little boys too much? Had he already been unwell when he finally decided to get married? Had his close friends William Chaytor and Christopher Pickering advised him that, as he needed a legitimate heir to inherit those of his properties which, unlike Marske, were in fact entailed, he should marry, albeit belatedly? Had he done so reluctantly, and was the Will now an attempt to regularise the legal aspect of his new marital status? None of these questions are explicitly explained in the document, although there are hints that he was not happy with his situation.

John Hutton III died in September 1782, a few days short of his fifty-second birthday. His grave was later discovered beneath box pews in 1992, near that of his father. It is marked by a ledger stone inscribed 'Here lies interred the body of John Hutton of Marske in the county of York Esq'r. who departed this life the 26th day of September 1782 aged 51.'[18] . His long and complicated Will[19] was proved in London in December 1783. Not only did it determine much of what would happen to his successors, but it also reveals his hopes for the future of his family. That he assumed he would have many descendants is clear from the lengthy details whereby he specifies who would inherit what and in what order. Sadly, none of that was to come to pass.

The Will begins by referring to his recent marriage to Anne, but he does not refer to her with any affection, which may suggest that the relationship was failing. He states that the covenant of jointure made for her future, in lieu of her right as a widow to a third of his wealth, had not yet been enacted. So he made provision for her as if that covenant was in place, but that was only for an annuity of £100. He also left her a legacy of £200 in cash, but he says that if she chooses not to accept the annuity and legacy, nothing was to be paid to her. This would appear to have been far from generous, and may have led to her subsequent difficult relations with their sons.

18 Letter from Sebastian Rowe, church architect, dated 27 February 1992.

19 National Archives PRO PROB 11/1111.

His Will appointed two trustees with the quite onerous responsibility of not only implementing his wishes, but looking after the many assets for the long period until all the boys successively reached the age of twenty-one.[20] Neither trustee was a relation, though both had clearly been closely involved with the affairs of the family for some years, and indeed had been the witnesses to John Hutton's marriage.

In the Will they are formally named as William Chaytor esquire of Spennithorne and Christopher Pickering gentleman of Crakehall House in Crakehall. Chaytor, who would much later become Timothy Hutton's father-in-law, was a distinguished lawyer, and would clearly make an excellent trustee. John Hutton III's connection with Christopher Pickering is unclear, although many years later Timothy Hutton had someone copy out from the Bedale parish registers the entry recording the burial in 1803 of Christopher Pickering of Crakehall.[21]

John Hutton III's Will directs that all his sons, including the eldest three sons who had been born out of wedlock and so were technically called Ling,[22] and had all been baptised as such, should bear the name Hutton and the coat of arms of the Hutton family.[23] This was certainly put into practise, as all records of them in later life called them Hutton.

Their father leaves the trustees money to provide for the maintenance and education of all the sons for up to £100 a year each. He leaves most of his estate, including Marske Hall and its historic contents, to John at his coming of age, and £5,000 each to James and Matthew at their comings of age. He gives lengthy instructions as to how these sums and inheritances were to be divided if any of them died young. Then how such were to be passed down between the sons, and then between the daughters, which he assumes the sons will produce. Ironically he emphatically stipulates that all such inheritances would be limited to their legitimate children. He even makes modest provision – though much more generous than that for his own widow – for the sons' potential widows!

20 NYCRO ZAW 155 Rentals & accounts of T. Hutton's estate during his minority 1783-95 [MIC 1762].

21 NYCRO ZAW/70/22/27, copy dated 23 March 1807.

22 NYCRO ZAW/70/22/26 is a piece of paper of 1807 onto which are copied the parish register entries of the baptisms in Marske Church of the children of John Hutton and Anne Ling. The burial of John Hutton III on 26 September 1782 is also noted on ZAW/70/22/24.

23 Arms granted 1 May 1584 – arms: gules, on a fess between 3 cushions argent, fringed & tasselled or, a cross humetté between 2 fleurs de lis of the field; crest: on a cushion argent placed lozenge-ways an open bible, the edges gilt with the words *odor vitae* inscribed. Burke's *History of the Landed Gentry*.

Although John Hutton III's eldest son John clearly did inherit the non-entailed Marske estate, despite his illegitimacy, it would seem his right to it came under doubt in 1810, when it was tested at law.[24] John Hutton III's Will draws attention to the fact that only Timothy, as the one legitimate son, was entitled to inherit the family's entailed property, which he, John Hutton III, had inherited from his father, John Hutton II, in 1768. Thus Timothy, on his majority, inherited Clifton-on-Ure, which John Hutton II had purchased in 1735, and the small estate of Walburn, in the parish of Downholme near Richmond, purchased by him in 1755. For this reason John Hutton III made no other financial provision for Timothy in his Will.

At John Hutton III's death in 1782, Anne was a young widow, still under thirty. She continued to live in Marske Hall, raising her four young sons, the eldest of whom was just eight years old. The youngest, Timothy, was not quite three, so presumably would have few, if any, memories of his father. The circumstances of the boys' childhoods must have been somewhat strange. They had the companionship of each other, for serious pursuits or for playing in the spacious grounds, and their large home included a long gallery, an ideal playground for indoor games. The household would include plenty of staff to attend to their needs. Nevertheless, there was no father, and what Hutton relations there were did not live close by. Their widowed mother, though clearly an able lady, was not from a background similar to that of her in-laws, the Huttons, and she may not have been very happy with the way the family's affairs had been left. Perhaps she received some support from her two sisters who lived nearby.

The boys' future fortunes presumably did not matter to them while they were very young. The eldest son John would one day be squire of the Marske estate, and Timothy as the only legitimate son had a separate destiny. But Matthew and James, although each having a £5,000 inheritance when reaching the age of twenty-one, would need other careers. Both joined the army.

It is likely that John Hutton III's youngest brother James, who lived at Aldburgh Hall near Masham, and his brother-in-law Henry Pulleine, who lived at Crakehall, helped with the running of the estate while the boys were young. John Hutton IV officially came of age in 1795, but was then still in London finishing his education. So Anne for the time being remained at Marske, still providing a home for her younger sons.

Anne Hutton seems at some stage to have inherited a small freehold property through her Westmorland family background, for when her

24 NYCRO ZAZ 70/22/29 Case & Counsel's opinion on John Hutton's title 8 October 1810.

eldest son John made his Will in 1839, he owned 'my house and Garth at Maulds Meaburn in the Parish of Crosby Ravensworth in the County of Westmoreland'.[25] However, for much of her widowhood she seems to have had little money to call her own. Although separate financial provision was made in her husband's Will for the boys' education, she had only been left a legacy of £200 and an annuity of £100.

The trustees of the family finances, William Chaytor and Christopher Pickering, seem to have treated Anne in a manner matching the somewhat cool tone of John Hutton III's Will. There is some evidence that she was made aware of the reduced circumstances of her widowhood, for among some papers relating to her is a letter[26] from William Chaytor and Christopher Pickering, dated 3 December 1784, telling her that they consider it necessary to dispose of various 'luxury' items, including the chaise and chaise horses, 'As Master Timothy Hutton is now gone from Marske....' Timothy would then be only five years old, so had he already been sent away to boarding school?

25 National Archives PRO PROB 11/1956/196.

26 NYCRO ZAW 93.

FORMATIVE YEARS

The early schooling of the Hutton boys was probably left in the capable hands of Richard Horne. Like Anne Hutton he was a native of Westmorland, who first having been perpetual curate of Downholme, served as rector of Marske until his death in 1803.[27] A close friend of John Hutton III, he would be something of a father figure to the boys. Their father's expressed wish that his trustees should ensure that the boys receive a good education resulted in all four sons being sent to Richmond School. Possibly he had even recommended this, as the excellent headmaster there was, as noted earlier, Anthony Temple, a contemporary of his at Coxwold School.

Boys like the Hutton brothers, who were private pupils from outside the town, had to board in Richmond. At the same time William Chaytor also had sons boarding there.[28] Older boys, especially those preparing for university, lived in the headmaster's home, Oglethorpe House. Younger boys boarded with one of the other masters. Possibly all four Hutton boys, plus the Chaytors, were boarded together. It is not known whether or not they all started at the school together, the only firm date we have is that Timothy's older brother John started there on 7 August 1787,[29] when he would be coming up to thirteen.

The friends and contacts Timothy made while at Richmond School were to establish the close links with the town that lasted all his life. John and Timothy certainly established a lifelong and very close friendship with a slightly older fellow pupil, James Tate (1771-1843), who would succeed Anthony Temple as the next Master of Richmond School. Tate's pupils included several who won prizes at university, and became known as 'Tate's Invincibles'.

As senior schoolboys, John and Timothy Hutton and James Tate joined a coterie of intellectual friends who, somewhat pretentiously, called themselves the Richmond Athenaeum. This club for intellectual pursuits met at Yorke House on The Green, the home of John and Elizabeth Yorke, who had been friends with the father of the Hutton brothers.

---

27 Raine, *Marske*, pp. 12-13, 20.

28 Recollections of James Arrowsmith, a Richmond upholsterer who copiously annotated his copy of Christopher Clarkson's *The History & Antiquities of Richmond in the County of York*, now in York Minster Library, [hereafter 'Arrowsmith'].

29 Wenham, L.P., *Letters of James Tate*, Yorkshire Archaeological Society Record Series (1966), [hereafter 'Wenham, *Letters of James Tate*'], p.82.

The Richmond artist George Cuit the elder (1743-1818), a man a generation older than Tate and the Hutton brothers, called himself the 'Major Domo' of the Athenaeum. Another interesting member was James Field Stanfield (1749-1824), a prominent campaigner for the Abolition of Slavery, and also one of the actors in Samuel Butler's theatre company, which regularly visited Richmond. James Tate and John Hutton were, in adult life, to continue to endorse the liberal political values upheld by this 'Athenaeum' group. George Cuit's son (who always used the spelling George Cuitt for his name), an exact contemporary of Timothy Hutton's and one of his closest friends, went to Richmond School at the same time and was also a member of the Athenaeum.

Anthony Temple, himself a classical scholar of no mean ability, sent at least thirty boys to university during his time as headmaster. James Tate went up to Sidney College, Cambridge – Temple's alma mater – and not only had a distinguished career as a schoolmaster and classicist, but ended it as a Canon of St Paul's Cathedral. John Hutton IV went up in 1791 to Christ's College, Cambridge, where his father had studied, and graduated in 1795. He then joined, first, the Inner Temple, then Gray's Inn.[30]

Timothy Hutton followed his eldest brother to Christ's College in 1796 but seems not to have graduated. Neither John nor Timothy Hutton went on a Grand Tour of Europe, but both were to lead the lives of well-educated and cultured gentlemen, entertaining intellectual friends and artists at their respective homes. They both kept up to date with scientific developments, particularly in agriculture. John greatly improved his estate at Marske, while Timothy created a fine estate at Clifton. John accrued at Marske such a valuable collection of books that he employed a full-time librarian, Michael Fryer, as one of his resident companions.

John Hutton III's elaborate hopes for his many anticipated grandchildren came to nought. John Hutton IV remained a bachelor. The two middle Hutton sons, James and Matthew, who each spent some time as army officers, both died young, James in 1803, and Matthew at Macclesfield in 1813. It would seem there was a gradual handing-over of the reins of the Marske estate to John Hutton IV after his coming of age in 1795. The Hutton relatives who had overseen the estate gradually faded out of the picture. Their father's youngest brother James died in 1798, and his brother-in-law Henry Pulleine in 1803.

30 Venn, *A Cambridge Alumni Database 1200-1900* – venn.lib.cam.ac.uk, [hereafter 'Venn *Alumni*'].

At some stage after Timothy's eldest brother John took up residence at Marske, their mother Anne moved into Richmond, probably in the very late-1790s. The town offered many social activities which attracted genteel widows, including the plays and assemblies, and perhaps she also enjoyed the race meetings which had meant much to her husband. She seems to have lived in Frenchgate, alongside many such widows. This was conveniently close to St Mary's Parish Church, and not far away from John and Timothy's old school friend James Tate and his family in Swale House. By 1820 she was certainly renting what is now No. 65 Frenchgate, from Alexander Smith, an innkeeper with an interest in racehorse breeding.[31] Earlier she may have lived elsewhere in Richmond, and she did move to another Frenchgate house towards the end of her life.

Anne Hutton was closely involved in the family life of James Tate, and became godmother to his second and third children, Margaret Wallis Tate in 1799 and, in 1801, James Tate the younger, who would follow his father as Master of Richmond School in 1833.[32] Both John and Timothy Hutton were also godparents to the same Tate children. Anne Hutton's two middle sons James and Matthew, who were both to die long before her, each made some financial provision for her in their Wills, and John and Timothy may also have contributed financially to the later years of her long widowhood.

Timothy Hutton returned home to Marske Hall from Christ's College, Cambridge in the late 1790s. We can assume that by now his mother had moved out, his eldest brother John had taken up residence as the young squire, and both the middle brothers Matthew and James would sometimes be in residence there. It would be at Marske Hall that Timothy came of age on 16 October 1800. Was there a lively party with all four brothers and their friends present? Sadly it is not recorded. Timothy Hutton, as the only legitimate son, could now take up ownership of the family's two entailed estates which, being some distance from Marske, had presumably been somewhat neglected in the lengthy period between his father's death in 1782 and his own majority.

Both estates, at Clifton-upon-Ure and Walburn, had been purchased by Timothy's grandfather, John Hutton II, and so inherited by Timothy's father in 1768. The Clifton-upon-Ure estate lies on the north bank of the river, two miles north, as the crow flies, of the small North Yorkshire market town

31 Wenham, L.P. (ed.), *Richmond Burgages Houses, North Yorkshire,* North Yorkshire County Record Office Publications No.16, (1978), p.51.

32 Wenham, Leslie P., *James Tate, Master of Richmond School, Yorkshire, and Canon of St Paul's Cathedral, London,* North Yorkshire County Record Office Publications No. 46, (1991), [hereafter 'Wenham, *James* Tate'], pp. 209, 426.

of Masham. The site's spectacular views down into the river provided the potential to transform it into a fashionable Georgian landscape.

The other estate, at Walburn, in the parish of Downholme, lies only about four-and-a-half miles south-west of the larger market town of Richmond, where Timothy already had so many connections. However, Walburn, in a more upland area, now consists mainly of the humps and bumps of a deserted medieval village,[33] and the only substantial intact building standing there was a fortified manor house lived in by a tenant farmer. Although Timothy would much later make repairs and improvements to Walburn Hall, its proximity to Marske – only some three miles away – was perhaps seen as a disadvantage.

33 Horne, Peter D., "Aerial Archaeology in Yorkshire, Recent Work by RCHME", *Yorkshire Archaeological Journal* vol. 66, (1994), pp.242-4, includes an aerial photograph of Walburn DMV.

PART TWO:
CLIFTON CASTLE

Genesis

Moving In

Further Developments

Household Staff

Agricultural Staff

Land Crops

Livestock

Weather

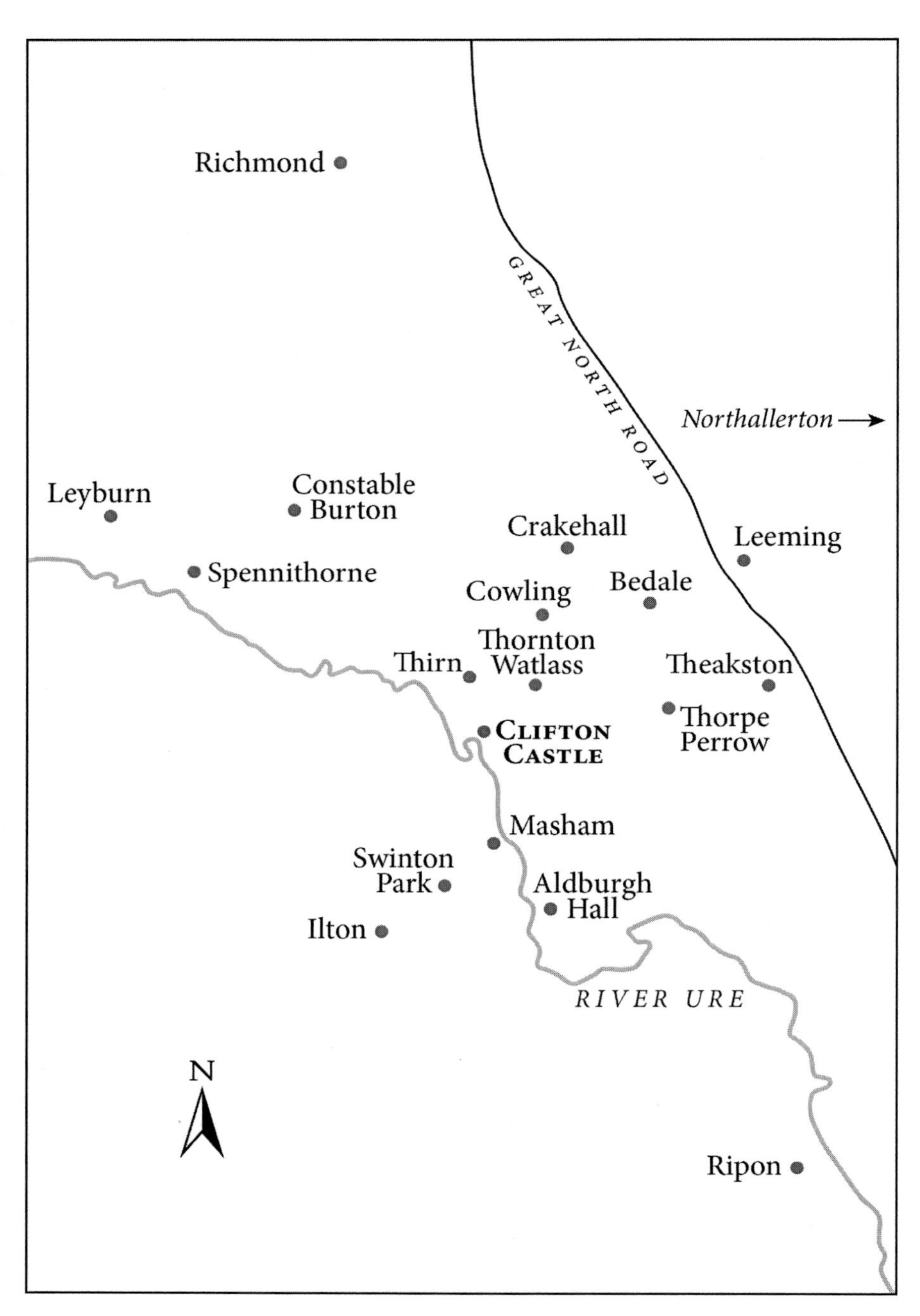

Places near Clifton Castle

GENESIS

Timothy Hutton's diaries do not cover the period when he must have made the decision as to where to make his adult home. Did he toy with choosing between his inherited properties at Clifton and Walburn? Or was there no contest, as it was clear to him that only Clifton offered the potential to create, not only an elegant house, but also a fashionably landscaped setting? At least we know that his choice of Clifton was very successful.

All that stood there in 1800 were the ruins of a small castle originally built by Geoffrey le Scrope, and described by John Leland as 'like a pele or castelet'. Late in the nineteenth century it was recorded[34] that a shilling of the reign of Edward II (1307-27) had been found embedded in the wood of an apple tree which was taken down about 1880, and this coin fits well with the castle's likely completion date of 1317.[35] Part of the old building seems to have continued in use as a dwelling, for Timothy's father had a male servant living there in 1780,[36] and in 1789 it was said to be the home of gentleman farmer Mr T Beckwith.[37]

The lack of documentary evidence about his earlier life means that we cannot be sure how Timothy planned to fund the transformation from ruined pele tower to handsome Georgian residence. Presumably income from his estates had been accumulated by the family's advisors during his minority. His eventual considerable income from his agricultural activities, and banking and other investments, lay far in the future. Perhaps it was something of a gamble, and the unease about whether he would manage to balance his financial books caused him to continue accumulating investment income, almost obsessively, right up to the end of his life.

The name that Timothy chose for his creation – Clifton Castle – reflected the site's history. His regard for that past is also demonstrated by his decision to have a record made of what the old building on the site looked like. For this he got his old mentor from the Richmond Athenaeum, the elder George Cuit, to paint it in watercolour in 1803.

34 Bulmer *op.cit.* p.611.

35 Licence to crenellate granted to Geoffrey le Scrope for Clifton-on-Ure on 25 September 1317.

36 John Hutton was taxed for 1 servant at Burton-upon-Ure, "Tax on male servants 1780".

37 Worsley, Giles, "Clifton Castle, Yorkshire", *Country Life*, 22 September 1988, p.160.

How Timothy chose the person to design his new house is also something of a mystery. He might have asked Cuit's old Richmond friend, the architect Thomas Harrison. However, by 1800, Harrison was successfully established with a large practice in Chester, and so was perhaps too busy to undertake a commission back in North Yorkshire. It was to a more local man that Timothy turned, John Foss (1745-1827), the Richmond stonemason-turned-architect.

Foss had acted as clerk of works for the construction of Middleton Lodge near Scotch Corner, under the supervision of the York architect John Carr, and had worked at Swinton Castle under the architect James Wyatt. He had also worked on his own account at Thorp Perrow for Mark Milbanke, as well as for many other local landowners known to Timothy. Their recommendations must have been sufficient to convince Timothy that Foss was the man for the task.

Timothy, as a cultured man himself, may also have had an input into the design. What resulted was certainly Foss's most successful composition, an elegant Palladian-style villa, though with more fashionable neoclassical decorative details. The foundation stone of the new house was laid on 8 September 1802,[38] and within a few months George Cuit would make another watercolour showing the new house going up alongside the ruins of the old castle.

Foss, though belonging to a generation older than Timothy, became a close friend. Timothy must have had the utmost faith in Foss's reliability, and that of his son William, who spent much time on site acting as clerk of works for the project, while his father was elsewhere attending also to his other commissions. That Timothy could safely leave the project in their capable hands is evident from what happened not long after the laying of the foundation stone, when building works were presumably getting into full swing.

The Hutton family in general, and it seems Timothy in particular, suffered a severe loss when his second eldest brother James died on 24 January 1803. Although Timothy's diaries do not survive for this period, it is clear from frequent diary references to the anniversary many years later that his grief was profound. In the summer of 1803, Timothy went for a three-week tour of the Highlands of Scotland. He was accompanied by George Cuitt the younger, who was his exact contemporary as they shared the same birthday, 16 October 1779. Perhaps Cuitt, as a dear friend,

38 Worsley, *op.cit.* pp.162-3, quoting John Cowell's memorandum of the works.

encouraged him to take the holiday, not only for its intrinsic interest, but also rather as therapy to try to assuage Timothy's grief.

Whatever the reasons for the trip, Timothy kept a separate daily diary of it. The Highlands of Scotland were becoming a fashionable destination for artists, poets and topographical writers, fascinated by the dramatic scenery. Neither Timothy nor Cuitt had been able to afford a Grand Tour of Europe, although Cuitt would be well aware of its attractions, his father having greatly benefited from the opportunity of experiencing such through generous and unexpected patronage.

The two young bachelors, with someone called Towery,[39] set off on Monday 18 July 1803, for Catterick Bridge, where they dined before taking the 'Telegraph' coach for Newcastle-upon-Tyne, which they reached in time for supper. Getting up at 5a.m. the next day, they took a chaise to Morpeth, where they got their breakfast. Heading further up the Great North Road for Alnwick, they were very disappointed with the castle there. The lodgings where they stayed in Berwick were dirty, but they found the New Inn at Dunbar very good.

By Wednesday 20 July they were admiring the architecture of Edinburgh New Town, before attending the theatre in the evening. The next day was spent at Leith Races, and the following day they explored the studios of artists and engravers in Edinburgh. On Saturday 23 July they left Edinburgh for Lanark, where they spent the night, and the next day travelled along the Clyde to see the lowest and most dramatic of the Falls of Clyde, the Corra Linn waterfall, then much famed as a natural wonder. The artist J M W Turner had made a pencil sketch of this, overlaid with watercolour, in 1801,[40] and Cuitt would later produce an etching of the waterfall.[41] Arriving in Glasgow on 25 July, Timothy and Cuitt found the hotels there better than those in Edinburgh. On 27 July they went on to Dunbarton, and paid five shillings for a boat ride on Loch Lomond.

Towery now headed home, leaving Timothy and George to their own devices, having to carry their 'nabsacks' on their own backs. Nevertheless on 28 July they walked eight miles before breakfast, thirteen miles to dinner, then another eight before supper and bed at Inveraray. Friday 29 July was very wet so they visited a whisky shop, though neither of them liked whisky!

39 It is not clear whether he was a friend or a manservant. He does not occur again in Timothy's diaries.

40 Baker, Christopher, *J.M. W. Turner, The Vaughan Bequest*, National Galleries of Scotland, (2018), p.40, picture exhibited under the terms of the Vaughan Bequest in January 2019.

41 Information from Peter Boughton.

Saturday 30 July saw them walking '12 long miles' to Bonawe near Taynuilt before breakfast, followed by a pleasant walk alongside Loch Awe. After another twelve miles they reached Oban, where they joined up with two other travellers going in a boat to Mull, and had a salmon supper at Galchayle. The last day of July saw them walking to Bagganubra along a very bad road which gave them sore feet. The food there was awful too!

On Monday 1 August, Timothy and George went to see Staffa, but the sea was rough and very frightening. They hired horses at four shillings each to take them to Aros on Skye, and then got the boat to Fort William, where they spent a few days. On several days following they got very wet in storms, and found the inns had whisky but little food. By Friday 5 August they had got themselves twenty-nine miles further to Fort Augustus. The next day, now tired of walking, they hired two horses and a man, paying seventeen shillings for the horses and sixpence for the man! Most impressed by the Falls of Foyers, they went on to Inverness, where they attended church on Sunday 7 August.

On Monday 8 August they took a chaise for the eighteen miles to Nairn, then ten miles to Forres, and twelve miles to Elgin where they stayed overnight, before looking round Elgin Cathedral – 'a grand ruin' – the next day. Their enthusiasm seems to have been waning by this stage of the trip, for they were disappointed by only being able to see the outside of Gordon Castle. It was now twelve miles to Cullen, another twelve miles to Banff to stay overnight, twelve more to Turriff, seventeen miles to Oldmeldrum, and eighteen miles along a bad road to Aberdeen, where there was 'nothing worth seeing'.

One hopes that Timothy felt better when he returned home on 12 August 1803, and was pleased with how well work was progressing on Clifton Castle. Perhaps the outside walls were now taking shape, in the beautiful honey-coloured ashlar sandstone said to have been transported from the neighbouring Swinton estate along the River Ure.[42]

When finished, the entrance front to Clifton Castle would have a central portico with four giant Ionic columns supporting a frieze and pediment. The left facade has a central bow, rising through the two storeys, providing the main ground-floor drawing room and first-floor boudoir above it with large windows from which to enjoy the view south towards Masham. That the drawing room was designed to be large enough for entertaining is borne out by a later reference, on Friday 7 November 1823: 'Scott the

42 Worsley, *op.cit.* p.163.

conjurer came to perform at Clifton. His tricks were excellent. We had him in the Bow Room. All the Servants came in.'

As work on the handsome exterior was completed, similarly elegant interiors could be fitted out. The most impressive feature is the staircase, set behind a screen of Ionic columns, taking an 'imperial' layout with two flights branching out from the lower section, below a large tripartite window which floods the space with light. John Foss may have been a provincial architect, but this composition is a tour-de-force. There are some beautiful doors created by local carpenters from Thornton Watlass, using fine mahogany imported through Hull, pleasing chimneypieces, and charmingly understated neoclassical plasterwork decorations on the ceilings by one William Wenham,[43] whose provenance is unknown.

All this magnificent work obviously took some years to complete. And in addition to creating his future home, Timothy had other matters to attend to. In the pediment of the entrance portico of the house is carved the untinctured Hutton family's coat of arms, first granted to Archbishop Matthew Hutton in 1584, which Timothy's father had been so insistent that all his sons used. At the time it was carved there was no Mrs Timothy Hutton whose arms could be impaled with those of Timothy. But that was outstanding business which he intended to put right.

43 *Ibid.*

MOVING IN

On 4 December 1804, at the age of twenty-five, Timothy married Elizabeth Chaytor of Spennithorne Hall in Spennithorne Church near Leyburn in Wensleydale,. Presumably the happy event was well celebrated with a party in Spennithorne Hall. Elizabeth was almost exactly the same age as Timothy, born six months before him on 17 April 1779. Their marriage was to last over fifty-four years.

Elizabeth proved to be a good choice for the life husband and wife would lead together. Timothy was an astute businessman, and well aware that several previous generations of the Hutton family had benefited from marrying ladies with money. Some years later he would record in a notebook the 'marriage portions' brought into the family by such wives: Barbara D'Arcy to Matthew Hutton in 1617, £1,500; Frances Stapleton to John Hutton in 1651, £1,500; Dorothy Dyke to John Hutton I in 1680, £2,100. We know from an indirect source[44] that Elizabeth Chaytor brought to their marriage £15,000, perhaps twenty times that sum in present-day money. Possibly her father William Chaytor, who had been one of Timothy's childhood trustees, was being generous to this union of two young people with whose lives he had already been so deeply involved.

When Timothy and Elizabeth married, Clifton Castle was far from habitable. He had, as a bachelor, probably in 1802, taken up residence in a smaller house nearby, called Clifton Lodge, and Elizabeth now moved in with him there. Soon after their marriage, Timothy purchased a Prayer Book to use when attending Thornton Watlass church, and he inscribed it with his name and 'Clifton Lodge 1805.'[45] This was to be their home for several years. Even after Clifton Castle was finished, Clifton Lodge continued to play a role in the household's life. Its 'garret' storey was removed in May 1825 when it was being refurbished to become ancillary accommodation for other family members, and it later housed members of staff and their families.

Few of Timothy's records survive from before 1810, so most details of the work of building Clifton Castle are missing from his story. It seems likely,

---

44 Wenham, *James Tate*, p.248.

45 Still in use in July 1955 according to letter written to L P Wenham by the then owner of Clifton Castle, signed Assheton Curzon-Herrick.

however, that there was a pause in the construction works, probably lasting a few years. This may have been due to some tension within the Hutton family. On 22 March 1807 Timothy had the entry of his marriage copied out from the Spennithorne parish registers.[46] This may have coincided with his accumulation of other genealogical information about his family, the precise purpose of which is unclear. Or he may have been trying to fend off challenges to his legal position, or that of his brothers. Their mother seems at some stage to have challenged her financial situation, and there is also the possibility that someone was casting doubt on whether the eldest brother, John, technically illegitimate, although acknowledged by their father, had been entitled to inherit the Marske estate.[47]

Work on Clifton Castle must have forged ahead in the period roughly 1808-1809 and, doubtless using some of Elizabeth's handsome dowry as well as whatever capital Timothy had accumulated, the couple were able to finalise their plans for what would be their home for nearly fifty years, and which they generously shared with friends and the many families to whom they were related.

Early in 1810, when Timothy's main diaries start, Clifton Castle was nearly ready for occupation. On Thursday 1 February 1810, Timothy recorded 'Mr. Foss and I at Clifton setting out the new road up to the house', and William Bucktrout, the Bedale house-painter, was at work decorating the house. Furniture had been ordered from the leading firm of cabinet-makers, Gillow and Co., who had a showroom in London but made most of their famously high-quality pieces in Lancaster. One lot had arrived on 24 January, and another wagon-load came on 5 February. Timothy sent the firm a draft for £259 3s. on 29 January, but he does not make it clear if this was the total bill. On 21 June the diary notes 'The furniture arrived from London'. Other furniture was made locally, as Timothy noted on Monday 1 February 1813: 'Walked to Watlass to W. Wright's to see the book case he is making for me.'

A very handsome bed made for Clifton Castle was given to the City of Leeds museums in 1963, and is now in the collection of Temple Newsam House. It seems to have been made by the London cabinetmaker Benjamin Evans, and is thought to date from *c.*1825. The canopy has very elaborate cornices of pierced acanthus plumes on anthemion fans, flanked by long S-scrolls, and is supported on cabled front pillars, all in mahogany, with beech back posts and underframing. The signature 'H. Simpson, Joiner,

46 NYCRO ZAZ 70/22/28.

47 NYCRO ZAZ 70/22/29 Case & Counsel's Opinion on John Hutton's title 8 October 1810.

Cliffton Castle, March 24 1896' relates to the replacement of the original hangings. Three window pelmets, also from the best Clifton Castle bedroom and matching the bed, were also given with it.[48]

Some pieces of the furniture they had been using in Clifton Lodge were moved across to Clifton Castle under Elizabeth's supervision on Monday 9 April 1810, but other items no longer required were auctioned later that week, raising £208 5s. 2d. As they began living in Clifton Castle that month, Timothy and Elizabeth found their new accommodation very cold. Presumably things improved as the weather warmed up and fires were lit more regularly.

A few months later they were feeling more at home, and could celebrate the successful completion of their major project. On Monday 4 June 1810 Timothy records: 'Gave the labourers their dinners & a dance after, being a sort of house warming, & in compliment to his majesty's birthday.' That the house itself was complete is implied by another diary note, for Tuesday 10 July 1810, when Timothy had to visit Northallerton for a meeting of the Quarter Sessions Court: 'Paid Chris[topher] Mitchell the property tax for Clifton ye year £25 6s 11d.' Another entry, dated Saturday 24 November 1810, confirms that Timothy had sent his groom, William Coultman, into Richmond with some old lead for John Metcalf. This may be a rare reference to some material from the medieval castle which had been kept but was no longer needed.

Finally in residence after such a prolonged period of frenetic activity, Timothy and Elizabeth could attend to other matters. At last there was space for their personal possessions, including clothes. Timothy at least – and one hopes Elizabeth too – had something of a spending spree. He noted on Sunday 1 July 1810 'Metcalf, the tailor, at Clifton', followed by, on Wednesday 12 September 1810, 'Got a box of clothes from Mr. Wright, London – breeches 7 pair, waistcoats 6, gaiters 4, do. short 2, coat 1.' Timothy seems, as was doubtless to be expected of a gentleman, to have been dressed by London outfitters. The only similar reference was made on Saturday 6 October 1827: 'Mr. Nightingale my tailor from London at Clifton.' However, footwear seems to have been obtained more locally, for on Tuesday 20 October 1812, Timothy noted 'Thos. Saddler of Crakehall at Clifton, ordered of him 2 pairs of shoes & one pair of boots.'

48 Taken from a fuller description in Gilbert, C., *Furniture at Temple Newsam & Lotherton Hall*, vol.1 (1975) pp.23-27 and 715.

FURTHER DEVELOPMENTS

The initial phase of the creation of a handsome home in a desirable setting may have been completed in 1810, but for many years further work was on-going, which presumably helped spread out the cost over a longer period. Subsidiary ranges were added to the house, service buildings constructed, grounds landscaped, and property elsewhere on the estate built or improved.

Even before Timothy and Elizabeth moved into the main house, plans had been agreed with John Foss for the construction of further buildings. Some were necessarily to be separate from the house, for example on 13 February 1810, 'In the morning drew a plan of the buildings to be erected at Clifton for the Cattle.' His cattle were close to Timothy's heart. Other additions adjoined the house, and by Saturday 15 January 1820 Timothy could note 'We got into our new apartments, the rooms over the Servants' Hall & store rooms.'

The Servants' Hall itself seems not to have been finished for another ten years. On Timothy's fifty-first birthday, Saturday 16 October 1830, he recorded, 'The servants & the labourers with those that were employed in building the Servants Hall had a supper & a dance, being the first day the room was used.' This was the room to be used for the bi-annual Rent Day dinners, each 29 June and 27 December, when all the tenants paid what rents were due.

Occasionally something recently built required an early repair: Wednesday 10 September 1823 'A man from Sheffield came to fix the stone in the staircase.' The house and its outranges relied on a large number of oil-lamps for artificial lighting, and a lot of oil was consumed by the household. On Saturday 31 March 1830, 'Sent the carts & Mr. Harker's waggon to Boroughbridge for 24 quarters of whale blubber.' Canal barges could reach Boroughbridge to bring foreign imports by sea via the Humber.

Timothy continued to buy furniture for Clifton Castle, often from house sales. As well as paintings given by his local artist friends, Julius Caesar Ibbetson and the younger George Cuitt, he bought others when opportunities arose. Timothy acquired ten pictures, for example, when he was in Liverpool in October 1817, and in October 1823 he purchased pictures, a fireplace and an all-important clock for the stables from a sale at Wycliffe-on-Tees. The stable clock was installed and put into working order by William Terry, the Richmond clock and watchmaker who was recommended to the Hutton family by James Tate on the grounds that Terry wound up the school clock![49]

At the sale in May 1826 of the furniture of old Mr Baines of West Tanfield, Timothy bought 'a marble slab being the fellow to the one I have in the hall; they were purchased at Mr. Dodsworth's sale at Crakehall in 1805.' Even as late as 1843 Timothy purchased a table on the 'first day of the sale of the furniture from Hornby'. This refers to Hornby Castle near Catterick, the seat of the Dukes of Leeds. Timothy had noted the death in London of the sixth Duke of Leeds on Tuesday 10 July 1838; he remained in contact with his son.

Work began on the grounds as soon as Clifton Castle itself was nearing completion. Again this continued for many years. Several large-scale projects, such as setting out roads, tree-planting on the estate, developing gardens near the house, went on concurrently. A kitchen garden, to produce fruit and vegetables for the household, was one of the first external developments. It was soon enhanced by a hothouse – on Tuesday 3 March 1818: 'Mr. Foss drew a plan of the Hot house for William Wright. We fixed upon the stove being in the back garden.' William Wright was the versatile village joiner in Thornton Watlass, who turned his capable hands to making many things for Clifton Castle, including this large wooden greenhouse. Much of the hothouse glass was extensively damaged by hail during a tremendous thunderstorm in June 1835.

The initial creation of the kitchen garden was quickly followed by a garden for growing flowers with which to decorate the house. On Monday 18 March 1811 Timothy reported, 'Set out the Flower Garden near to the Kitchen Garden.' Clearly sufficiently keen on this project to be involved with the practical work himself, he spent several days in the next few weeks working in the Flower Garden, planting shrubs 'that came from Thompson's', and laying down gravel in the walkways between the beds.

Some choice trees were planted near the house. These included a large holly which was, with difficulty, cut out from its former place on the estate, and brought by nine horses on Saturday 10 October 1812 to be planted at the south-east corner of the house. Six walnuts were planted in the bank in front of the house early in April 1814. Other existing trees on the estate had to be removed to open up vistas from the new house. For example, in May

49 Letter from James Tate to John Hutton headed St Hilary's Day (13 January) 1818, on which day Terry took up office as Mayor of Richmond.

1815, John Foss was given the task of deciding which trees should be taken down to improve the view of Masham Bridge.

By June 1819 the labourers were creating scenic walks near the river, and at the end of May 1821 'the thatched house near the Low Ness' was being finished. This building does not survive, but two other little garden follies, known as 'huts', were added elsewhere in the grounds, one of which still has a heather-thatched roof.

Further trees arrived in December 1828, including more hollies for planting behind the garden, and several interesting fruit trees from Lee & Co. of Hammersmith, London, for the large garden: 'One Orleans plum, one violet d[itt]o, one Goliath d[itt]o, one Hemskirk apricot, one Breda d[itt]o, one Florence d[itt]o. The violet plum is the Reine Claude.' Trees continued to be planted on the estate in the 1830s. Spanish chestnuts and elms were ordered from York, in November 1835, and a scarlet horse chestnut was planted near the river in 1837.

To make exotic iced puddings using the estate's fruits, an ice-house was created, which was ready to be filled with ice in early January 1827. It took ninety-three cartloads of ice to fill it! There were various ponds in the gardens, and a stock of fish, including tench and perch, arrived from a relative in June 1830. A gate lodge was built 1826-7, with stone for the pillars of its entrance portico coming from Ellington Firth on the Swinton estate, and another lodge at High Gates in 1837.

HOUSEHOLD STAFF

All Timothy Hutton's personal records show him to have been a conscientious and benevolent employer. His diaries record a great deal about the many individuals whose livelihoods and lives were intertwined with his own, and in some cases his regret when they moved to other posts. Some of the fullest details come from a notebook labelled 'Servants Book', which starts in 1808, when Timothy was still living at Clifton Lodge.[50] Here he records, not only the names of servants and the dates of their entering his service, but what they were paid, what uniforms he supplied, and in some cases where they had previously been employed. Several of these references show that staff were moving to and from employment with various members of Timothy's circle.

The earliest such reference is 'Joseph Miller came to live with T. Hutton after the death of W. Milbank Esq're. in the year 1802 March 8th'.[51] The phrase 'came to live with' occurs elsewhere,[52] and indicates a personal servant of some status who lived and worked closely with his employer. Timothy, still a young bachelor in 1802, would be pleased to recruit an adult manservant such as Miller, of whose qualities he would already know. Miller too was a bachelor in 1802, for Timothy's diary entry for 29 December 1808 notes: 'Joseph Miller left the service of T. Hutton to be married to Ann Todd late a servant to Mrs. Hutton of Clifton.'

Elizabeth had brought her own staff with her when she married. As a well-to-do young lady she would be used to reliable attendants, skilled in helping with her hair and clothes among other duties. Timothy would presumably now have some overall responsibility for her personal staff, but this does not show in the records he kept, which relate mainly to male servants. Perhaps Elizabeth oversaw the employment of the female staff, both personal and household. A rare reference to a female employee is noted on Wednesday 6 February 1805: 'Mary Collison came to Clifton as Dairy Maid.' Long before Timothy and Elizabeth moved into their new

50 Apparently kept with Timothy Hutton's diaries in the library of Clifton Castle. Details from it were copied by L P Wenham.

51 William Milbanke had owned Thorp Perrow, one of the estates near to Clifton. He was succeeded by his son Mark, a small boy in 1802.

52 For example on Saturday 25 August 1810: 'James Whaley came to live with me at Clifton, wages £36 15s.'

house, the development of Clifton Castle required the hiring of many staff for both indoor and outdoor work.

It would seem that Joseph Miller had risen up from being a manservant to acting as butler, for on the same day that Timothy records Miller's departure in 1808, he also noted: 'Thos. Spence came to live with T. Hutton at Clifton Lodge to be the Butler at 30 guineas a year and to find his own clothes. His last years service was with Mr. Retfern of Langton.' Butlers seem to have moved around between neighbouring families, for Timothy noted on Friday 6 February 1818: 'Abraham Exelby came to offer himself to be my butler. Wrote to Mr. Milbanke for Abraham Exelby's character.'

A butler was the most senior member of a gentleman's household staff, but some had worked their way up the ladder from footman to underbutler. This is indicated when, several years later, Timothy recorded on 12 May 1824: 'Robert Reynolds aged 30 came to live with me as Footman, he has for the last nine years lived with Lord Darlington in the capacity of Under Butler. Wages for the year ending May 13th 1825, £20 0s 0d, for hats £1 3s 0d, to have two suits of clothes and one Great Coat for two years.'

Reynolds seems not to have been an acceptable employee, for Timothy noted on Monday 1 November 1824, 'Rob't. Reynolds the Footman quitted my service.' He was immediately replaced, for two staff appointments were noted on the following Wednesday: 'John Kilner came to live with me as Butler and Thos. Selby as Footman.' Kilner sadly died, 'about 5 o'clock', on Monday 1 October 1827. Such was his status as butler that Timothy attended his funeral in person. His entry for Wednesday 3 October is: 'Attended poor Kilner's funeral at Watlass Church. His brother from Cockmanthorpe[53] the only relation at his funeral.'

After Kilner there seems to have been rather a high turnover of butlers: 'Chris'r. Rennison (Butler) arrived at Clifton from York 22nd May 1838. 35 years of age. Wages for the year £35 0s 0d. and to have the yeast.' Butlers oversaw the brewing of beer for a household, and yeast was a by-product of the brewing process. Selling it for bread-making would be a profitable sideline. Rennison clearly, however, did not stay, and it would seem that demand for butlers meant that they could ask for higher wages: 'Wm. Creaser (Butler) came to Clifton July 16 1839, about 30 years of age. His last place with Mr. Leatham of Heath nr. Wakefield. Wages for the year forty pounds without perquisites except part of the yeast if he can brew what is not wanted for the use of the house.'

53 This should probably be Copmanthorpe, near York.

Sadly, Creaser's stay was even shorter. Timothy had to note on Monday 14 October 1839: 'William Creaser late my Butler left my service this morning. He was an excellent servant and I was sorry to part with him.' Creaser apparently moved to Leeds, for on Thursday 31 October 1839 Timothy wrote, 'Got a letter from Dr. Hobson of Leeds for the character of my late Butler which I replied to.' It would seem Timothy had sought a recommendation in seeking a new butler. He wrote to Mrs Lucas of Ripon, a lady from whom he had in the past obtained wine, 'respecting a butler'.

Doubtless the news of a vacancy with a good employer travelled quickly round the circles of those anxious to upgrade their position, even for a post for which there was a high demand. Certainly it did not take long for Timothy to make an appointment. On Wednesday 23 October 1839, 'Charles Douthwaite came to offer himself to me as Butler, and I engaged him provided his late master gives him a suitable character.' This obviously proved satisfactory, for on Saturday 9 November 1839 Timothy noted in his diary, 'My butler Charles Douthwaite came to Clifton.'

In the 'Servants Book' Timothy wrote a fuller entry: 'Charles Douthwaite came to Clifton as Butler November 9th 1839 his last service was with Mr. Denison of Kilnwick Percy as Footman forty pounds wages for the year without perquisites except part of the yeast if he can manage the ale.' A young man of about twenty-three when he was appointed, Charles Douthwaite remained with Timothy for some years, although he suffered from, but survived, smallpox in 1844. Later that year he witnessed a version of Timothy's Will, but left his employment soon afterwards.

The next butler was called Bennison. By the time of his appointment Timothy was also having to run the Marske estate, after his brother John's death. One of Bennison's tasks was to go over to Marske with Timothy to investigate the wine stocks in the cellars, and also the fine collection of gold and silver 'plate' acquired over the years by the Hutton family, the care of such utensils falling within a butler's duties.

As butler, Bennison was succeeded by Joseph Simpson, a local lad born in Thornton Watlass, possibly to a tenant of Timothy's. He had worked his way up the household ladder, having originally been appointed in a quite lowly capacity on 13 May 1841, when he was only fifteen.[54] His starting wages were £10 a year, though Timothy noted that he would increase that by £2 the following year 'if he behaves well.' He obviously did behave well, for by 1851 he had achieved the coveted post of butler.[55] He became

54 1841 census.

55 1851 census.

Timothy's right-hand man later in their respective lives. When Timothy was an old man, paying his last visit to London in the summer of 1862, he 'Took Joseph to take care of me.' Joseph Simpson was one of the five senior staff at Clifton who were each left £100 in Timothy's Will.

After his marriage it would seem that Timothy treated himself and his new wife to a greater degree of luxury than he had himself as a bachelor, even before they moved into Clifton Castle. Not only did he employ grooms to look after the horses used for riding, but there were now other horses trained to pull the various conveyances he bought. Two horses to pull Timothy and Elizabeth's carriage were even brought up from London in 1842. His conveyances presumably bore the Hutton coat of arms, and the coaching staff wore livery which identified them as his entourage.

The coachman enjoyed a higher status than a groom, his wages usually being paid in guineas, whilst those of the groom were in pounds. On 5 June 1810: 'William Coultman came to Clifton to live with T. Hutton to be the groom at 17 pounds a year, and liverys, to be one month off in the year in the Local Militia.' The 'liverys' consisted of three suits of clothes, to ensure that he would always look smart. To keep him warm when travelling outdoors in winter, he was supplied with a new greatcoat every two years. In Timothy's 'Servants Book' is an undated summary, headed 'A Statement of Price for Timothy Hutton Esq. Liveries':

For the Coachman	£	s	d
Blue Coat	2	10	0
Vest		14	6
Small clothes	1	2	0
Gaiters		12	0
Driving Jacket	1	7	6
Moleskin do		12	0
do Overalls		9	6
Drawers		3	3
Singlets		5	6
Buckskin Smallclothes	1	10	0
Great Coat	3	14	0
Livery Buttons & Edging extra			

For the Footman	£	s	d
Coat	2	7	6
Vest		14	0
Small clothes		13	0
Jean Jacket		13	0
Drawers		3	3
Buckles for Smallclothes extra			

It is not known how soon after his marriage in 1804 Timothy acquired a coach and the necessary staff, but a coachman was certainly in post by the summer of 1806: 'John Clarke hired to be Coachman to T. Hutton June 5th 1806, at 17 Guineas and liverys. Entered into T. Hutton's service about ye 12th of June 1806.' John Clarke became a much trusted employee, for on 22 November 1810 he was sent 'to Leyburn to get £60 to pay the servants wages with', and on 13 February 1817 was despatched, again to the Hutton family's bank in Leyburn, 'to get some old coin exchanged for the new coin. The new coin issued this day by order of the Mint for the first time.' This was the very day the whole country experienced a most significant event, the Great Recoinage, when all old coins were called in and exchanged for newly-minted ones.

John Clarke ran various errands for Timothy. As well as being honest, he must have been able to conduct himself well. He was sent to the colonel with Timothy's resignation from the Masham volunteers. Sadly, John Clarke almost blotted his copybook for, when receiving his year's wages of seventeen guineas in June 1813, he asked for a rise, 'which I would not agree to.' Perhaps he was prone to having ideas above his station, for he became a freemason in the Richmond Lodge in 1820, where he was proposed not by his employer, but the innkeeper of the King's Head Hotel in Richmond. Leaving Timothy's employment a few years later, Clarke may have gone to work at that establishment, which was then a flourishing business probably able to pay more than Timothy's seventeen guineas. Certainly his former colleague, Simon Chandler, who had worked on the husbandry side of the Clifton estate, had moved there to work a few years earlier.

By Sunday 21 May 1826 there was a new coachman: 'Joseph Thorpe (my coachman) drove for the first time on the saddle since he came to Clifton. The horses went remarkably well.' Yet by late 1827 he too had left, for on the last day of that year Timothy 'engaged Christopher Mudd to be my coachman for 20 guineas per annm. [He] to find his hats & boots.' The yearly rate had gone up, but the 'perks' had gone down.

Christopher Mudd would seem to have been about twenty-one on his appointment, and as yet unmarried, though he later married a widow with children, and had others with her. His employment was to be abruptly terminated on Saturday 23 May 1835: 'Mudd quitted my service being compelled to do so in consequence of Margaret Brotherton being with child to him and he a married man with 7 children. He was an excellent servant and a grievous disappointment to me having to part with him.'

Timothy's regard for Christopher seems, however, to have led to his being reprieved, for he continues to appear in the diaries. In the 1841 census he features as aged thirty-five living in one of the staff lodgings at Clifton Lodge with his wife Mary [40], and children William [12], James [10], Christopher [7], Mary [5], Leonard [4] and a baby daughter. His daughter Margaret had died in February 1837 during an influenza epidemic, and Mary was also to die, in May 1843.

Not only was Christopher Mudd forgiven for his transgression, he later became one of Timothy's senior employees. In this capacity he was to move into much grander accommodation, Burton House at Low Burton. On Saturday 15 May 1847 Timothy noted 'C. Mudd and his family left the Lodge & went to Low Burton to the house Mr. Prest occupied.' By the 1850s Christopher Mudd was described as living there with the occupation of farm bailiff.[56] He was given leave in February 1855 to attend the funeral of his brother Leonard near Peterborough. On Sunday 8 April that year he received news of another family bereavement: 'A letter came to C. Mudd to say his son Christopher died at Sidney on the 10th January.' Christopher Mudd was still in Timothy's employment when his master died, and was among the senior staff bequeathed £100 in Timothy's Will.

A new coachman had to be appointed when Christopher Mudd took up a more superior position at Clifton: 'Thomas Robinson. Coachman &c. Novr. 23rd 1839 settled with the above to this day and agreed with him for the next year for £18 and a hat.' This was a lower wage than that on which Christopher Mudd had been appointed in 1827, possibly because Thomas Robinson can only have been about nineteen when he joined Timothy's service.[57] Even so, he remained faithfully in Timothy's employment till the latter died, and like Christopher Mudd was left £100 in his Will.

Thomas Robinson lived in one of the gatehouses at the entrance to the Clifton Castle estate, and a further note recorded: 'Novr. 23rd 1847 paid to

56 Whellan & Co., *History and Topography of the City of York and The North Riding of Yorkshire*, vol.ii, (1859), p.368.

57 His age is given as thirty-one on the 1851 census.

Thos. Robinson for his wife attending to the Gate at the Lodge at the rate of £5 pr. annum and £2 for coats.' Timothy seems to have had a particularly soft spot for Thomas Robinson's son John, who perhaps showed particular ability. In a codicil to his Will Timothy stated:

> *And in as much as I have in part educated John Robinson the son of my servant the said Thomas Robinson, and not wishing to have his education neglected, I therefore give and bequeath to the said Thomas Robinson the sum of One hundred pounds to be by him placed out at interest or otherwise made use of for the benefit and advantage of his said son the said John Robinson generally and in such manner as the said Thomas Robinson may think fit.*

Staff of a more junior level were required to look after the horses in the stables. One lad, Robert Oliver, came with a promising pedigree of employment, having worked for a leading name in the racehorse training world. Perhaps he felt unhappy moving away from that environment, even though Timothy provided good clothing:

> 'Robert Oliver. Novr. 4th 1841 came to Clifton, engaged him to assist in the stables, he last lived with Dawson the trainer in Coverdale. Wages eight pounds for the year, two suits of clothes, Stable dress, Gaiters, one hat and one greatcoat for two years. About 18 or 19 years of age but does not appear to be so much.'

In the next entry, one can almost detect the sadness in Timothy's voice: '1843 March 14th The above [Robert Oliver] left my service unknown to me in the night, on the 18th he returned for his wages for 18 weeks and four days and I paid him £5 7s 0d.' If any stable staff were absent, the needs of the horses had to be covered by other people, even if that came at a hefty price, rather like hiring agency staff today: 'Robert Hall 14th May 1859 Eighteen weeks and five days helping in the stables at 1/- pr. day. Pd. this day £6 11s 0d.'

As Timothy developed the surroundings of Clifton Castle, an increasing number and variety of skilled staff had to be employed. He took a particularly close interest in the formation of the gardens near the house, and thus in the gardeners he employed. Skilled gardeners were clearly in great demand in the early-nineteenth century, commanding relatively high salaries. Such men moved around, either to attain higher wages as their reputations grew, or to acquire more experience.

Timothy's first reference to a gardener occurs very early on in his records, in his 'Servants Book': 'Rich'd. Smales came to live with T. Hutton Nov'r. 28th 1808 to be the gardener. Wages 26 Guineas pr. Anm.' It was clearly a blow when, on Friday 23 October 1812, 'The gardener set off for Yarm to be upon permanent duty with the [Militia] volunteers.'

It is likely that the immediate successor to Richard Smales was Philip Jackson, who Giles Worsley credits with laying out Timothy Hutton's orchard about 1816.[58] Certainly he features in Timothy's diary. Like the butler Joseph Miller and Elizabeth's servant Ann Todd, in 1808, Jackson married a fellow member of staff on Wednesday 18 May 1825: 'Philip Jackson (my gardener) and Jane Storrow (my housekeeper) were married. They went to the Lodge in the evening.' The entry shows that, as a married couple, they were eligible for one of the units of staff accommodation in Clifton Lodge.

Philip Jackson and his wife must have moved on to pastures new before 1835. However, he not only kept in touch with Timothy, but remained in his high regard, for on 3 June 1835 'Jackson (my late gardener)' stayed overnight at Clifton. Shortly after this visit, Timothy appointed a new gardener, a Scotsman, John Chalmers: 'Engaged the above as Gardener on the 26th of July 1835 at 30 guineas pr. annum. He came to Clifton on the 29th of July. 25 years of age. The last 3 years as under gardener at Brough Hall Catterick, before he was in the gardens at Mrs. Maxwell near Dunfries. Was born at Castle Douglas.'

John Chalmers seems to have had particular expertise in the successful planting of trees. For example, on Monday 16 November 1835: 'The gardener and his men planted out the Spanish Chesnuts [*sic*] and Elms I got from York. Some by the side of the River betwixt the Quarry Close and some behind the garden on the other side of the Gill.' This was followed later, on Saturday 25 March 1837, 'A scarlet horsechestnut planted below the hut[59] near the river', and on Thursday 20 April 1837: 'Got more trees planted in the Park.'

Perhaps this work resulted in Chalmers gaining a reputation for tree planting, and thus being 'head-hunted' by another estate. Two years later, on Monday 28 October 1839, his successor was also on the move: 'Robert Burn the gardener left Clifton this day.' He was replaced quickly, but the employment terms were having to be bettered. On Saturday 9 November

58 Worsley, *op.cit.*

59 A small thatched folly, at least three of which were constructed in the grounds of Clifton Castle. One which survives is still referred to as a 'hut'.

1839 Timothy noted: 'The Gardener, George Stobbart, came with his family to the Lodge.'

Stobbart is one of Timothy's staff for whom the 'Servants Book' provides details of his contract:

> 'George Stobbart Gardner came to the Lodge on the 9th Nov'r. 1839, our agreement is one pound pr. week and vegetables from the garden for the use of himself & family he has a wife and one child. His house is included in the agreement. The above was gardener to the Rev'd. John Orde of Wensley.'

George Stobbart and his wife Sarah, both aged twenty-five, were living at Clifton Lodge at the 1841 census, with their young children, John aged two, and ten-month-old George, who had been born after Stobbart's appointment.

Despite the family being allowed to have a share of some of the garden produce, the Stobbarts also moved on, for on Saturday 29 November 1851: 'George Greensides (my gardener) died here half past eight o'clock in the evening aged 30.' On 3rd December, Timothy 'Went to the funeral of poor Greensides.' Despite his relative youth, Greensides had possibly been unwell for some time and thus may have needed some assistance, for the 1851 census shows James Nicholson, gardener, aged twenty, living in Clifton Lodge. Ten years later, Timothy had a thirty-three-year-old single man as his gardener, Edward Gaun, who was still with him and sufficiently highly regarded to be left £100 when Timothy died.

As noted earlier, fewer of the female staff are named, although they held posts ranging from highly responsible housekeepers to women who worked in the fields. On Tuesday 3 July 1810, 'Mrs. Parmley the housekeeper came to Clifton', and she must have been succeeded by Jane Storrow who became Mrs Jackson in 1825. It is not clear whether Jane was kept on as housekeeper after her marriage, but a few years later another one was appointed: 'Wednesday 2 December 1829 Mrs Mackey our new housekeeper arrived.' She seems not to have been a success, for by Wednesday 30 December that year 'Mrs Mackey quitted our service. We sent her to Tanfield Hall.'

There must have been other housekeepers, but at the end of his life Timothy was employing Anne Cordukes, who was left £100 when he died. She was described as a twenty-seven-year old York-born lady's maid in the

1851 census. Obviously kept on after Elizabeth's death, she had become Timothy's housekeeper by the 1861 census.

Timothy seems to have taken pleasure in his employees marrying. In addition to the examples noted earlier, he recorded on Saturday 10 May 1845: 'Mrs. Pickering married this morning at Watlass Church.' Hannah Pickering, a thirty-year old female servant, was living in Clifton Castle in the 1841 census.

Inevitably there were sadder events to record in the diaries. On Monday 28 December 1835: 'Mary Lumley our kitchen-maid was buried at Watlass', and on Wednesday 13 July 1853 'Jane Marley one of my labourers was taken ill in the hayfield & died soon after she was taken home to Lowburton.'

The women servants seem to have been paid half-yearly, unlike the men who had to wait a whole year for their wages. Timothy noted on Friday 24 November 1843: 'Call'd at the Bank at Leyburn to get some money to pay the women servants half yrs wages', and again, on Thursday 13 May 1847, 'Paid the women servants ½ yrs wages.'

Unmarried members of the domestic household staff lived close to the Huttons in Clifton Castle itself. Census returns give a picture of their numbers. In 1841 there were three resident male servants, aged between twenty-five and fifteen, and five female servants aged between thirty and twenty. By 1851 there were still three men, but the number of females had increased to eight. Ten years later, when Timothy was a widower, there were five men and seven women.

We have seen how some of the more senior staff were accommodated in Clifton Lodge, where Timothy and Elizabeth had resided before Clifton Castle was ready for occupation. Following a period when it had become the home of Clervaux Chaytor, Elizabeth's brother, and his family, Clifton Lodge had been divided up into apartments so as to house several staff families, including those with families of young children. Some married staff also occupied separate properties elsewhere on the Clifton Castle estate.

AGRICULTURAL STAFF

Many staff were required on the estate farmland, of different kinds and status. There was clearly a differentiation, judging by their different rates of pay, between the skills of 'a servant in husbandry' and a 'farming servant'. The latter earned four guineas a year more than the former. Simon Chandler, described as a servant in husbandry, quit Timothy's service on Sunday 13 May 1810. He had been taken on in 1808 at Martinmas, the feast day of St Martin on 11 November, when such workmen were traditionally hired. He had served a full year up to November 1809, and so by the following May was due wages for a further half year, which were £8 8s 0d. Timothy notes that he was leaving in order to work at the King's Head Hotel in Richmond for the licensee, John Yarker. John Coultman, presumably a relation of the groom William Coultman, was hired at the higher rate, coming 'to live with T. Hutton as Farming Servant from May Day 1810 to May Day 1811 at 20 guineas for the year.'

Some of the agricultural staff were appointed to a specific task, though might later diversify. On Sunday 3 June 1810 'Robt. Pattison came to hire to me to look after the cattle, the terms were one month upon trial.' Timothy had, over the previous few years, built up a herd of very well-bred cattle. Robert Pattison started work ten days after their initial meeting, and turned out to be a mature employee who could be entrusted with a wide variety of tasks. On 21 February 1812 he was sent 'with a horse & cart to Leyburn to take Miss Moore's harp.' He visited Richmond on two days in Spring 1815, first to collect a picture, and subsequently eight bushels of tares. Tares were a type of kale, increasingly being used for animal feed. It was obviously the seed of such which was bought, for it was sown the following day. Eight bushels of seed must suggest a large area of land being used for this crop.

Reliable worker that old Pattison must have been, he was nevertheless able to astonish his employer – on Monday 18 December 1815: 'My servant Robert Pattison got married to Mary Gatenby, a servant at the Farm House. The bridegroom in his 63rd year & the bride in her 23rd year.' The couple moved into Clifton Lodge, and had a son, Richard. Robert remained a loyal employee at Clifton until he died aged eighty on 18 January 1839, and Timothy had a handsome tombstone erected to his memory, still situated in Thornton Watlass churchyard just west of the church. Timothy let his widow Mary, and son Richard, now aged eighteen and training to be a whitesmith, a worker in lighter metalwork than that produced by a blacksmith, continue to live at Clifton Lodge. Mary appears as still living there not only on the censuses for 1841 and 1851, but even for that of 1861, by which time she was in her seventies. Her name was added to Robert's tombstone when she died on 22 August 1866 at the age of seventy-five.

Employees were sometimes taken on at a very young age, particularly if their family was already established and well-regarded on the Clifton estate. William Dodsworth, a farmer who was probably already a tenant when Timothy took the estate over, had two sons, Henry and John, who were to follow their father into Timothy's employment while still boys. Timothy noted: 'Henry Dodsworth (Aged 13 on the 11th May) Hired by his Father William Dodsworth to live with me from the 22nd of April 1811 to ye 13th of May 1812 for £7 7s 0d', and 'May ye 19th 1812 Paid to William Dodsworth for the use of his son Henry Dodsworth one years wage due on the 13th Inst. £7 7s 0d.'

Even at such a tender age, Henry clearly worked hard, and the following year, when he was now fifteen, Timothy recorded: '1813 May, Took Henry Dodsworth into the Stables in April last past and hired him to serve me for one year for 5 guineas and two suits of clothes and a hat. The agreement was made by his Father and me on the 12 inst. Tim'y. Hutton.' Henry continued to progress, for on 13 May 1815 he was paid retrospectively for the year just served, and promoted for the ensuing year: 'Henry Dodsworth one years wage due this day £7 7s 0d Hired Henry Dodsworth for £8 8s 0d and three suits of clothes.'

Henry's progress up the employment ladder meant that he received not only higher annual wages, but also more impressive livery. By 29 May 1818, when Henry was twenty, Timothy 'Agreed with Henry Dodsworth to serve me from the 13th of May last past to the 13th of May 1819 for sixteen pounds, two coats, two pair of breeches, two waistcoats and two cotton jackets, one guinea per annum for hats, one great coat in two years.' But Henry was destined for even greater things: 'Henry Dodsworth May 13th 1822 paid the above one year's wages £17 1s 0d agreed with the same for one year ending May 13th 1823 for £25 and to find his own clothes. And one guinea a year if he pays proper attention to the ale and brewing.' By now it would seem Henry was helping his father, who had been appointed as Timothy's brewer on Leap Year Day 1816: 'Saw the whole process of brewing. Expect we shall have better ale than the last brewer made for me.'

William's younger son John was also taken into the workforce, and at such an age that it was his father, not the boy, who was paid his meagre earnings: 'John Dodsworth, the son of Wm. Dodsworth, 11 years old last Michaelmas, came to live with me on the 13th of May 1818. No agreement for wage. May 14th 1819 gave Wm. Dodsworth for the use of his son John £3 3s 0d.' As young John was living in, he was presumably already destined to work in the house. Here there was a team of manservants employed, and although John, as a boy, would be joining the lowest of the tiers, there was potential for him to progress up the ranks, and eventually earn a relatively high wage.

William Dodsworth is one of the few staff who can be specifically placed in their home, for on Thursday 7 August 1817: 'Dodsworth's family got into the new house called Birktree House.' But William was versatile, and also turned his hand to a variety of tasks. He went to collect wine from Ripon, taking with him the money for payment, and took the luggage ahead when Elizabeth was journeying to Redcar for the summer of 1819.

It has been seen that Timothy Hutton recorded how much his staff were paid, sometimes where they came from or why they left him, and in the case of the Dodsworth family, how boys entered into service. Reference has also been made to the traditional practise of employing agricultural workers for a year, usually from Martinmas in November. Timothy's diaries reflect some changes which resulted from the shortage of agricultural labourers caused by the Napoleonic wars. Hirings might be held also in May, at the start of the busy summer season, as shown by the entry for 10 May 1818, concerning John Hunter, who 'quitted my service this day having to attend the Hiring at Thirsk tomorrow, I gave him leave to go'. In July 1810 Thomas Spence was paid £16 19s 3½d 'for one half year and two weeks wage', presumably having been kept on the extra couple of weeks to help with hay-making.

Another detail of how staff were taken on is provided by an entry in the 'Servants Book' from Martinmas 1828: 'William Peacock or Pickering Peacock – Thos. Wilson engaged the above at the Hiring Bedale to live at Clifton. Wages for the year £14, gave Wilson 5/- for the Man's Godspenny.' The 'godspenny' which had to be reimbursed was a coin given as a mark of good faith when hiring a servant. This entry is also unusual in that Timothy seems unclear about the name of the employee: perhaps he went by two names.

The deaths and illnesses of tenants and staff frequently feature in Timothy's diaries. On Sunday 10 May 1812 he noted 'John Simpson, the son of Richard Simpson of Thirn [a hamlet on the estate one mile north of Clifton Castle], died. His death was occasioned by a mortification taking place in his hand which spread to his heart.' Less than a year later, on Saturday 13 February 1813, 'William Whaley [perhaps the brother of James Whaley who had been appointed manservant in 1810] died this morning about 8 o'clock at this house. Sent William Coultman [the groom] to inform William Whaley's mother of his death.

Some of the deaths were more dramatic, such as the entry for Wednesday 14 February 1821:

> 'On our return [from Spennithorne] Mrs Storrow (my housekeeper) met us at the door & inform'd she believed Abraham was drowned in the river near the Mill. We had all the menservants out to past eleven o'clock. They could not find him. This day three years ago Abraham came to live with me.'

The following day: 'Poor Abraham was found opposite the Island towards the low end of the deep. He was taken to one of the cottages at the Mill to have the Coroner's Inquest upon him. From thence he was moved to Snape.' And on the Friday: 'Abraham was buried this afternoon at Well. Sent Harry and Storrow to attend his funeral.' The burial register for Well gives his name as Abraham Exelby, aged forty. His home must have been at Snape, a small village lying about three miles east of Clifton Castle, and situated within the ecclesiastical parish of Well. He had come from Thorp Perrow to Clifton Castle, as butler, in 1818.

Another entry, written on Friday 18 October 1822, also tells a sad story: 'Stephen Metcalf died this afternoon at Masham. He had been upwards of twenty years servant & labourer at Clifton. Seven children living; his wife died last year.' Metcalf would seem to have been one of Timothy's first employees when he took over the Clifton estate. On Thursday 7 April 1831 another labourer died: 'Thomas Barwick of Thirn died this day at 2 o'clock. One of the day labourers at Clifton betwixt twenty & thirty years.' On the following Saturday: 'Most of the men were off work in the afternoon. They went to attend Barwick's funeral. He was buried near the Anabaptist Chapel at Masham.'

Another entry, for 25 June 1838, reads, 'Robert Brown, many years a labourer at Clifton, died on Saturday morning, and was buried this afternoon at Watlass.' Timothy's note of Thursday 20 June 1861 records: 'Sam Tunks one of my farming men died at the Lodge". The census taken earlier that year includes Samuel Tunks, aged 46, agricultural labourer, among the Clifton Lodge residents. In 1851 he had been living there with his wife Hannah and one-year-old daughter Mary Ann who, it would seem, had died before 1861.

Some of the workers and tenants became too old or infirm to continue in employment, although they remained within the estate 'family'. On Wednesday 15 January 1823 'Jenkins Dinsdale died at half past 11 o'clock in the night at Mary Buckles. He had been many years chargeable to this township.' The following Friday, 'Old Jenkins was buried this afternoon. The labourers & some of the servants assisted in taking him to church.'

Another reference to the death of a person who had been 'on the parish' appeared earlier, on Christmas Day 1813: 'Thomas Metcalf of Rookwith died, a pauper belonging to Clifton.' Sometimes it was the dependents who were left who had to resort to the Poor Law. On Thursday 23 February 1837 'Thomas Buckle one of my labourers died.' Two days later, 'Rode to Bedale and attended before the Magistrates respecting the settlement of the widow and children of the late Thomas Buckle of Thirn.'

Fortunately Timothy also provides more cheerful anecdotes about his staff. On Thursday 19 July 1821, he recorded: 'The Coronation of George the Fourth...... Gave the labourers bread, cheese and ale in the evening.' Then on Thursday 19 September 1822, 'We dined early being Masham Races & most of the servants had leave to go to Masham'; on Christmas Day 1834: 'All the labourers men and women dined at Clifton'; and on New Year's Day 1837, 'Had the labourers children &c. to dine in the Servants Hall.' The Coronation of William IV on Thursday 25 June 1838 was also marked by Timothy: 'gave the workmen 1/- each and the women and children 6d each.'

Timothy Hutton's individual tenants are not always easy to identify. In some entries they are brought together as a single group, paying their rents twice each year, at the end of June and in Christmas week, such important events in the finances of the Clifton Castle estate being marked by a Rent Day dinner. For example, on Thursday 28 June 1810: 'The Rent Day at Clifton. Had all my tenants to dine with me.' Elsewhere they are referred to individually, either as a name, or a place, for example, Tuesday 20 February 1855: 'James Hutchinson of Helwith [on the Marske estate] died this morning.'

Some of the outdoor staff lived in the estate hamlet of Thirn, where Timothy improved its housing – on Thursday 9 May 1811 he 'sent John Clarke to Gilbertscar to order some slate for 2 houses in Thirn.' Timothy not only improved property already within the Clifton Castle estate, but in many cases made improvements to newly acquired lands and properties. In April 1834, for instance, he bought Haregill Lodge at Ellingstring near Ripon and, closer to Masham, acquired High Burton and later Low Burton. In early August 1837 Timothy negotiated with Mr Humphries, agent for Mark Milbanke, to buy High Burton Farm, for what seems the very large sum of £14,000. To fund this purchase he not only took out a mortgage, but sold some land at Hunton to the Wyvills of Constable Burton and to Lord Bolton. Relevant to his acquisition of High Burton Farm is an undated etching by George Cuitt, entitled *The Remains of a chapel at High Burton near Masham, Yorks,* which depicts a tumbledown stone building, with dilapidated thatched roof, apparently being used as a hay barn, and a horned cow drinking in what is presumably the River Ure.

High Burton Farm's sitting tenant was George Outhwaite, who Timothy went to see as soon as the finances were sorted out in May 1838. Subsequent improvements to the farmhouse included sinking a cellar, presumably to make the house less damp. This work Timothy inspected on Thursday 9 April 1840, and he planted three elm trees on the road leading up to the house in November 1840. George Outhwaite moved into 'the New House at Highburton' on Tuesday 15 December 1840, and had many years enjoying this new abode, before he died, as Timothy noted, on Monday 22 January 1855.

LAND CROPS

Successive generations of the Hutton family attempted to improve their estates, and Timothy's eldest brother John was a notable agricultural improver on his Marske estate. The so-called Agricultural Revolution saw new techniques applied to farming in order to produce more food. This was needed to feed both the burgeoning populations now living in towns, and also for animals, including those which worked the land. Timothy was already growing new crops with which to feed his animals when his diaries start, and these also detail how he manured and drained his land.

Timothy took a close interest in the day-to-day work carried out on his estate, regularly going out into the fields, and speaking to the labourers, who included women as well as men. Perhaps he even helped in the fields at busy times. He notes the dates when various crops were sown, or the hay-making finished, and cereal crops, beans and potatoes were harvested.

His interest in turnips, however, bordered on the obsessive! He defined them as Swedish turnips, which we now call swedes, but these were grown not as vegetables for humans. Instead they were intended as winter feed for cattle and sheep, which were being over-wintered in increasing numbers. When he had noted the turnip seed had been sown, his records show that he returned to the field a few days later to see if they were yet showing!

When the turnip seedlings were thinned out, these 'thinnings' were transplanted to replace those that had failed to germinate. So the crop yield was clearly very important. Except for the sowing, which was done by men, the turnips were largely nurtured by the women labourers, who first cleared the land where the crop rotation indicated the seeds should next be sown, and then hoed round them, and eventually dug them up.

Timothy notes the time spent on his various crops, such as for their sowing or harvesting, and noted the yield in good or bad seasons. For instance 1847 was the best crop of hay he had as yet experienced for both quantity and quality. His appreciation of the efforts involved in achieving good crops is demonstrated by the entry for Saturday 7 September 1822: 'finished cutting the beans, gave the servants & labourers a dance.'

The farming operation was surprisingly intensive. For example, they began sowing turnips on 19 June 1810, finished the turnip sowing at noon two days later, and in the afternoon started threshing oats. This continued the whole of the next day, the horses being used to power a threshing device. The last of the hay was brought in on 9 August, and on 20 September the men ploughed for the sowing of winter wheat. Where the potatoes had been lifted by early November, more wheat was then sown.

The weather inevitably determined whether sowings or harvestings were early or late. In 1811, for example, the sowing of turnips began six weeks earlier than in 1810. Timothy tells us in great detail about the harvesting of oats in 1812. On Tuesday 20 October, 'Wind & sun in the forenoon, got some oats led.' 'Led' is the term used in the Yorkshire Dales for material being transported. The entry for the same day continues, 'A little rain at 12 o'clock but not so much as to prevent our getting some oats led in the afternoon.' The next day was very fine and Timothy, having finished getting in the rest of his oats by noon, was able to send his horses over to a neighbour to help him take advantage of the good weather to get some of his corn in.

October 1816 saw a week of fine weather mid-month. On the Monday, 'The days very fine. Got some wheat led for the first time this season. Got all the corn cut.' By the Saturday, 'Got all my corn led.' Usually it was possible to start cutting wheat in September, occasionally in August. Beans were sown in April and cut in September or October, to be stored in a stack like the hay which was harvested in late June or the first half of July. Wheat was sown immediately the bean field had been ploughed, perhaps in November.

Timothy's own animals did not produce sufficient manure to enrich all his arable fields, and at the end of October 1827 he purchased twenty-one loads of it for £9. Later, in the early 1850s, he started growing crops as 'green manure'. He referred to this as 'guano', but as he sowed it, this was clearly not the rich fertilizer based on bird droppings from caves in South America of that name, which was by the mid-nineteenth century being imported by steam ships.

In February 1834 Timothy visited Cleasby, near Darlington, to see a draining plough, 'which I much approve of and intend having one made.' At the end of November the new plough was ready, and was brought to Clifton by cart. It was tried out on his land a few days later. Ploughing was a hard task for both men and horses, and new machines for the purpose were particularly desirable. Possibly it was this machine which Timothy went to see at work on Thursday 2 March 1837: 'Went to see the men ploughing in the Great Close, part of which is intended for turnips and potatoes and the remainder for open fallow.' In March 1841 he walked to an outlying part of the Clifton Castle estate, where 'the men were sowing oats on the turnip land', and nearby, a few weeks later, 'the labourers were setting potatoes.'

Many agricultural societies were established in the early Victorian period, to help raise farming standards in many ways.[60] The most famous of these and still in existence is the Yorkshire Agricultural Society, founded in 1837, which hosts each July what has become known as the Great Yorkshire Show. It is now permanently based in Harrogate, but for many years the show was staged in a different location each time. At such shows, ploughing competitions were held, and new machines exhibited. On Wednesday 16 March 1842 Timothy 'Rode to Thornton Steward [between Masham and Leyburn] to see the ploughing, premiums being offered for the best work, in two classes one for men and one for boys under the age of 18'. Timothy attended another, similar competition held at Jervaulx in November 1849.

On Friday 29 September 1843 he 'went to see the agricultural implements &c exhibited at Mr. Jaques's Farm near Easby.' Richard Machel Jaques of Easby, near Richmond, owned ironstone mines in Cleveland, and pioneered the production of iron suitable for the stresses the new farm machines exerted on the material. In the summer of 1844 Timothy visited local farmers who had invested in a 'Clodcrusher' machine, a type of roller developed at Beverley in the East Riding. It worked well on land after a dry season, and was surprisingly good on rough ground too.

The following year Timothy invested in more machinery. Tuesday 11 November 1845: 'At Clifton all the day and went twice to the Boat Close to the subsoil plough work which is lent to me on trial by Scurah of Crakehall, likewise a strong four-horse plough. Like both & intend purchasing them.'[61] The subsoil plough was at work on the Clifton Castle estate by mid-January 1846. By the 1850s Timothy was travelling to other parts of Yorkshire to see new threshing machines powered by steam, but he seems to have held back from such a dramatic step as investing in one of these.

60 Evans, Eric J., *The Forging of the Modern State, Early Industrial Britain 1783-1870*, Longman, (1983), pp.130-1.

61 White, William, *History, Gazetteer, and Directory of the East and North Ridings of Yorkshire*, (1840), p.580, lists Joseph Scurah as the village blacksmith at Crakehall near Bedale.

LIVESTOCK

Timothy's diaries frequently mention animals. Horses were used for riding, pulling carriages and in agricultural work. He farmed cattle and sheep, and took a keen interest in the scientific breeding of such animals to improve their quality. He bought and sold animals at annual fairs, and some of his animals were also prepared for the agricultural shows of which he was so fond.

Somewhat surprisingly, in view of his grandfather's achievements in the breeding and training of racehorses, the fewest references are to horses. On 9 February 1810 Timothy went to Bedale and bought a black horse, bred by Jeffery Wood of Askrigg, for £100. Four months later he sent his coachman, John Clarke, to Boroughbridge with a male horse to sell, raising 20 guineas. Sadder news was recorded in November 1817, when on consecutive days the old grey horse, followed by the old coach horse, were shot and buried in the Quarry Hole.

A later coachman, Christopher Mudd, who had just been appointed, was sent to Northallerton to sell a horse in February 1828, raising £37 5s 0d, and in September 1831 Timothy himself attended the sale in Aiskew of T. Swan's horses, buying a grey mare for £45 11s 6d. Mudd was also sent to Boroughbridge Fair with a brown colt in June 1835. Timothy's last equine transaction seems to have been buying a pony at the Masham Cattle Show in September 1860.

Timothy's interest in the breeding of better stock is shown by his keeping of a special notebook in which he carefully recorded the genealogy of his shorthorn cattle. This information, which dates from before his surviving diaries begin, shows that he began buying quality cattle before he had even started building Clifton Castle. The material starts with mention of a cow which Timothy named 'Wilkinson', after his tenant Ralph Wilkinson of Walburn Hall, who had bred the cow. He was to name several cattle after the person who had bred them, or the home of the breeder. Timothy proudly noted that 'Wilkinson' had 'Got the Premium' at the Halfpenny House show in 1801. She had a daughter Timothy named 'Hester' in 1803, and another, 'Bessy Bell', in 1804.

In 1802 Timothy bought a cow at Darlington, which he describes as 'the great red cow'. It had been bred at nearby Neasham, and Timothy named it

'Neesom'. 'Neesom' had several good calves, including 'Lucy' in 1803, and a bull calf named 'Volunteer' in 1804. For the years 1802-6 Timothy details the bulls used for his calves, and this makes it clear that he was using the finest animals then available. Another cow bought by Timothy was 'Newton', named after its breeder Mr Charge of Archdeacon Newton near Darlington, which had been fathered by 'Mr. Charles Colling's Grey Bull'. There are several references to Charles Colling (1751-1836), the renowned breeder of Ketton near Darlington, whose most famous animal was the Ketton Ox, after which a pub in Yarm is named. Colling's bulls were so highly regarded that they cost a lot of money to hire – on 20 December 1804 Timothy paid £42 to use one of them for a single season. 'Newton' produced 'Cicely' at Clifton Lodge in 1803, by Mr Charge's grey bull, and 'Cicely' later had a white and red bull calf named 'John'.

Timothy bought two cows directly from Charles Colling, both the offspring of the latter's 'Grey Bull', and from both of which cows Timothy subsequently bred. One cow he named 'Mrs Colling', who in 1804 had a bull calf given the name 'Ned', who later became Timothy's stock bull, and in 1806 a calf called 'Salley'. The other of Colling's cows Timothy called 'Ketton', who in 1804 produced a white calf 'Mary Gray', and the following year another heifer, for which Timothy used the old term a 'quey'.

Timothy later owned a red and white bull, 'Robin', who was hired out for the season to Lord Grantham of Newby Hall in February 1810, on condition it did not service more than forty cows. Most cows produced one calf at a time, but a cow called 'Countess' successfully calved two calves in October that year. Sometimes Timothy produced a cow which could be sold for a reasonable amount of money. He sold one to Mr Place of Bedale for £30 in 1821.

Timothy was interested in new breeds of cattle. In November 1823, when Ayrshires had newly been brought into England as dairy cows, Timothy's herdsman, Wilson, purchased two for him. Later, on Tuesday 20 November 1832, Timothy went with Wilson to East Witton Fair, where they sold two steers, and bought two more Ayrshire heifers. A couple of years later, the number of cattle at Clifton Castle must have considerably increased for, on Tuesday 30 September 1834, Timothy and Wilson travelled to Westmorland and purchased thirty Galloway heifers at Brough Hill Fair, then a major annual event for the buying and selling of cattle, sheep and horses.

Timothy regularly attended fairs for the sale or purchase of animals at many market towns, though most were more local than Brough Hill. Two fairs in a fortnight were held at Bedale in May 1835, 'well attended by purchasers and a good show of cattle', and Timothy sold a cow which was near calving for £10 9s. Both Richmond and Reeth also had cattle shows by the mid-1830s. On Monday 23 September 1839 Timothy bought twelve Scotch heifers at £7 5s each. Still keen to improve his cattle, he bought two calves at a cattle sale at Jervaulx the following month.

The 'Durham breed' of cattle at Northallerton Agricultural Show received an admiring entry in Timothy's diary in August 1840. Timothy was pleased with his sale of three fat heifers at Masham Fair in September 1844 as they went for nearly £43. His continued interest in cattle shows saw him visiting those at York in 1848 and 1853, and at Darlington from 1855. The advent of rail travel meant that he could more easily visit shows and sales further afield.

Diary entries sometimes record the dates when the cows were brought inside due to cold weather. In 1811 they were able to remain outside until frost and snow on the ground brought them in as late as 5 December. In 1816 hard frost started much earlier, and the cows had to be brought in on 10 November.

Timothy seems to have taken a more 'hands on' interest in his sheep. Again he bought animals to improve his flock as well as selling those he bred. He regularly had sheep bought and sold at Bedale Fair. As with his cattle, there are occasions when he sold on his sheep to people he knew, as on Thursday 11 April 1811, when Edward Carter, the landowner in Theakston who not long afterwards would become Timothy Hutton's brother-in-law by marrying Elizabeth's sister, 'bought six Spanish sheep and five lambs of me.'

For the purpose of achieving quality sheep Timothy, like farmers today, carefully chose a tup [ram] to mate with his flock. The choice had to be made in late summer to produce lambs the following spring. On Thursday 18 September 1828 Timothy called on George Outhwaite, the farmer at High Burton near Masham, and negotiated with him the use of one of his tups at the price of 2s 6d for each ewe it served. Again as today, some years the price of livestock was depressingly poor. The following year, Timothy commented on Thursday 17 September: 'A very great quantity of sheep were shown at Masham. Little business was done, there were few buyers & money scarce.'

In April 1830 he spent the morning with the herdsman dressing the sheep's feet against foot rot, and on 19 May that year commented that they were able to start clipping the sheep which had been fed on turnips in the winter. In September 1832 he sold sixteen wethers [year-old sheep] at

Masham Sheep Fair for £1 6s each, and four fat ewes at £2 10s each. He also bought ten gimmers [female sheep in their second year which have not yet had a lamb] at £1 13s each.

Timothy and the men got the sheep washed on 10 May 1834, and clipped forty-eight of them on 22nd, ready for the Sheep Fair at Masham. The ewes were put to the tup on 6 October 1835. Forty-nine sheep were sheared on 23 May 1836, and in the September the wool was weighed and sold in Masham at 1s 6d per lb. In 1840 they began washing the sheep rather earlier, on 27 April, and finished shearing on 23 May. By this time Timothy was going to watch the washing and clipping work, rather than helping, but he went to Leyburn on Friday 16 June 1854 and bought eighty-two half-bred sheep.

Thomas Mudd, the farm foreman, went up by train to Newcastle in April 1860 in order to travel to Penrith for the fair there on the 23rd, and came back having bought eighty sheep. By 7 May the sheep had arrived at the Marske estate, which Timothy was now running since the death of his brother John in 1841, and Timothy went to have a look at them: 'much I am pleased with them, 80 & all well.'

Timothy was still visiting the local sheep and cattle fairs until a year or so before his death in 1863. Even as late in his life as the Masham Sheep Fair on Wednesday 17 September 1862, he went there with Mudd, who 'bought 122 lambs, half Scot & half English.' On Wednesday 5 June two years earlier Timothy visited Pepper Hall,[62] noting 'A sale there of farming stock', but he seems not to have purchased anything.

Timothy seems not to have kept pigs, but on Wednesday 20 February 1828 he walked into Masham 'to see a very large pig fed by John Lightfoot[63] which weighed upwards of 44 stone without head & feet'. This was the era when it was fashionable to produce huge animals, particularly cattle.

Timothy seems to have used at least one dog for working with his animals. On Saturday 3 August 1833 he rode to Marske 'to see some dogs tried belonging to Kit Wilson. I bought one for six pounds'. The word 'tried' presumably means what is now termed a sheepdog trial. Christopher Wilson was the village joiner and postman in Marske.

62 Now called Pepper Arden Hall, at South Cowton. Shortly afterwards a 'model farm' would be constructed adjacent to the house.

63 The publican and wine merchant of the King's Head Hotel in that town.

WEATHER

Like all farmers – and gardeners – today, Timothy was very reliant on the weather. His diaries reflect this, providing interesting details of the weather in North Yorkshire. Indeed, many of the entries are very similar to modern news reports – the worst this, the most severe that since......... For example, on 17 January 1811, 'A very great flood in the Ure, the water higher than before seen it', or 1 February 1817, 'The day extremely fine. I never remember such weather at this season of the year. Finer than I ever remember [it] to have been in April.'

Snow features frequently in the diaries. The early part of 1812 saw snow reported from early March to 7 May. In January 1814 Timothy had been with his brother John in Marske, and they were anxious to get from there to Spennithorne for Timothy's father-in-law's birthday party on 22nd. Timothy and John struggled to get there through snowdrifts. Hoping to return to Marske the following day, they set out from Spennithorne, each with one of their servants to help, but were unable to get further than half-way to Leyburn and had to turn back. A four-hour journey on 24 January, during which they had to dismantle some fences in order to cut through fields, finally got them back to Marske. Snow-melt inevitably resulted in floods, and an early fall of snow in November 1816 resulted in anxiety about the ability of the River Ure's banks to hold the water off Timothy's Clifton land. All was well, 'but very near.'

The winter of 1819/1820 was severe. An extremely cold day on 21 October 1819 saw an early covering of snow, and on 23 December Timothy's diary entry records that six inches of snow lay on the ground. This was the date that Timothy's tenants assembled at the house and paid their rent. A country estate such as Clifton Castle depended heavily on its rental income, and to encourage prompt payment many landlords provided hospitality as an incentive. Clearly deep snow was not allowed to stand in the way of either the settling of dues or the associated festivities. The diary entry continues, 'The rent day at Clifton. Had all the tenants to dine.'

The bad weather continued into January 1820. On the 19th his sister-in-law and a friend, who had been staying with the Huttons, left Clifton after breakfast: 'So much snow had fallen in the night they were obliged to have four horses to take them to Spennithorne.' Heavy snow occurred again in early February 1823, making it very difficult to travel either on foot or horseback. Timothy commented that it was almost impossible to cover the short distance to Masham.

Winter snow continued to cause problems. On Monday 26 January 1829: 'Snow all the forenoon, a great quantity now on the ground. The river [Ure] is in many places frozen over.' Just over a year later, on Friday 5 February 1830, 'Mrs. Hutton [who had been at Marske] arrived at home about 6 o'clock being so much snow near to Downholme the horse could not drag the carriage & the post boy had to go to Leyburn for another pair of horses.' The year 1837 saw a prolonged period of snow late in the winter, in March and April, whereas it came early in 1843, on 17th October: 'From five to six inches deep of snow in the morning. Many of the trees, particularly the oak, broke with the snow.'

Sometimes old weather lore was noted. On Saturday 25 January 1817: 'St. Paul. If St. Paul be fine and clear, we shall have a happy year. Such was the day.' This was followed by the good February day mentioned above.

As in 1947 and 2018, the severe winter of 1819/20 was followed by a hot summer in 1820. Monday 26 June 1820: 'The day hot. The thermometer up to 80 [degrees Fahrenheit] the last 3 days.' The hot weather caused problems on 7 May 1826:

> 'Sultry all the morning. Began to thunder about 2 o'clock & continued till after six, the lightning was dreadful & the rain fell in torrents. The overflow of water down to the house was beyond description, considerably higher than yesterday. The torrent down the bank in front of the house was tremendous: for sometime I feared a portion of the hill would be taken away but happily no serious injury as might have been expected.'

Other unseasonably high rainfall caused further problems. On Wednesday 3 October 1821, 'River very high. A boy from Ellington [about a mile across the Ure from Clifton] with three horses trying to cross the river at Brigwath were drowned. He was returning with his cart from leading coals.' The following day: 'The boy & horses not found; some parts of the cart were found opposite Black Dub Bank cast up with the wreck.' Another two days later: 'The poor boy that was drowned on Wednesday was found in the river nearly opposite Clifton.' Sometimes Timothy himself came to grief in wet conditions. On Friday 18 July 1828, while riding home from Theakston via Snape, he 'got the Pony boged [*sic*] and my self very wet and dirty, having to wade a considerable distance through some water.'

On Wednesday 10 June 1835 'Towards evening a most tremendous thunderstorm at Clifton. The hail broke a great quantity of glass in the hot house.' Worse occurred on 23 April 1847 when a thunderstorm killed a boy and two racehorses training on Middleham Moor. The wind also caused problems later that year. On Saturday 1 December 1821, 'The wind extremely high the whole of last night....... A dreadful accident at Newton House occasioned by [the storm] betwixt three & four o'clock in the morning, one of the chimneys was blown down & kill'd Miss Russell (Lady Darlington's niece) in bed.' A few years later, Timothy visited the rebuilt house again, on Tuesday 26 October 1830: 'Rode in the gig to Newton House to call upon Lord Cleveland.'[64]

Stormy winds again caused damage on Saturday 13 January 1827: 'The wind very high in the night. Several trees blown down in the plantations, particularly larch & spruce fir, & several stacks in the neighbourhood blown over.' Again on Monday 7 January 1839, 'The highest wind ever known, it rose in the night and continued all the day. Considerable damage done all over [this] part of the country to buildings, trees and stacks.' This was followed two days later by a comment about his neighbour's estate of Swinton, just south of Masham: 'The damage done to the timber in the park at Swinton is beyond description.'

64 The discrepancy of names is due to the third Earl of Darlington becoming the first Duke of Cleveland. See 'VANE , William Henry' in 'Cast of Characters'. Newton House had to be demolished after the extreme storm damage, and was replaced by a mansion designed 1822-3 by the Durham architect Ignatius Bonomi.

PART THREE: TIMOTHY HUTTON AT WORK AND PLAY

Social Life

Travel and Communications

Militia

Courts

Parliamentary Elections

Ecclesiastical Matters

Medical Matters

Education of the Poor

Sporting Activities

Food and Liquor

Freemasonry

Mercers, Grocers and Haberdashers

SOCIAL LIFE

Timothy Hutton was not only a man who enjoyed many cultural activities, he was also very sociable. He seems to have gone on his own to many of the intriguing events he attended, and he only occasionally mentions what Elizabeth was doing, such as 'Mrs. Hutton went to Richmond to see the fashions' on 29 May 1821 and again on 12 June 1823. That early-nineteenth century Richmond hosted fashion shows should not be a surprise, for the town was then still an important social centre, a place where many fashionable Georgian social events took place.

Richmond was the venue for many of Timothy's leisure pursuits. The town held race meetings, assemblies and drama performances when the North York Militia were mustering there, and Timothy, as an officer in the Milita, enjoyed many of these events in this capacity. His diary entries for the second week of October 1810, during that autumn's muster, illustrate this well. He attended each of the three days of the Richmond races, taking his wife and her two sisters with him, in his new carriage, up to the racecourse on the edge of the town. Tuesday 9th: 'The first race day at Richmond'; Wednesday 10th: 'Mrs. Hutton, the two Miss Chaytors & Self went to the stand [the Grandstand] & in the evening to the Assemblies'; and ending with the sad note on Thursday 11th: 'The new carriage very much scratched. Went with the ladies to the stand.'

Timothy was particularly interested in plays, and on at least six occasions attended performances at what is now called the Georgian Theatre Royal, which had been established by Samuel Butler in 1788. Timothy's diary entry for Friday 11 May 1810 describes a typical day for an officer during the North York Militia muster in Richmond: 'On the moor in the morning. Inspected by Col. Pulleine. Col. Strawbenzie dined with me at Yarkers.[65] In the evening went to the Theatre to hear Mrs. Inchbauld.'[66]

Timothy attended two more performances at the theatre in the latter part of the following year. On Thursday 26 September 1811 he noted: 'Rode

65 The King's Head Hotel in Richmond, where Michael Yarker was the licensee *c.*1799-1823.

66 This Mrs Inchbald may not have been the famous actress Elizabeth, but her sister-in-law, the wife of her brother George. George is known to have been with Samuel Butler's company of players in 1796 – see Rosenfeld, Sybil, *The Georgian Theatre of Richmond, Yorkshire, and its circuit,* The Society for Theatre Research, London, York, (1984), p.52.

to Richmond [from Marske] ...... went to ye Play..... slept at Yarkers.' A few weeks later he took Elizabeth to the Richmond theatre: Friday 1 November 'Mrs. Hutton & I went to Richmond to see a play', wording which seems to imply that the purpose of going to Richmond was to attend the theatre.

After the death of Samuel Butler in 1812, Richmond Corporation encouraged the troupe of actors continued by Butler's widow, and then his son, Samuel Butler junior, by supporting performances at the Richmond theatre. Timothy's diaries show that on several occasions he attended the theatre in the company of senior members of the Corporation. He made two visits to the theatre, a decade apart, with a friend he refers to as 'Mr. Smith'. This was George Smith, Mayor of Richmond in 1815 and 1827. On Saturday 15 October 1814, Timothy 'Rode to Richmond, dined with my mother, got tea with Mr. Smith & went with him to the play. Returned to Mr. Smith's to supper and stop'd all night there'. On Monday 8 November 1824: 'In the evening Smith & me went to the play.'

Further evidence of Corporation support for the theatre is provided in Timothy's diary entry for Tuesday 27 October 1829: 'Rode to Richmond & dined with the Worshipful the Mayor (Wm. Thompson) at the King's Head. Thirty nine I believe sat down to dinner..... Went to the Theatre in the evening to see Kean perform: was much pleased with him. Slept at the King's Head.' Despite Timothy's praise of Kean's performance, the theatre was increasingly in decline, and although Kean was a star, fewer people were attending.

Timothy attended plays closer to home than Richmond on the rare occasions when such entertainment was available, enjoying 'the Play' at Masham with George Cuitt in January 1840. However, throughout his life he had visited theatres when travelling further afield. He saw the popular actor Charles Mathews on stage in York on 13 March 1812 and, on Monday 15 July 1816, in Newcastle on his way to Scotland, he saw 'Miss O'Neil'[67] take the part of Mrs. Oakley in *The Jealous Wife*. In 1810 and 1819 he attended London's Covent Garden Theatre, and was at the Leeds theatre in 1835. The advent of railways meant he could travel much more easily, and he went to Manchester in 1857 where, among his activities, he attended the theatre, spent two days at an exhibition, and went to Peel Park to see the statue of Queen Victoria.

The diaries from his younger years show many attendances at balls and assemblies, not only in Richmond but sometimes in Bedale, and occasionally

67 Eliza O'Neill was a leading actress, based in Covent Garden.

at either his own home or those of his neighbours. On Wednesday 1 January 1812 he 'Gave a dance in the evening to neighbouring families.' There was even an attendance at a New Year's Eve Fancy Dress Ball at Richmond: 'upwards of two hundred people assembled there' on Monday 31 December 1832, when Timothy and Elizabeth were in their fifties. Richmond was in very upbeat mood that year, following the long-anticipated passing of the Act to reform parliament.

Timothy enjoyed music. On Friday 24 May 1816 he went to a military concert performed at Lightfoot's [The King's Head] in Masham by the North York [Militia] Band, and booked them to give a concert in Richmond Market Place the following evening for five guineas. The band was given breakfast at Clifton on their way home: 'They played us a few tunes.' The Masham Band played on the evening of 8 August 1831 outside Clifton Castle, and presumably played inside when back there on 28 December that year. The following Boxing Day 'The Hunton Band and Well Band met at Clifton and gave us some musick [*sic*].' The Masham Band was back at Clifton for a morning concert on Monday 6 June 1842.

While in York in February 1832, he heard 'Signor Paganini' [the famous virtuoso Italian violinist Niccolò Paganini (1782-1840)]. He attended a concert in York after going to the races there in October 1838. On 24 May 1836 he 'Went to Masham Church to the Oratorio', and on 10 December 1840 it was 'The Oratorio at Bedale.' On Wednesday 16 December 1857 he recorded: 'At Dr. Mark's morning concert at Leyburn & most highly gratified with the performance of the boys, about 40 of them all under the age of 15.' Almost the last entry in Timothy's diaries is on Wednesday 7 January 1863: 'The morning concert at Bedale, a very good meeting.'

A number of diary entries cover 'one-off' events, although Timothy gives a frustrating lack of detail in some cases. What can be the interpretation of his entry for Tuesday 24 May 1814: 'Mrs. Hutton, Miss Chaytor and self went to Ripon to Mr. Lucares to dinner, saw the illumination at Ripon in the evening.' Surely a May evening would not lend itself to such?

Timothy was intrigued by conjurors. In fact he stayed on in Bedale, after a meeting on Wednesday 18 February 1818, in order 'to see the conjurer, Mr. Ingleby.' Ingleby was sufficiently impressive for Timothy to take Elizabeth to Masham to watch his performance on 22 May 1821. Another conjuror, called Scott, was brought to Clifton Castle to give a performance on 7 November 1823: 'His tricks were excellent. We had him in the Bow Room. All the servants came in.' On Saturday 24 May 1856 Timothy was in Richmond to see 'Professor Bernado Eagle and his daughter, clairvoyant lady, much pleased and surprised.' George Barnardo Eagle was a celebrated magician, and his daughter Georgiana became a psychic to Queen Victoria!

Hot-air balloon displays were fashionable in the 1820s and 1830s, and on 18 October 1825 Timothy rode to Richmond to see a balloon launched. A similar spectacle very nearly turned into a disaster on Saturday 28 June 1834. A hot-air balloon, launched at Ripon at 7.30p.m., became visible from Clifton Castle about 8p.m., and caused a lot of excitement. Timothy got on his pony to ride after it, and saw it come down at Rookwith, a few miles to the north. Two local boys, the sons of the blacksmith, crept inside the collapsed balloon and were nearly suffocated with the gas. Timothy sent for the Masham surgeon, Richard Hutchinson, who bled them profusely, and with great difficulty resuscitated them, one of the boys, John Horner, being particularly ill: 'We rubbed his wrists, chest and legs, the latter we had in hot water. Applied vinegar and water to his face and temples. I did not get home till one o'clock.' Timothy returned to Rookwith the next day, and was relieved to find that both boys were recovering well.

Less traumatic journeys include seaside visits to Redcar. Elizabeth Hutton went there, with her mother and sister, but without Timothy, in September 1811, and in the summer of 1819 Elizabeth took three local children to stay there for several weeks. Timothy joined them for part of their stay, and recorded bathing in the sea, riding on Redcar's beautiful sands, and seeing the lifeboat launched. In May 1820 Timothy visited the spa wells at Croft-on-Tees, 'and had a warm bath.'

Displays of wild animals were clearly a much-relished treat for Timothy, and he mentions several. He went to Crakehall on 21 November 1820 'to see a show of Wild Beasts', and on Saturday 29 June 1822 went to Richmond with Elizabeth, and her sister-in-law and the latter's children, 'to see a collection of wild beasts.' Timothy and George Cuitt enjoyed Wombwell's Menagerie at Masham on 4 December 1840: 'was most highly gratified with all the animals being in so fine a state.' On Wednesday 21 June 1843 it was the turn of Isaac A. Van Amburgh (1811-85), the American animal trainer, to visit Richmond with 'his lion and tiger &c &c.' On 23 May 1846 Elizabeth accompanied him for a morning visit to Bedale 'to see a grand procession of carriages drawn by elephants, camels and horses.'

Timothy's frequent attendance at fairs held in various towns for the purpose of showing, buying and selling agricultural animals has already been mentioned. The present-day association of the noun 'fair' with travelling amusements and sideshows does not reflect its former significance. A fair was a privilege granted by a medieval charter, enabling the place to hold a trading event lasting two, three or even four days, with stalls of general commodities, but particularly focussed on the sale of animals.

Some places had several fairs a year, for instance Richmond had three, and Timothy attended its Palm Sunday Eve Fair in 1821. Like this one, most of the fairs Timothy attended have now lapsed, but one which does survive is the famous Appleby Horse Fair held each June in Cumbria, and which he went to in 1837. The other fairs he visited included Northallerton[68], Middleham Moor[69], to Masham[70], Bedale[71], Leyburn[72] and Askrigg[73].

Timothy belonged to several respected local societies, such as the Richmond Scientific Institution, established by his eldest brother John, to further knowledge of modern scientific developments, particularly as they affected agriculture. Members met on Thursdays in the lending library room of the Richmond printer John Bell in Finkle Street,[74] and once a year held a dinner at the King's Head Hotel when up to twenty-eight members might dine together. On Thursday 23 April 1812 [the annual general meeting] Timothy noted in his diary 'Rode to Richmond & dined at the Scientifick [*sic*] meeting which was very well attended. Mr. Hutton was chosen President & I had the honour to be chosen Vice President.'

It would seem that Timothy rarely missed the opportunity of a convivial dinner. He frequently travelled to Richmond for such events, for example to dine with the mayor, the freemasons, the Company of Mercers, Grocers and Haberdashers, or his fellow officers in the North York Militia. These gatherings were, of course, only open to men. Often he names his companions, for example on 13 September 1817: 'Rode with Mr. Foss to Richmond. I dined with my brother at the Market Club.'

Timothy also had links with Ripon, as Clifton Castle was in that area, so sometimes travelled to dine there. Thursday 2 February 1816: 'Rode to Ripon. Mr. Baines went with me from Masham. We dined with Mr. Morton the Mayor; 97 sat down to dinner', and Monday 29 January 1821: 'Went to Ripon. I dined at the Town Hall with a large party of gentlemen of the

68 February 1813 and 1840 and 1842.

69 November 1839, 1840, 1841, 1842, 1846, 1854, 1856 and 1858.

70 September 1832 and 1853, Easter Fairs in April 1834 and 1845.

71 May 1834, July 1838, 1840 and 1845, Christmas Fairs in December 1836, 1841, 1855 and 1857.

72 May 1849

73 July 1858.

74 Wenham, *James Tate*, pp. 308, 423.

town & neighbourhood being the anniversary of the King's accession to the throne.' George IV had come to the throne the previous year, so it was his first anniversary.

TRAVEL AND COMMUNICATIONS

Timothy's busy lifestyle meant that he travelled a great deal. This was often on business, and on his own, sometimes in the company of friends or colleagues. Such journeys he continued until an old man. Or a journey might be for family reasons, a christening here, a funeral there. Such trips were routine affairs, doubtless not worthy of the term 'travel' in his eyes. Yet thoughout his life Timothy took a keen interest in the many revolutionary changes he observed in the means of travel and communications.

His diaries record only one foreign trip. In the summer of 1826 he undertook a tour of France and Italy. He took with him two of the sons of the late Revd John Fisher, who had been Rector of Marske until his untimely death. These were John Hutton Fisher, named in tribute to Timothy's eldest brother, the boy always being known as Hutton Fisher, and his younger brother William Fisher.

There were, however, several significant holiday-type journeys in the British Isles. Some of these were fairly close to home, such as visits to the seaside at Redcar with his wife and her sister. Even so, the majority of Timothy's expeditions were made without Elizabeth.

Timothy's Scottish holiday in 1803, when he was still a bachelor, was the first of his many recorded trips. On Wednesday 14 March 1810 he and two male friends left Clifton after breakfast, heading first to Ripon and Boroughbridge, where they got a chaise to York. Arriving at 3.30p.m. they dined, went to a play, and stayed overnight. Up early the next morning they caught a 5a.m. stage coach, had breakfast at Ferrybridge, and dined at Doncaster. They left there at 2p.m. and reached Sheffield for supper and another overnight stay. Leaving by the 3.30a.m. mail coach, they reached Derby for breakfast, and there visited the china manufactory and silk mill, before going via Litchfield to Birmingham.

On Saturday 17 March they visited Clay's Manufactory in Birmingham before heading for Warwick and visiting the castle and church there. After sleeping at Shipston, they visited the park and gardens at Blenheim, before seeing most of the colleges in Oxford. Early the next morning they visited Nuneham Courtenay, to see Lord Harcourt's collection of paintings, and, after travelling through Henley and Maidenhead, reached London towards evening on Monday 19 March. After dinner they were able to see the second half of the play at Covent Garden Theatre. The building had been rebuilt after a fire in 1808, but Timothy found it disappointing.

Other theatre visits followed on the Tuesday and the Thursday, and on Saturday 24th they watched a juggler and went to a very good oyster shop in Fleet Street. As well as spending Wednesday 28th, Saturday 31st and Tuesday 1st April doing the equivalent of looking longingly in car showrooms, the group also fitted in a coach ride out to Kew where they were 'much gratify'd' with the palace. Walking back into London, they went to the opera that evening. After a final theatrical performance at the Lyceum on Monday 2nd, they headed back north, leaving London in the Carlisle Coach at 7.30p.m. on Tuesday 3rd. After travelling all the next day and night, Timothy arrived back home at Clifton at 5a.m. on Thursday 5 April.

Timothy and Elizabeth shared an interest in the fashionable experience of 'sublime' dramatic landscapes in places such as Scotland, and she accompanied him on some trips there. Timothy, Elizabeth, and one of Timothy's male friends, Dixon, whose Christian name is never given, went on a tour of Scotland from late June to early August 1812. Twenty pages of incredibly detailed accounts survive from this trip, which ran up a total bill of over £206! A map of Scotland cost 8s 6d and a pencil 6d. Various amounts of plaid were bought, costing £2 3s 4d, a pair of shoes for Elizabeth cost 6s 6d, and a haircut for Timothy cost 1s. Tips to those opening churches were usually around 1/-, chambermaids received a similar tip, waiters somewhat more. Dinner, bed and breakfast was between £1 and £2, having boots cleaned was 2d. Attending the theatre in the country cost 6s, but 12s in Edinburgh, plus 1s for the man who kept their seats there.

The following year there were two trips. In early March, Timothy set off on his own for London (Drury Lane Theatre one evening, the opera the next) and a week later got to Bath, where again he saw a play. Then by chaise to Plymouth Dock to see the Dockyard, and went on board the *Queen Charlotte*, a Royal Navy flagship. Returning to Bath via Exeter, Timothy arrived in Birmingham at 9.30p.m. on Friday 2 April. The next day, the first on the return journey, the coach overturned near the toll bar at Sheffield, and Timothy hurt his shoulder. After a final overnight stop in Leeds, he got home in the evening of Sunday 4 April, and immediately sent for his friend, the highly-regarded Masham surgeon John Baines, to look at his shoulder.

By the last day of August, and presumably fully recovered from this accident, Timothy, Elizabeth and her elder sister set off in the carriage after breakfast. They were heading for the Lake District, travelling there through the Craven area of Yorkshire. They took four horses and two menservants with them. They returned to Clifton on 14 September 1813.

The same threesome set off for another Scottish tour on Monday 4 July 1814: 'Mrs. Hutton, Miss Chaytor and self set off from Clifton at 7 in the morning.' They spent the first night at Bishop Auckland, paid a brief visit to the 'rather disappointing' castle in Durham, before reaching Newcastle-upon-Tyne via Falla's Nursery at Gateshead. After dinner they 'went to see the Northumberland Glass House.'

The next day, Wednesday 6th, they arrived in Alnwick, where the people were 'very busy preparing for the Illumination of Friday evening.' 'The Castle at Alnwick is magnificent, but gaudy, ... the furnishing of the Castle the worst I ever saw.' The following day the country was enjoying a somewhat premature Day of Thanksgiving for the Peace in Europe.

Through Berwick the party continued to Dunbar on Friday 8th, and there met up with James and Margaret Tate, who were staying at the home of one of Tate's favourite 'Invincibles', Hon. Charles Fox Maitland, 4th son of Lord Lauderdale. Reaching Edinburgh on 9th, the Hutton party visited a lapidary in the Old Town before breakfast on Monday 11th, and on 12th they visited the gardens at Dalkeith.

A trip to Hopetoun House on 13th did not achieve entry as they had hoped: 'The house at Hopetown is not shown to strangers. The front of the building not so elegant as I had expected, having always understood that Hopetown House was one of the best speciments of Grecian architecture we had in the Island.' Timothy was more impressed by Lord Elgin's house on the opposite side of the Firth (Broomhall, in Fife), which had been designed by his acquaintance, the successful Richmond-born architect, Thomas Harrison of Chester.

The hectic sight-seeing pace continued on Thursday 14 July when the party reached Linlithgow, saw the castle and church – 'well worth seeing' – before heading to Stirling, where they paid an evening visit to the castle, from which the view was grand. On Saturday 16th the party met up with the somewhat controversial politician James Stuart, who showed them Callander and Brachlinn Falls Bridge, and took them on a boat trip to see 'fine, wild scenery': 'The Trossachs are sublime.' Of Stuart, Timothy said, 'I was very pleased with him & likewise his venerable mother to whom I gave a kiss when we parted.'

The tour continued at a hectic pace, with several more days spent visiting the sights, including seeing the largest larch tree in Scotland, then to Perth, and Scone, Dunblane, Stirling, arriving at Glasgow on Saturday 23 July.

On Sunday 24th they attended the English church there in the morning and afternoon, and on Monday 25th left Glasgow at 8.30a.m. for Greenock. Timothy daringly took a steamboat the twenty-six miles by river, while the ladies undertook the twenty-two miles more conservatively by road in a carriage. At Greenock they watched part of the West India fleet.

Tuesday 26 July saw the party struggling to find accommodation at Androssan, where it was both the sea-bathing season and the races at Irvine. Timothy was complimentary about the achievements of Lord Eglintown, who was developing a pier to form a harbour at Androssan, and also lodging houses there.

On Wednesday 27th Timothy bathed in the sea at Ayr, and was pleased to find a very good inn there: 'the best we had been at, the charges very reasonable', compared with the bad beds costing 12s at Ardrossan. On Thursday 28th they went to Cummock and Farquhar, and the following day to Dumfries, where Timothy walked down the side of the river and 'got some of the rock which is composed of limestone, granite, sandstone spar or marcosite.' The party set off home, via Carlisle, Penrith and Sedbergh, arriving back at Spennithorne on Tuesday 2 August, and on Wednesday 3rd 'Mrs. Hutton & I arrived at Clifton at 11 o'clock am.' In July 1816 Timothy and a couple of men friends spent another fortnight in Scotland, and in the summer of 1823 Timothy and Elizabeth had a lengthy English tour, visiting London, Salisbury, Bath, Gloucester, Cheltenham, Malvern, Birmingham, Derby, Worcester, Lichfield and Sheffield.

The earlier Scottish steamboat trip had whetted Timothy's appetite for experiencing many more new transport opportunities. On Friday 2 May 1828 he headed south to Selby, caught a steamboat to Hull, and the next day landed at Goole for breakfast, seeing the new dock and warehouse 'which are in my opinion very complete.' Goole was indeed completely new, an industrial town developed earlier in the 1820s by the Aire and Calder Navigation company for the transport of coal, forming the country's furthest inland port, which had only opened in 1826.

A trip to London in 1831 saw a combination of forms of transportation old and new. On Monday 9th May Timothy set off from Bedale in the 'Courier' coach, dining in Leeds, then travelling through Sheffield, Nottingham, Leicester and Northampton, reaching London on the afternoon of 10th. He stayed at the Tavistock Hotel in Covent Garden. On Thursday 19th he enjoyed a day at Epsom Races, and on Saturday 21st he started heading back, boarding the Middlesbrough steamboat at 10pm.

He was on the steamboat all of Sunday 22nd, and on Monday 23rd, with the wind against them slowing the journey. As the stock of coal was getting low, they put into Bridlington Quay to take on extra coal. Setting off after dinner they cast anchor off Hartlepool for the night. At daybreak on Tuesday 24th a pilot came on board to steer the boat up the Tees, and they arrived at Middlesbrough at 4a.m. Timothy took the 'Railway' coach the four miles to Stockton, got a chaise to Darlington, where he met the 'Telegraph' coach which took him to Leeming Bar, and there his coachman met him in his carriage.

There was a further short trip to Scotland in October 1836, mainly visiting cattle shows, and then a gap – perhaps as Timothy and Elizabeth settled into a more sedate middle age. The trips to London in 1846-8 were for medical, rather than pleasure reasons. He made his final trip to London, as a widower, in the summer of 1862. On the morning of Monday 28th July he met up with his Middleham friend Thomas Topham at Bedale Station, and the train got them to the Portland Hotel about 10p.m.: 'Took Joseph to take care of me.'

The next day, Topham left them but Timothy and his faithful butler Joseph Simpson visited 'the Exhibition', the Great London Exposition. Its international displays were so impressive that they spent the next day there as well. On Thursday 31st Timothy and Joseph visited Kew '& much pleased with it', then on Friday 1st August Topham rejoined them and he and Timothy revisited the exhibition: 'a half crown day, much to be preferred to a shilling day.' On Saturday 2nd they left London by the 10a.m. train: 'I arrived home before 8 o'clock.' The railways had reduced the time needed to travel between London and Yorkshire to one day.

Although Timothy's diaries give many explicit details of his own personal transport arrangements, and other details are implicit, he does not always give us a complete picture of what must have required far more organisation than modern-day ability to jump into a car and head off near or far. Horses for riding must have been kept as a matter of course without being mentioned, and details of his employees show that, after his marriage, coachmen were employed as well as grooms. But information about the actual vehicles he owned is sporadic and incomplete.

There are, however, some amusing parallels with the modern practise of an almost recreational viewing of new cars, and of trading in an old vehicle for a new. While in London in March 1810 we know that Timothy and his friend Dixon spent several days browsing the gigs and other coaches on sale in Little Queen Street, Tottenham Court Road, 'Tatersdale's' and Whitechapel.

Timothy's diaries do not inform us whether he actually ordered a new vehicle in London, or if this was mere 'window shopping' with a view to placing an order more locally subsequently. However, we do know that later that year he did indeed own a new carriage, for he was somewhat annoyed that his new carriage was scratched in the melee of taking his wife and her two sisters up to the grandstand on Richmond Racecourse in Richmond. On Wednesday 13 March 1811 Timothy reports that 'Mr. Williamson ye Coachmaker, Ripon' was at Clifton, but does not say whether it was to repair the scratches incurred at the races or to supply another new vehicle.

It was on Saturday 6 July 1822 that we first have details of a specific purchase: 'Bought a gig.....£18.' On Thursday 23 October 1823 Timothy 'Went in the gig to Wycliff to attend the sale. Bought the fireplace.' Presumably he did not bring it home in the gig as this was a light vehicle used for relative speed. After touring the continent in the summer of 1826, Timothy's thoughts turned to renewing his vehicle, and at last gives us more intriguing information about the transaction. Wednesday 6 December 1826: 'I ordered a carriage of Myers (the coachmaker at York) called a briskie for which I am to pay £155 & he will allow £45 for my old carriage.' The term 'briskie' does not seem to have survived, although it implies speed.

It would appear, however, to have served Timothy well for many years. There is a long period without references to purchasing new vehicles until, in the middle of his hectic round of engagements as High Sheriff of Yorkshire, on Friday 26 July 1844 he casually notes, without further elaboration, 'The new chariot arrived at Clifton.' He gives more details of a later transaction, on Thursday 8 July 1852, when he took with him a younger man and one with businesslike knowledge for moral support in the deal. 'Left Clifton at ½ past 6 & met Mr. C.L. Bradley at Catterick Bridge, got post horses there & went to Darlington, bought a carriage there of Stephen Carlton for which I gave £130 and the old carriage and to have double harness sent to me in the agreement.' Presumably the harness was quite a valuable 'perk' to have negotiated.

The vast improvements in travel experienced during Timothy Hutton's lifetime were also reflected in the available means of communication. The Huttons were in the fortunate position of having staff they could despatch with an urgent message, such as news of a death. In the background there was also a postal service, which was prompt, if expensive. It was the recipients who paid the postage, rather than the senders, before Rowland

Hill's Penny Post became available in 1840. The exception to prepayment was if letters needed to be sent abroad. On Thursday 22 May 1825, Timothy 'Wrote to Mr. Smith in Paris and took the letter to the Post Office in Masham to pay the postage.'

National news travelled north slowly in the period covered by the early diaries, and much faster later on. On Wednesday 13 May 1812 Timothy noted: 'Heard at Richmond of the assassination of the Hon. Spencer Percival (Chancelor [*sic*] of the Exchequer) in the lobby of the House of Commons.' Percival was actually the Prime Minister, the dreadful event had taken place about 5.15p.m. on Monday 11th.

In January 1820 news of two events of great national significance reached Timothy only days apart. His diary for Wednesday 26th noted 'Got the acc[oun]t of the Duke of Kent's death. He died on Sunday last at Sidmouth in Devonshire.' That Duke's baby daughter would, of course, seventeen years later, become Queen Victoria. The Duke's father died a few days later: Saturday 29th 'His Majesty King George the Third died at Windsor at half past 8 o'clock in the morning.' What follows is again significant: Tuesday 1 February 'The account of the king's death came to Richmond.' Thus it seems that in 1820 Richmond, an important borough, only heard of the death of the country's longest-reigning male monarch three days after Timothy did so.

Communications were thankfully much speedier over thirty years later when, on Thursday 11 May 1852, Timothy could note in his diary 'Received an account of the death of Major Dodsworth. He died at Hastings at half past two o'clock. The account came to Thornton Hall by Telegraph.' The memorial to John Smith Dodsworth in Thornton Watlass Church confirms that this was the actual date he died, but states more specifically that he died at St Leonards-on-Sea.

Later that year, Timothy again heard promptly of a national event, on Thursday 24 September 1852: 'The Duke of Wellington died yesterday aged 84.' A few years later still, Timothy could be a party to, and easily travel by train to attend, an event concerning another national figure: Saturday 30 August 1856 'Went to Leeds..... to witness the presentation of a Sword to the Earl of Cardigan, I being an early subscriber.' The hero of the Charge of the Light Brigade had property in Leeds, hence the location of the presentation, the jewelled sword having been commissioned by a group of his friends in Yorkshire.

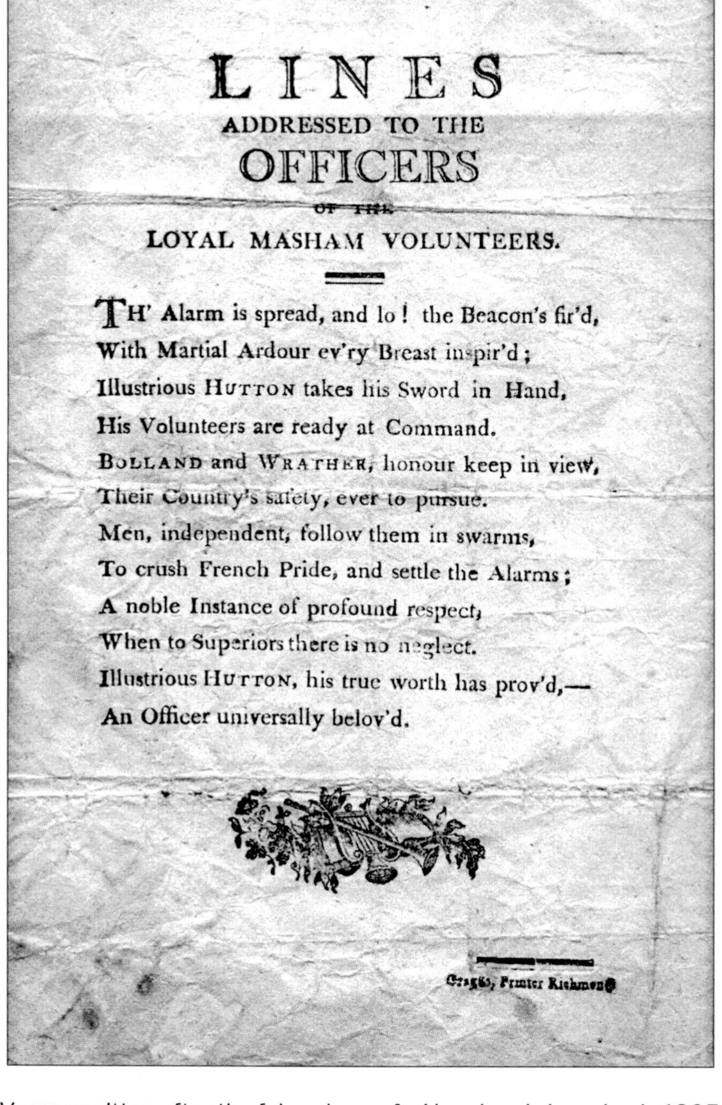

LINES

ADDRESSED TO THE

OFFICERS

OF THE

LOYAL MASHAM VOLUNTEERS.

TH' Alarm is spread, and lo! the Beacon's fir'd,
With Martial Ardour ev'ry Breast inspir'd;
Illustrious HUTTON takes his Sword in Hand,
His Volunteers are ready at Command.
BOLLAND and WRATHER, honour keep in view,
Their Country's safety, ever to pursue.
Men, independent, follow them in swarms,
To crush French Pride, and settle the Alarms;
A noble Instance of profound respect,
When to Superiors there is no neglect.
Illustrious HUTTON, his true worth has prov'd,—
An Officer universally belov'd.

Craggs, Printer Richmond.

Verses written after the false alarm of a Napoleonic invasion in 1805. In a private collection.

MILITIA

In the early-nineteenth century each county had to provide and pay for a number of militiamen aged between eighteen and forty-five, and to provide them annually with several weeks of training. This was organised by the lord lieutenant of each county. Officers were also recruited from amongst the local aristocrats and gentry, their rank being allocated according to their wealth. The men were called up according to a parish ballot, and their unavoidable absence could be hard for families and employers to cope with. Timothy himself had to accept the loss of some of his staff to this cause: in 1810 his groom William Coultman had to have one month off a year to serve in the militia, and in 1812 his gardener Richard Smales was greatly missed when he set off for Yarm to be on permanent duty with the militia.

The Richmondshire Battalion of the North York Militia was based in Richmond, and its men had training exercises up on the moorland to the north-west of the town. There was also a section known as the Loyal Masham Volunteers. Timothy Hutton was one of the lesser officers, at first in Masham, and then with the Richmondshire. The numbers of men required for this part-time army were increased as the threat of invasion intensified, and Timothy's diaries provide a detailed account of the time devoted to these activities, and the logistics of recruitment and training.

Sometimes there was an unscheduled emergency which the militia had to deal with. On Saturday 16 March 1805 he records 'Informed that the beacons [which signalled invasion] had been lit in the night. Took the alarm & call'd the volunteers out at Masham & went with all possible speed to Thirsk where we found the alarm was false.' In tribute to this, the Richmond postmaster Robinson William Craggs, who was used to printing news bills, was asked to produce a doggerel ditty commemorating Timothy's part in the event.

The officers' role was two-fold. They had to supervise the training given to the men by the professional non-commissioned officers in the daytime, and they also had to attend the numerous morale-boosting social activities held in the evening, accompanied by their wives. The schedule was daunting. Timothy left Clifton Castle, into which he and Elizabeth had only just moved, for Richmond on the evening of Sunday 22 April 1810. He stayed in the town on Monday 23rd for parades in the Market Place in both the morning and evening. On the Tuesday and Wednesday mornings he was up on the moor with the soldiers.

Elizabeth travelled over to Richmond later on the Wednesday for the couple to attend the evening ball, and she returned to Clifton on Thursday afternoon. Timothy followed her after the evening parade, getting home at 10p.m., but returned to Richmond on the evening of Friday 27th ready to go back on the moor with the men the next morning. He was with them for more training each morning of the following week. On the evening of Wednesday 2 May he dined at the Town Hall, and on Thursday 3rd 'The whole of the officers dined with the Mayor of Richmond.'

The muster continued for the whole of the following week except that heavy rain on the Tuesday meant the exercise was cancelled. The players were in town that week, and he saw Mrs Inchbald at the Theatre on Friday 11 May after the senior officers had inspected the men earlier in the day. He seems to have had a couple of weeks' break, before on Tuesday 29 May leaving Clifton before 5a.m. to get to Richmond for breakfast at 7.30a.m., followed by going on the moor for another inspection.

On 17 May 1810, James Tate wrote to an old friend from his youth, John Disney, son-in-law to the former rector of Richmond, Archdeacon Francis Blackburne. Disney had become leader of the Unitarian movement, and Tate was updating him on Richmond news: 'Timothy Hutton, Lieutenant Colonel of the Second North York Locals, went away on Saturday. John Hutton, Lieutenant Colonel of the Firsts, and war-like figure he cuts, has just left us.'[75]

The conclusion of the annual training did not mean the tasks were over for the year. Timothy rode to Bedale on Friday 10 June 1810 for 'A meeting of the Deputy Lieutenants to take in the returns of those liable to serve in ye militia', and was back there in the morning of Thursday 27 September 'to ballot for the militia'. Each parish had to provide its quota of men by balloting those eligible. The following afternoon twenty-five officers were entertained to a dinner by the militia's commandant, Timothy's brother-in-law Col. Chaytor of Croft, to update them on progress. Timothy went to the theatre again afterwards.

The following year the muster took place a little later, beginning in May. On Wednesday 15 May, based in Richmond, he rose at 6a.m., set off for the moor with the soldiers at 8a.m., and got back into Richmond at noon. He

75 Wenham, *James Tate*, p.259.

was up on the moor the next three mornings, and on the Friday travelled back to Clifton for 4.30p.m. But after staying just one night, he had to return to Richmond early on the Saturday morning for another session on the moor. On the Sunday he rode out to Kiplin to see the inspection of the troop based there, but later that day, back in Richmond, he walked in the evening into the castle yard, where the militia was then based, with the governor, Mr Redshaw.

On Monday 20 May a new phase of the training began, firing ball cartridge up near the Richmond Beacon. The following two days were spent up on the nearby racecourse where the soldiers were being exercised. By the Friday the operation had moved to the other side of the Beacon for more firing of ball cartridge. On Sunday 26 May he attended Richmond parish church with the soldiers before the final inspection of the Richmondshire Battalion on the Monday, culminating with a dinner for eighty-seven at the Town Hall.

Tuesday 28 May was wet and most of the men, presumably thankfully, left Richmond, but he had to deal with a court martial, when William Warde was sentenced to be confined for four months. In the evening 'Returned to Clifton in ye carriage with Mrs. Hutton.'

By the following summer, Timothy had realised that his involvement with both battalions was too much, and he resigned from the Mashamshire Volunteers. However, he not only continued with the Richmondshire Battalion, but was appointed major by the lieutenant-colonel of the North York Militia, Turner Straubenzie of Spennithorne, on 10 April 1813. Now his involvement seems to have fallen to manageable levels.

He rode to Bedale on Thursday 27 February 1817 for a meeting of the deputy lieutenants to swear men in for the militia, but mostly he merely dined with his fellow officers. Elizabeth accompanied him to Richmond on Friday 21 June 1821, 'The Regiment were inspected before dinner, we went to see them & were highly delighted; the day was extremely fine'. They both attended the officers' ball that evening.

Both Hutton brothers retained friendships with some of the established officers they had worked with in the militia. Captain Simon Thomas Mewburn was one such man, who was later remembered as being 'a frequent visitor to Marske Hall in good old John Hutton's days.'[76] Mewburn had had a number of roles, for example he was quartermaster of the North York Militia, and had also served as steward to the owner of Richmond

76 Wenham, Leslie P. (ed.), *Richmond, Yorkshire, in the 1830s*, privately published, (1977), p.62.

Castle, the Duke of Richmond. In this capacity he oversaw the clearing of debris in the castle yard prior to the erection of the North York Militia barracks there in the 1850s.

Timothy recorded in his diary on Thursday 30 April 1846, 'Got a letter from Mr. I. Fisher to say poor Mewburn died last night at 8 o'clock.' Isaac Fisher was an old friend of Timothy's who acted as head of the Richmond branch of the family bank, and he had obviously heard there the news which would be of great interest and concern to many people in the town. Mewburn was buried at Croft-on-Tees church on 6 May 1846, at the age of sixty-six.

By the 1850s, Timothy was sufficiently senior to be fraternising with the then full colonel, the seventh Duke of Leeds of Hornby Castle near Catterick. He went up to the moor again on Tuesday 7 June 1853 to see what was now called the North Riding Rifle Corps reviewed by Lt. Gen. Arbuthnot: 'The officers and men did their work well and were highly complimented by the General.' Timothy continued with the Rifles, travelling to Leyburn and York as well as Richmond to see them.

COURTS

As Justices of the Peace for the North Riding of Yorkshire, both Timothy Hutton and his eldest brother John adjudicated on a number of courts and sessions. The highest level of these was the York Assizes, which dealt with serious cases referred to it by lower courts. An elegant Assize Court building had been constructed in the 1770s, to a design by the architect John Carr, in the 'Eye of York' around York Castle, the most obvious medieval remains of which is Clifford's Tower. Facing the Assize Court building was a matching block, built as the Female Prison in the early-1780s, also by John Carr, and between the two the County Gaol, later known as the Debtors' Prison, of 1701-5, probably by the Yorkshire Baroque architect William Wakefield. The former Female Prison and Debtors' Prison now form the Castle Museum, but the Assize Court building still fulfills its original purpose, its two court rooms now used for the York Crown Court. In the basements of all the blocks are cells where the prisoners were confined.

The Eye of York was an area not within any of the three historical North, East and West Ridings, hence its use for courts serving the whole of Yorkshire. The Assizes provided a spectacle popular with Georgian society, particularly if any capital sentences were handed down. Public executions had been held at the York Tyburn on the Knavesmire until 1802, when they had been moved to the Castle where they could be carried out more discreetly behind the Assize Court. Hangings did, however, continue to generate a frisson of excitement, and a few people did manage to get viewing places for them.[77]

The Assizes sat twice a year, in the Spring, for the Lent Assizes, and later for the Summer Assizes, and on occasion additionally for some special reason. In advance of each season, that year's High Sheriff of Yorkshire summoned a Grand Jury of twenty-four land-owning gentlemen, and arranged for one of them to act as foreman. Timothy served on a Grand Jury many times, and thus spent a lot of time at York Castle, even more so in the year he took his turn as High Sheriff in 1844. His brother John had served similarly in 1825. Each High Sheriff appointed a chaplain for

77 Royal Commission on Historical Monuments, *An Inventory of the Historical Monuments in the City of York, vol. ii, The Defences,* (1972) [hereafter RCHM].

his year of office. John had had James Tate as his chaplain, and Timothy nominated his cousin-once-removed Robert Pulleine.

Timothy's first diary entry mentioning serving on such a York jury occurs on Tuesday 7 March 1820: 'Got a letter this morning from York to attend on a Special Jury in the cause of the King against Hunt & others. The Trial to come on on [*sic*] Thursday ye 16th inst.' His fellow jurors were to include his brother John, and his brother-in-law Col. William Chaytor of Croft. Others were from Scarborough and Wakefield, and the foreman was from near Hull. There were ten defendants, accused of inciting unrest in a huge crowd.

Timothy was duly in position to be sworn in as a Special Juror for the first day of the trial, which lasted from 9a.m. and was only adjourned at 6p.m. The next day it again started at 9a.m. and went on until after 7p.m. They sat all day on the Saturday until 6p.m., and were then adjourned until 9a.m. on Monday 20 March. That fourth day lasted until after 6p.m., by which time the court had heard the examination of the witnesses for the prosecution. On Tuesday 21st, the subject of the trial, Hunt, made his defence. Timothy was in court all day the following Wednesday, Thursday and Friday, and on Saturday from 9a.m. until 7.30p.m., by which time the defence's witnesses had been heard, and the judge's summing up had begun.

On the final day, Monday 27 March, the jury retired just before noon, and returned to give their verdict at 4.30p.m., finding four men not guilty, and the others guilty of unlawfully, maliciously and seditiously meeting and assembling. The accused were already under recognizance to appear at the Assizes the following term. Timothy's patience was wearing thin, and he commented 'Received only a guinea each of our attendance the 10 days. I gave mine to Mr. Honley the Governor of the Castle for the prisoners. My brother & Col. Chaytor & I believe some one beside to the Infirmary at York.'

For the Assizes proper, a Grand Jury of twenty-four was sworn, as there could be two courts sitting needing twelve men each. Timothy records being in York at the end of July 1827 for such, and being sworn as a juror, but gives no details of his time in court at this session, so perhaps he wasn't called. For the week 23 to 27 March 1829, however, he gives slightly more information, listing the twenty-four jurors, who had Sir Bellingham Graham of Norton Conyers, near Ripon, as their foreman. Timothy gives details of the social events associated with these Assizes, listing where each day's dinner was held, adding that he attended a ball on the Monday evening, a play on the Tuesday evening, and a concert on the Wednesday evening. However, no details are provided of the cases, and he concludes by noting that the business was all finished before midday on the Friday, so Timothy left York at 2p.m. and got home about 6.30p.m.

In the 1830s he seems to pay more attention to the Assizes. On Saturday 4 July 1835 he recorded receiving a letter from Mr Roundell, that year's High Sheriff, requesting 'my attendance on the Grand Jury at York on the 20 inst. which I accepted.' He was in York from 20 to 22 July on that occasion. A similar letter arrived the following year on Sunday 7 February from Major Yarburgh, and Timothy was on the Grand Jury a full week, travelling to York on Sunday 28 February and returning on Saturday 5 March.

There was a lot of pomp associated with the Assizes. A pair of senior judges, who travelled from Assize Court to Assize Court on the Northern Circuit, when arriving at York were met by the High Sheriff on the western outskirts of the city at Dringhouses, and escorted from there to their official lodgings. A special coach, kept for the annual occasion, with attendants in elaborate liveries riding atop, transported the judges from their lodgings to the Castle with great pomp, a tradition that continued into the twentieth century. Before each Assizes started, the judges and Grand Jury processed to York Minster for a service, at which the all-important sermon was preached by the High Sheriff's chosen chaplain.

The High Sheriff for 1837 was Timothy's friend and neighbour, Mark Milbanke of Thorp Perrow, and Timothy served on the Grand Jury for the summer sitting. He travelled to York on Tuesday 11 July, and went to the Minster on Wednesday 12th to hear Revd George Foord Clarke, Rector of Thornton Watlass, preach. Timothy was in York until Saturday 15 July. He again served on the Grand Jury at York in March 1838, July 1840 and March 1841. Then in 1844 it was his turn to be High Sheriff, responsible for organising the sittings and grand juries, and hosting the evening social events.

Timothy recorded his year of office in considerable detail. His appointment began on Thursday 1 February 1844, and he spent the next two days in York, with he and his Under Sheriff being sworn in, before he returned to Clifton by the three o'clock train from York, arriving at Clifton Castle just after 6p.m. His Under Sheriff was William Gray, of Gray's Court in York, the house next to the National Trust's Treasurer's House, which had in the early-eighteenth century been the home of Jaques Sterne, uncle of the novelist Laurence Sterne. William Gray was a self-made man who, conscious of his own good fortune, undertook many philanthropic acts in York, and became a friend of

William Wilberforce.[78] He was a generation older than Timothy, and indeed was to die the following year in 1845, but Timothy doubtless would consider him a kindred spirit as they worked together.

On Friday 9 February 1844 Timothy called on Revd Robert Pulleine at Spennithorne, where Pulleine was then curate, and asked him to be his chaplain for the year. On Friday 8 March, Timothy and Elizabeth set off for the Lent Assizes in York, where they had lodgings at Mort's in Coney Street, near where lodged the assize judges, who were imminently expected. However, this was one of the occasions when the judicial best-laid plans met a hitch, for on the Saturday a message reached York that the judges were unable to get through their business in Durham, and would be arriving a day later than expected.

The judges did indeed get to York early that Sunday morning, arriving just in time to have breakfast before the Minster service, and the party dined at the Deanery in the evening. The two judges that Lent Assizes were Mr Justice Coltman, and Robert Rolfe, later Baron Cranworth, baron of the court of exchequer and a well-liked judge. Each judge sat in one of the two court rooms, so two lots of cases were tried.

The following day, Monday 11 March, Timothy and Robert Pulleine collected Mr Justice Coltman and took him to York Castle, where the Assizes were held, for him to open the Commission. They then handed the judge over to the City of York Sheriff, who took him to York's Guildhall, also to open the Commission there. At 12 noon Timothy took both judges to the courts at the Castle.

Later, Timothy hosted the Grand Jury to dinner at the Black Swan Hotel, and then went with Elizabeth, and the rest of their party, to that evening's ball. The days from Tuesday to Saturday followed a similar pattern, taking the judges from their lodgings to the courts, dining with the Grand Jury at a different pub, followed by a concert on the Wednesday and an attendance at a play on the Thursday. Sunday saw another Minster service and another dinner at the Deanery.

The courts sat each day of the following week. The Hutton party again went to the play on the Friday. On the Saturday, the two justices each finished their cases, Rolfe concluding his by 2p.m., which enabled him to catch the 3p.m. train to Liverpool, and Coltman finished at 10p.m. Timothy's session in York concluded on the Sunday with his attending prayers and dining at the Castle.

78 Wenham, L. Peter, *Gray's Court, York (St. John's College)*, York [undated, *c*.1963].

Typically of his character, Timothy took a compassionate interest in the fate of some of those miscreants who appeared at the Assizes, particularly those receiving a death sentence. Timothy's diary entry for Thursday 18 April 1844 has him in London, visiting the Home Office:

> 'I went there to make inquiry respecting George Lowther who was sentenced to be executed for murder at the last Assizes and I had the satisfaction to hear he had got a respit [sic] until further signification of Her Majesty's pleasure. Consquently he will be transported for life. I left London at 9 o'clock.'

The next day, 'Got to York at ½ past 6, after breakfast went to the Castle, and found all right. Saw Lowther who is now removed from the condemned cell.'

By 17 June 1844 Timothy was making arrangements for that year's Summer Assizes, writing letters asking friends and acquaintances among his fellow JPs to sit on the Grand Jury. On Monday 8 July he noted 'The Servants & horses went to York', and he and Elizabeth followed the next day, arriving in York in time for dinner. On Wednesday 10th 'Went to meet the two Judges at Dringhouses. The Lord Chief Baron [of the exchequer] Sir Fred. Pollock Knt. & Sir Cresswell Cresswell Knt.'

Frederick Pollock, a Londoner of humble origins, was one of a family of brothers who all attained high office. He was considered to unite a retentive memory, great natural acumen, and tact in the management of juries, with a profound knowledge of the common law.[79] Cresswell, formerly Cresswell Easterby, born into a prosperous merchant family with links to Newcastle-upon-Tyne, started his career in mercantile cases. Later he became the first judge of the newly-established divorce court, hearing over a thousand cases over six years and, perhaps somewhat ironically as he was a bachelor, earning a high reputation for the quality of his divorce case judgements. He was counted 'as one of the most creative legal figures of the high Victorian age.'[80]

On Thursday 11 July 1844 Timothy escorted the two judges to the Castle, went to the Minster afterwards, and dined with the Grand Jury at the Black Swan. On Friday 12th he dined with the judges then attended 'the Play' in the evening. He was at the Castle all day on the Saturday, and on the Sunday 'Took the judges to the Cathedral. We took the Sacrament.' The

79 oxforddnb.com.

80 *ibid.*

Assizes continued all the following week, so they were all at the Minster again on Sunday 21st. The judicial business continued into Wednesday 24th, when 'Mrs. Hutton & me left York after four o'clock.'

Another special session of the Assizes took place late in 1844, sitting from Wednesday 27 November until Saturday 14 December. This time Timothy refers to two cases. Tuesday 10 December 1844: 'William Kendrew was tried for the murder of Mr. Inchbald and found guilty, the trial lasted all the day.' A trial which was widely reported in the national press, it concerned the shooting of Inchbald, a wealthy retired merchant who farmed near Boroughbridge, by twenty-two-year-old labourer and poacher Kendrew, who pleaded guilty and was sentenced to execution by hanging.

The second case from the same Assizes, noted by Timothy in his diary, was another where he seems to have pleaded for clemency. Wednesday 25 December 1844: 'Got a letter from the Secretary of State's Office respecting William Potter's sentence being commuted to transportation for life.' Presumably this was welcome news on Christmas Day.

Timothy's year of office as High Sheriff of Yorkshire was drawing to a close, but there were still some official functions to attend in connection with it. On Thursday 16 January 1845 he was in York to dine at the De Grey Rooms, a handsome newly-erected building intended for grand functions, situated in the recently-laid-out street of St Leonard's. There were a hundred and fifty guests, hosted by the Sheriff of York. Timothy was impressed: 'a very satisfactory meeting to me.'

In July 1845 Timothy and Elizabeth were back in York for Timothy to sit on the jury of a Nisi Prius Court, a special sitting of the Assizes to hear a pre-trial for a case to be heard in London. He was in court for Wednesday 16th and Thursday 17th. In the evening of the 17th Timothy and Elizabeth were among the guests who dined with the Lord Mayor and Lady Mayoress of York in the city's grand early-Georgian Mansion House: 'Forty eight sat down to dinner in the Large Room. The two Judges and the High Sheriff and his Lady dined there.'

On 13 October 1845, after Timothy had attended a meeting in York of railway investers, he called upon the Lord Mayor 'and made arrangements with him as to settling the account of the expense of my Sheriffalty [*sic*].' It would seem that it was not the done thing to be too prompt in seeking to recoup the considerable amount of money laid out in fulfilling such an office for a year.

Timothy continued to be invited to attend various official functions in York. His immediate successor as High Sheriff invited him to serve on the 1845 Grand Jury, and he was in York for the Lent Assizes from Friday 6 March to Thursday 12 March. On Thursday 17 December 1846 he was invited to dine with the Lord Mayor, George Hudson, 'the Railway King': 'upwards of five hundred dined in the Guild Hall'. The following day he took breakfast with the then High Sheriff and his lady at their lodgings. He served on the Grand Jury again for the Summer Assizes 1848, and for the last time in July 1850.

Meanwhile, more locally, Timothy served on various local courts, and also took a particular interest in setting up a local police force. London, and then other major centres, commonly established such, but it was more difficult in the countryside. One approach was for rural areas to set up a body to raise funds to bring malefactors to court, and Timothy's brother John had, in 1819, set up the Marske Association for the Prosecution of Felons. Many cases dealt with matters such as poaching; Timothy was involved with a case against five men found poaching at High Burton Farm in 1837.

Timothy's diary entry for Tuesday 12 January 1841 notes 'Rode to Bedale & attended a meeting of the gentlemen of the district to form an association to have a police for the district.' This was followed on Monday 25th by 'Walked to Masham & attended a meeting at the Schoolhouse where Capt. Harcourt [of Swinton Park] was President respecting having a police officer in Masham and to act in the whole parish.' It was agreed to have a police officer for the parish of Masham on 10 February. Similar meetings were also held in Bedale.

PARLIAMENTARY ELECTIONS

From medieval times the county of Yorkshire was treated as one constituency, represented in the House of Commons by two 'knights of the shires'. There were also burgess members from those boroughs whose charters had given them a seat or seats in parliament, Richmond being such a borough, having been granted two members by the charter of Queen Elizabeth I in 1576.

Elections for the two county MPs were held in York itself, voting being by the relatively few electors wealthy enough to be eligible. The voting process was not then by secret ballot, but highly visible, with the names of those voting, and for whom their votes were cast, being recorded in a poll book. If there were only two candidates, there was no need for a vote. The grassy central area of the 'Eye' of York, in York Castle, was where the parliamentary elections for the whole of the county took place, and were declared, until after the 1832 Reform Act. Those for the North Riding were still declared there until 1882.[81]

Timothy Hutton's first reference to a county election consists of two lengthy entries in October 1812. Monday 12th:

> 'Left Boroughbridge about 6 o'clock & got to York before 9am. The nomination day at York for the County. Lord Milton nominated by Sir F. Wood & seconded by Mr. Wrightson; Mr. Wortley by Sir Mark Sykes & seconded by Mr. Bethell; Mr. Lascelles by Mr. Ploomer & seconded by Mr. Wynn Bellasyse. The show of hands were [sic] in favour of Mr. Lascelles & Mr. Wortley. Lord Milton demanded a poll.'

Timothy must have returned home later that day, before beginning a strenuous day of canvassing for Lascelles, which, it transpired, was unnecessary. The following day, Tuesday 13th,

> 'Set off from Clifton before 6 o'clock for Hunton to canvass for Mr. Lascelles & Mr. Wortley. Call'd at Patrick Brompton in my way & got a promise from Mr. Hatton & son of their votes, call'd after upon Mr. Rigge who intended favouring Mr. Lascelles. Went to Hunton

81 RCHM, pp.82-4.

> & got a promise of 13 votes as under – Auton, Thos.; Bonson, Thos.; Calvert, Duke; Hodgson, John; Outhwaite, Chris'r.; Petch, Leo'd.; Petch, Thos.; Pearson, Matthew; Hall, John; Askew, Robt.; Clarkson, John; Pickersgill & Farvell, Joseph. Rode to Hauxwell & got breakfast with Mr. Gale; return'd home after. At ye [masonic] Lodge in the evening where I met Mr. Wise who had been at Bedale canvassing & had got a promise of 12 votes. Votes promised to me at Thirn – William Dodsworth, William Dunn, William Jeff & Joseph Horner.
>
> Hunton – 13, P. Brompton – 2, Thirn & Clifton -5, Walburn – 1, total 21.
>
> After Mr. Wise had return'd home he sent me word that he had receiv'd an account of Mr. Wortley having declined standing, in consequence of which it puts a stop to any further proceeding, there being no one (at present) to oppose Lord Milton & Mr. Lascelles. Upwards of thirty six thousand pounds was subscribed to carry forward the contest for Mr. Lascelles before we left York.'

Thus the election was uncontested, and Viscount Milton and the Hon. Henry Lascelles, later the second Lord Harewood, sat as the two members for Yorkshire.[82] There were two further uncontested elections which are not mentioned in Timothy Hutton's diaries: in 1818 the MPs being Viscount Milton again, plus James Archibald Stuart Wortley, Esq., later Baron Wharncliffe, and in 1820, after the accession of George IV, Milton and Wortley again.

In 1821 an Act of Parliament increased the number of county MPs for Yorkshire to four. The first election for this number was in 1826, and the four returned were Viscount Milton, Hon. William Duncombe [the son of Lord Feversham of Helmsley], Richard Fountayne Wilson Esq. of Ingmanthorpe, and John Marshall Esq. of Leeds, a merchant and manufacturer involved in the linen industry.

There was originally a further candidate, Richard Bethell, who eventually withdrew, but not before the anticipated election had cost the other candidates £250,000.[83] There is just one brief reference to this in the diaries, on Monday 22 May 1826: 'Got a letter from..... Mr. Fountayne Wilson.... to request me to be one of his committee at York at the approaching election.'

82 Park, G.R., *Parliamentary Representation of Yorkshire,* (1886), p.28.
83 *ibid.*

As Timothy was about to embark on a two-month tour of Europe, it was a good thing there would be no election.

The last contested election before the parliamentary voting system was substantially changed by the 1832 Reform Act took place in 1830. There was a two-day poll with five candidates – Viscount Morpeth of Castle Howard, Henry Brougham Esq.,[84] Hon. William Duncombe, Richard Bethell Esq., and Martin Stapylton Esq. Timothy's entry for Thursday 5 August 1830 records that he was in York: 'The day of election for the County. Five candidates started. They began to poll at half past five o'clock. I voted for Duncombe & Bethell...... Took supper..... with Mr. Duncombe's committee.' Morpeth, Brougham, Duncombe and Bethell all polled over 1,000 votes, but Stapylton, who had proposed himself, only received 94.

In 1831 there was one last election before the 1832 changes, but this time it was uncontested. The 1832 Reform Act gave each of the three Ridings of Yorkshire – North, East and West – two members, and representation for the first time to some new industrial towns. Instead of just one voting place, York, there were now other, nearer, locations, such as Northallerton.

John Hutton, and James Tate, and thus by implication Timothy, were among those on the Whig side of Georgian politics who campaigned strongly for the Reform of Parliament, and in particular wished for changes to widen the franchise. This was only partially successful, and it remained only well-to-do males who were eligible to vote, though there was an enhanced definition of freeholders. Nevertheless, the first parliamentary election after the change, late in 1832, caused widespread interest, and Timothy Hutton was much involved in the process.

He worked hard on behalf of William Duncombe, on Wednesday 21 November riding to meet him in Northallerton, where Duncombe 'addressed the freeholders. The meeting well attended', and on Saturday 24th 'Rode to Richmond.... The friends of the Hon. Wm. Duncombe met him at the King's Head.' On Thursday 29th, Duncombe's agent, Charles Hammond, 'came to breakfast after which I sent my coachman with him to canvass for Mr. Duncombe at Clifton, Thirn, Rookwith, Newton-in-the-Willows & Patrick Brompton.' The following day, 'After breakfast Mr. Hammond went to Swinton, Aldbrough & Well', and the next day, Saturday 1 December 1832, 'Mr. Hammond left Clifton after breakfast & went to Bedale, from thence to Scruton &c. & home.'

84 Later, as the first Baron Brougham, he served as Lord Chancellor, and also invented the carriage which bears his name.

On Monday 17 December 1832 Timothy was in York all day, witnessing who had been nominated to stand for the two North Riding seats: 'Mr. Duncombe, Mr. Cayley, Mr. Ramsden and Mr. Stapylton.' The election was on Thursday 20th: 'The election at Northallerton for the North Riding. Left Clifton at 7 o'clock for Northallerton & took with me 6 voters, Geo. Harker, Wm. Blackburn, John Tindell, Frank Scott, Wm. Dunn & Joseph Horner.' The following day: 'Rode to Richmond. Found Duncombe's friends in high spirits as to the result of the election. Ramsden behind Cayley and Duncombe beyond the reach of either.'

On Monday 24 December 1832, Timothy 'Attended Mr. Duncombe to the York Castle Yard, the High Sheriff declared the numbers to be as follows: Mr. Duncombe 4,885, Mr. Cayley 3,287, Mr. Ramsden 2,895, Mr. Stapylton 602.' There were 9,539 registered voters, and 8,581 had voted.[85] Doubtless Edward Stillingfleet Cayley of Wyedale near Scarborough also had a celebratory party, but it was Duncombe's that Timothy enjoyed that evening. Timothy noted 'Dined with Mr. Duncombe and a large party of his friends at the George Inn [in Coney Street, York]. We dined at 2 o'clock and separated at ½ past 6.'

Early in the new year of 1833 there were other celebrations on Timothy's home patch. Thursday 3 January: 'Rode to Northallerton to meet Mr. Duncombe at dinner' and on Tuesday 8th 'Attended the Duncombe dinner at Leyburn. The Hon. T.O. Powlett in the chair. Self vice-President. Thirty sat down to dinner. Put to bed at 10 o'clock.' So it sounds like quite a good evening!

Early in 1835 there was another contested election. The process began just before Christmas 1834. On Tuesday 23 December Timothy 'Set off for York at 8 o'clock. Dined with Mr. Duncombe's friends, 130 of us dined.' On the last day of 1834 he met up with Duncombe's agent Charles Hammond, and the following day Hammond began canvassing the tenants of the Swinton estate. On Friday 2 January 1835, Timothy rode to Northallerton to meet Duncombe and another of the candidates, James Walker of Sand Hutton, while Hammond went to canvass in Masham. The following day Hammond went canvassing in Bedale, and Timothy went to Richmond to meet up with Duncombe and Walker: 'the two addressed the freeholders from the King's Head Inn. Mr. Duncombe was introduced by Mr. Fox and Mr. Walker by me.' Duncombe and Walker canvassed Hawes early the next week, and on Wednesday 7 January 1835 Duncombe and Walker met

85 Park, *op.cit.*

up in Masham, and the third candidate, Cayley, was there also. Duncombe and Cayley were elected; Walker, who was not, had been seconded in his nomination by Timothy.

The first two general elections of Queen Victoria's reign, in 1837 and another early in 1841, were uncontested, with Duncombe and Cayley remaining as the members of parliament for the North Riding. Of the latter result, Timothy commented 'in my opinion, the election will be void', referring, it would seem, to the impending death of Lord Feversham. As this meant that Duncombe inherited his barony, he could not continue to sit in the House of Commons. He was succeeded by his younger brother, Hon. Octavius Duncombe, who sat with Cayley, now the senior member, for two further uncontested elections in 1847 and 1852.

Timothy did not restrict his interest to North Riding representation. On 14 December 1848, he went to Ripon, 'it being the election for the West Riding', the city of Ripon being just across the boundary from the North Riding. This was a by-election due to one of the MPs, Lord Morpeth, becoming the eighth Earl of Carlisle. Timothy had some land just across the border in the West Riding, and so had a vote there also.

None of the aforementioned election campaigns have mentioned a political bias, despite the Hutton family's general sympathy for the more radical, or Whig, side, although William Duncombe was considered a Tory. However, in the later-1830s there had begun a change in political definitions, and Timothy became involved with the establishment of a Conservative Association at Bedale in March 1838. He was chosen chairman, with Thomas Other as agent.

In the Spring of 1857 there was a general election, and so on Wednesday 1 April Timothy went to York for the North Riding nominations. Octavius Duncombe and Edward Cayley were now joined as candidates by John Charles Dundas. Timothy's diary noted 'The show of hands for Duncombe and Dundas. Poll demanded for Cayley.' Richmond and Leyburn were now polling centres for the North Riding election. On the 4th Timothy travelled early to Richmond, voting for Duncombe and Cayley, and at noon left Richmond to take his tenant at Walburn Hall, the elderly John Armitage, in his carriage to Leyburn to cast the same votes. Duncombe and Cayley were successful, Dundas lost by a few votes. He would later serve many years as an MP, following on from several earlier members of the family, and would also be succeeded by others.

At the 1859 election, the North Riding was uncontested, with Cayley and another of William Duncombe's sons, William Ernest Duncombe, taking the seats. The West Riding had an election between three candidates, and Timothy's choice, James Stuart Wortley, lost.

The last election to feature in Timothy's diaries was a by-election for one North Riding seat in March 1862 due to the death of Cayley in the February. The contest was between William John Sawrey Morritt of Rokeby Park, and Frederick Acclom Milbanke of Thorp Perrow. As Thorp Perrow was Clifton's neighbouring estate, it is interesting that Timothy went to Leyburn on Thursday 20 March to vote for Morritt.

ECCLESIASTICAL MATTERS

As an establishment figure, Timothy Hutton was involved in many church matters, concerning many churches. His diaries include many interesting references to contemporary ecclesiastical issues, such as the long-overdue repairs being undertaken to many church buildings and the erection of new churches. More mundane details cover the arrangements for services, including funerals and marriages, and the methods of filling various parish appointments. As a parishioner he had a close relationship with Thornton Watlass church, and as squire of Walburn he had a direct responsibility for Downholme church, followed later additionally for Marske church.

Some of the offices Timothy held required his presence at special services, such as those in York Minster connected with the Assizes, or as a freemason. Church attendances were also part of his role in the North York Militia. Most of these were in Richmond church, but while in the town during the training muster on Sunday 29 April 1810, he noted 'Walk'd to Easby Church to hear Mr. Thistlethwaite preach.'

Timothy's reason for particularly wishing to hear this preacher was that Revd William Thistlethwaite had been a pupil at Richmond Grammar School under Anthony Temple, at the same time as the Hutton brothers. Furthermore, Timothy would also know other members of the family, and was perhaps keen to hear news of them. From 1808 until his death in 1838, William Thistlethwaite was rector of St George's Church at Bolton in Lancashire. His father, Robert, had been vicar of Kirkby Fleetham until his death in 1790, but previously he had served as steward to the Wharton family of Gilling West, who provided his widow with a house there until she died in 1817. Another son of Revd Robert Thistlethwaite, Robert, joined the Foot Guards and is recorded as causing a disturbance at Richmond Theatre soon after it opened in 1788. The son of Timothy's contemporary, Revd William Thistlethwaite, also called William, was a 'Tate Invincible' and later became a professor of Greek in Cephalonia.[86]

Many new churches were erected in the nineteenth century. The first to be mentioned in Timothy's diary was that at East Witton, where the small

86 Wenham, Leslie P., *The History of Richmond School*, (1958), [hereafter 'Wenham, *History of Richmond School*'], p.58; Wenham, *James Tate* p.26; 'John Shaw's Journal', a manuscript in the collection of Richmondshire Museum; Bowman, T. & A., *Guide to Richmond and Neighbourhood* (1836), p.45.

church of St Martin, in the old village site at Lowthorpe, was replaced by a larger building dedicated to St John the Evangelist. This was built at one end of the new planned village which had recently been laid out by the Earl of Ailesbury.[87]

Timothy noted on Friday 27 April 1810: 'At 12 o'clock set off for East Witton & return'd to Jervaulx to dinner after setting out the new church or rather examining the old one to make a report to the bishop. Of the party were Mr. Brand of Wath, clerk, Mr. Costabadie of Wensley do., Mr. Baines of Tanfield, do., Mr. Brears of Middleham, Mr. Chaytor of Spennithorne & Timothy Hutton.' Jervaulx Abbey was one of the seats of the Earl of Ailesbury. The three clerics were accompanied by three local landowners.

The work to complete the new church must have begun apace, for Timothy was able to record on Thursday 1 October 1812: 'East Witton Church was consecrated by Dr. Law, Lord Bishop of Chester.' The Richmondshire area at that time lay within the diocese of Chester. The Bishop of Chester must have spent much time travelling across the Pennines into North Yorkshire for such happy events. An even longer journey for him was noted by Timothy on Wednesday 6 August 1817: 'The new church at Barningham was this day consecrated by Dr. Law.'

The diocese of Ripon was carved out of that of Chester in 1836, the first Bishop of Ripon being Revd Charles Thomas Longley, who held the post for twenty years. Timothy records on Friday 23 November 1838: 'The Bishop of Ripon and Mrs. Longley his wife call'd & lunched here', and not long after, on Monday 24 February 1840, 'Dined at Swinton.... met the Bishop of Ripon & his lady, Mr. & Mrs. York, Mr. & Mrs. Peter Ewart, Sir John & Lady Johnstone & Capt. Wyvill.'

Bishop Longley was also kept busy consecrating new churches in the area. Timothy attended such events at Crakehall on Saturday 11 April 1840, Healey on Tuesday 10 October 1848, Burrill on Thursday 11 September 1856, and Hawes on Tuesday 13 July 1858. In addition to the building of new churches, the Victorian period saw many new parsonages constructed, and Timothy notes that one was being built for the new church at Healey in 1858.

Timothy's lifetime saw the repair, rather than the replacement, of more significant ancient church buildings. Churches received regular 'Visitations' or inspections, every few years, and on Thursday 12 September 1822 the Bishop of Chester appeared in person to carry this out at Clifton Castle's

87 Hatcher, Jane, *Richmondshire Architecture*, privately published, (1990), pp. 82,84.

parish church at Thornton Watlass. Timothy noted: 'Went to breakfast at the Rectory Watlass. The Bishop of Chester arrived at 12 o'clock to see the Church. He expressed his pleasure at seeing the church in such good order. He requested the churchwardens would get two new books – a Bible & a Prayer Book & a new bell when we can afford to purchase one.'

Masham was sufficiently near to Clifton Castle for Timothy to have a close interest in the church there. He went to see the new organ opened on 13 May 1832, and watched a new vicarage being constructed in 1834/5. He notes on Sunday 27 December 1840, 'Mrs. Chaytor and Mrs. Cuitt walk'd to Masham to hear Mr. Waddington's farewell sermon'. Subsequently, on Thursday 20 May 1841, 'Mr. Riddell call'd before I got home he is the [new] Vicar of Masham.'

Revd Thomas Riddell was to be vicar of Masham for fifteen years. There is a memorial plaque commemorating him on the south chancel wall in Masham church, he died in 1855. He was succeeded by Thomas Hedley, and on Wednesday 4 March 1857 Timothy went 'To Masham to see Mr. Hedley with respect to some alterations he wants to make in that part of the Church where I have a pew.'

Other diary references to major repairs and improvements to other parish churches include, on Monday 23 May 1853, 'Went to Well to see the Church now undergoing great change', and on Thursday 10 November 1853: 'Saw the Church [at Burneston] which has undergone a great change & much improved.'

The most frequent church references in Timothy's diaries are to Thornton Watlass church, of which Timothy was churchwarden for part of the time. He paid the tithes due half-yearly (£8 5s), until they were commutated in the 1830s, a process which required several meetings. There are records of regular attendances, such as the household going to church there on Ash Wednesday, Good Friday and Christmas Day, and 'one-off' events such as the rector giving a charity sermon 'for the benefit of the Poor Irish' on Sunday 7 July 1822 – over £11 was collected.

The rector of Thornton Watlass, Revd George Foord Clarke, sought money to provide new pews for the church in June 1816. Timothy gave ten guineas to provide a family pew for Clifton Castle, and noted in August 1820 'Sat in the new pew for the first time.' Other repairs and improvements to the church had been completed in May 1820.

Revd Clarke was succeeded as rector of Thornton Watlass in 1842 by Reginald Courtenay, an Oxford man and a barrister as well as a priest.

Timothy had an additional link with this rector, for in the same year that Courtenay took up his appointment in Thornton Watlass, he married into the Beresford family of Bedale, who were friends of Timothy's. Towards the end of his life, on Saturday 21 December 1862, Timothy donated £5 towards the 'subscription for linen & some plate for the Communion Table' of his parish church.

Other church matters of particular concern to Timothy Hutton related to Downholme church, of which living he was patron. Timothy's eldest brother John held the equivalent position at Marske church, and this became Timothy's responsibility also after John's death. The brothers' friend James Tate had been incumbent of both churches, and when Tate left Richmond for London in 1833, there were thus vacancies at both. Both positions were initially filled by appointing the then curate of Marske, William Kendall, as incumbent for both. When Kendall died in 1855, he was succeeded by his cousin at Downholme, and at Marske by Thomas William Robson, the son of Timothy's old friend Thomas Robson of Holtby.

Downholme church is an ancient building situated a short distance from the village, and Timothy was responsible for repairs which were identified as being required when the Archdeacon of Richmond, John Headlam, carried out an official Visitation there. In 1841 there are several diary entries concerning getting these seen to. As part of the works, pitch pine pews were installed in the nave, and a family pew, of slightly better quality wood, was placed in the north side of the chancel. The family pew has since been moved to the back of the church.

In 1854 Timothy commissioned stained glass for the east window of the church. On Monday 8 January 1855, he 'Stoped [*sic*] at Downholm [*sic*] to see the painted glass in the East Window only finished yesterday' and Friday 21 September, 'Went to Downholm to see the window in the Church and much pleased with it.' A parsonage, now called the Old Vicarage, was built by Timothy on the edge of the village of Downholme in 1858.

During the 1840s, Timothy started taking more interest in historical and antiquarian matters, relating not only to his own family but also to the newly-developing fashion for the study of churches and other antiquities. An unusual diary entry for his support for such a cause, further afield than his own immediate environs, occurred on Tuesday 10 February 1852: 'Wrote to the Rev'd. G. Coopland of York & enclosed a five pound note for the restoration of St. Margaret's Church[88] in York.'

88 A medieval church with a fine Norman portal, but situated in what was in the nineteenth century a very impoverished part of York. It is now the York Early Music Centre.

An entry which foretold of Timothy's increasing interest in antiquarian matters was made on Friday 22 September 1843: 'Mr. Rain and Mr. Greenwell came to Marske to look for some papers.' Revd William Greenwell (1820-1918), in 1843 quite a young cleric, would later become highly-respected in the early days of archaeology, particularly for his excavations of prehistoric barrows. Before long he was to achieve greater ecclesiastical prominence as a young Canon of Durham Cathedral from 1854.[89]

Greenwell seems to have made only the one visit to Timothy, but 'Mr. Rain' would become a regular visitor to both Clifton Castle and Marske Hall. A noted antiquarian, and librarian to the Dean and Chapter of Durham, Revd James Raine (1791-1858) had also been a pupil at Richmond School, and remained a friend of and frequent correspondent with his old mentor James Tate. Furthermore, Raine married the eldest sister of George Peacock, one of Tate's most distinguished 'Invincibles', and they had a son, also Revd James Raine, who became Chancellor of York Minster. The elder Raine founded the Surtees Society, named after his friend Robert Surtees, author of the *History of Durham*, and both Raines edited many of the society's scholarly publications.

Timothy clearly enjoyed the company of both Raines, and James Raine junior would in 1860 publish an important work recording much of the Hutton family's history, largely based on his father's work.[90] On Friday 24 September 1852 Timothy noted: 'Mr. Js. Raine of Durham came to luncheon & stay'd to dinner', and on Tuesday 7 October 1852, 'Mr. Raine Jr. (from Durham) came to lunch [at Marske] & stayed all night.' On Tuesday 6 September 1853 Timothy went to Richmond and 'attended a meeting at the Town Hall, the Architectural Society. Met Mr. Raine & others there.' The following day 'Mr. Raine & his son came to Marske.' These minor variations of spelling are typical of Timothy Hutton's diaries.

Sometimes one or other Raine stayed for several days. On Monday 2 January 1854 'Mr. James Raine jr. came', meeting their mutual old friend Revd Warner Ottley when he called that day. It was Monday 9 January before Timothy noted 'Mr. J. Raine left Clifton.' James Raine senior arrived at Marske on Tuesday 25 September 1855, the following day visiting

89 Greenwell's far greater claim to fame might in some people's eyes be as the inventor of 'Greenwell's Glory', an artificial fly, originally a wet-fly, but later a dry-fly, still popular with anglers hoping to catch brown trout in northern rivers. Although Timothy's diaries do not specifically mention he himself going fly-fishing, he certainly granted permission for other men to use his waters, and so perhaps was able to discuss the merits of the fly with Greenwell.

90 Raine, *Marske.*

Grinton and Marrick churches, before leaving Marske three days later. James Raine junior continued to visit Timothy after the death of the elder Raine in 1858, and the pattern of visiting historic sites continued, as on Wednesday 28 March 1860: 'Took Mr. Raine to see Jervaulx Abbey.' A more personal note was made on Sunday 24 August 1862: 'Mr. Raine went with me to Downholme Church and we received Sacrament.'

MEDICAL MATTERS

Timothy Hutton's diaries contain a modicum of information on medical issues, mainly those concerning incidental events, such as accidents and/or deaths affecting friends and tenants, rather than family members. His own medical concerns mainly occur later in his life. However, there is one period, when Timothy was in his forties, that some unspecified ailment seems to have troubled him. His diary for Friday 19 November 1824 records: 'Mr. Campbell came in the forenoon & put three leeches on my left temple to remove an unpleasant sensation on that side of my head which produced the desired effect.' Again on Wednesday 11 July 1827 'Mr. Campbell was at Clifton in the afternoon & put some leeches on my temples.' Archibald Campbell (*c.*1775-1837) was a surgeon in Bedale, and Timothy's medical man from the 1820s until Campbell's death.

These references to Archibald Campbell in Timothy's diaries may, or may not, be connected with the implications of a letter[91] which James Tate wrote from Richmond to Timothy on 28 March 1827:

> 'My dear Sir, Forgive me expressing the anxiety which I feel in common with many others, in respect of your health and of the very unsatisfactory accounts which we hear of it. So many instances have occurred, within my knowledge, of the fatal effects of letting illness pass on from one stage to another without taking the very best advice and acting upon it; that I cannot help as a friend but beg of you to think of this in time. Every human aid and every thing that human skill and knowledge can do for your relief, God has placed at your command. Is it right then to neglect the means of preserving health; when health itself is one of the talents entrusted to our care? You believe, I know you do, the sacred responsibility under which we live. You have great power to do good: you do not want the inclination. For your own sake then and for the sake of all who are interested in your valuable life, fail not with promptness to take the very best human means for its preservation. I pray God to bless you, and remain affectionately yours, James Tate.'

91 In the library of Clifton Castle in 1944-5 and copied out by Peter Wenham by kind permission of Lady Curzon Howe; copy now in the author's possession.

Archibald Campbell's death was clearly a cause of sadness to Timothy. He recorded in his diary on Monday 13 February 1837: 'Mr. Campbell died at 10 minutes past 3 this morning', and on Wednesday 22nd 'Went to Bedale..... and attended poor Campbell's funeral.... he was buried in the church.' Campbell's successor as Timothy's preferred Bedale surgeon was John Buckle, who first appears in the diaries when he extracted a couple of Timothy's teeth in the late-1830s. There is no further reference to his own health problems until, on 17 September 1844, Timothy noted 'Buckle came to look at my toe and applied caustic to it.'

There are few references to Timothy's eldest brother John's health, although in January 1817 Timothy commented that his wife Elizabeth had stayed with John at Marske as 'He was so very ill.' No further details were forthcoming. Then, in the late-1830s, John's health began to fail. James Tate, writing to John Hutton on 7 August 1839, expresses pleasure that he has heard in a letter from Timothy that John had been as far as Wensley, and in another letter of 21 September that John had been to Croft, presumably to take the waters at the spa there.

Timothy's diaries give no information of the nature of John's illness, before noting his death on 14 August 1841, and funeral on 23rd. However, he obliquely refers to it with the remark on 15 December 1841: 'Mrs. Hutton came from Marske having been upwards of twelve months from Clifton.' Certainly Elizabeth is shown on the 1841 Census as being at Marske Hall and not Clifton Castle, where Timothy was on his own. So it would seem she had moved to Markse Hall to help look after her brother-in-law.

By 1846 Timothy's eyesight was causing him concern. In April of that year, he and John Buckle travelled by train to London to consult with the leading eye surgeon, Benjamin Travers (1783-1858). The comment 'The result was very satisfactory to both of us' is very uninformative! In the summer of 1846, two more teeth were extracted, then in January 1847 Timothy was back in London to see 'Mr. Travers to consult him about my eyes.' On Tuesday 23 February that year he was again in London, and 'Consulted Mr. Alexander Junr.'

Afterwards he went to see the funeral procession of the third Duke of Northumberland, who had died at Alnwick. The availability of railway transport meant that the duke's body was taken to London so that he could be buried in the family vault in Westminster Abbey. Timothy was himself making several train journeys to and from London, for on 25 August 1847 he consulted Dr Prout, the chemist and physician who specialised in the chemistry of digestion, and who also identified different types of kidney stone. There is no follow-up to this entry.

Early in April 1848 Timothy and John Buckle travelled to London and, on Mr Travers's recommendation, went to see 'Mr. Alexander the oculist.' They then sought out lodgings at No. 4 Albermarle Street, and returned home. On Monday 17 April 1848, Timothy, Elizabeth and her sister caught the early train from Northallerton to London, reaching the lodgings at 9p.m. On Tuesday 2 May 'Mr. Alexander operated on my eye about two o'clock in the afternoon.'

This is likely to have been a cataract removal. On Sunday 7 May, 'Mr. Alexander came and removed the bandages from my eyes & all going on well.' The nursing ministrations of the two Chaytor ladies seem to have been helpful, for on Monday 29 May 1848, 'With great satisfaction to myself, Mrs. Hutton & I left London for Clifton where we arrived before nine o'clock.'

The references to the two generations of 'Mr. Alexander' are interesting. The elder was Henry Alexander (died 1859), a London-based general surgeon, and Fellow of the Royal College of Surgeons. He became particularly well-known for his successful cataract operations, and was appointed oculist to Queen Victoria. It would seem that it was he who performed the operation on Timothy. His son, Charles Alexander, not a Fellow of the RCS but who later became assistant surgeon to the Royal Infirmary for Diseases of the Eye, seems to have been the person with whom Timothy had his preliminary consultation. The disadvantage of cataract operations at this time was that no artificial lens was implanted, so the patient had to wear heavy 'pebble' glasses.[92] Timothy's eye operation was duly followed up when he was again in London, on Tuesday 1 October 1850: 'went .... to try to get suited with spectacles.' Timothy is indeed shown wearing spectacles in his photographic portrait taken when he was an old man.

Regrettably, at the end of May 1855, John Buckle's son died. Timothy recorded: 'Call'd upon Mr. & Mrs. Buckle to condole with them on the death of their son William', and he went to Bedale to attend William's funeral on 2 June. Even when over eighty, Timothy makes few references to his health. But on Thursday 5 April 1860 he noted 'Having a troublesome cough I sent for Buckle. He came & dined with me. He did not think much of my cold, but I did, and I have no doubt its bronchitis.' However, the next day, 'My cold became much easier towards morning.' Timothy made no

92 *The Lancet* for 1826 vol. *x* p.419 describes Henry Alexander's remarkable technique for performing cataract operations; Plarr's *Lives of the Fellows of the Royal College of Surgeons* are available online at 'lives@rcseng.ac.uk'.

further mention of his health, and kept his diary up almost to his death in January 1863.

Timothy's diaries chart almost nothing about the health of his wife Elizabeth, so we cannot know whether she enjoyed such a robust constitution that she was never ill, or perhaps suffered so much ill-health that it was an everyday occurrence. There is, however, one entry, made shortly after the death of Timothy's eldest brother John, when both Timothy and Elizabeth seem to have been distraught with grief. On Saturday 4 September 1841, the two of them rode into Richmond after lunch, and Elizabeth suffered a very bad nosebleed, possibly brought on not only by the stress of John's death itself, but also the need to share with Timothy the load of dealing with John's affairs.[93] She was 'so much alarmed with it' that Timothy sent for two Richmond doctors, Henry Blegborough[94] and Richard Bowes[95]. Dr Blegborough's account book[96] shows that he charged his usual consultation fee of two guineas, and a further two guineas for a check-up a few weeks later, both of which were marked 'Paid'. Timothy makes no further reference to the episode, so presumably Elizabeth suffered no more such attacks.

Timothy's earlier diary entries contain a number of interesting references to the medical conditions of others, some reflecting his position as a caring squire. On Wednesday 4 June 1828 his entry records: 'Rode to Masham in the morning to make arrangements respecting the blind boy, going to the Blind Asylum at Liverpool. He may be admitted to the institution on the 1st of July.' The School for the Blind in Liverpool was the first of its kind in the United Kingdom, having been founded in 1791. However, the Masham boy's move there seems not to have been a success, for on Tuesday 9 December that year:

> 'Got a letter from Mr. Ayrton of Chester to inform me that Banks the blind boy was very ill at Liverpool & the doctors recommended he

93 Timothy's diary entry for Thursday 2 September 1841: 'Examined some of my late Brother's Papers & Mrs. Hutton with me.'

94 Henry Blegborough (1779-1865) was the second generation of Richmond medical practitioners of that name, his father being Henry Blegborough (*c*1735-1810) who was Mayor of Richmond when the Green Bridge was rebuilt. The account book survives of Henry Blegborough junior.

95 Richard Bowes (1809-92) was also a member of a Richmond medical dynasty, being one of three brothers who were the third generation of the family to practise in the town. Richard's father, Christopher, had had a career as a naval surgeon on slave ships before returning to live and work in Richmond.

96 Deposited by the author in Richmondshire Museum.

> should be removed from the Asylum. I went to Masham & showed Mr. Burrill the letter, he sent for Mr. Metcalf the overseer & they agreed to send to the boy's parents who are living at Bradford & to desire the father would go to Liverpool to see his son.'

This shows a surprising compassion on behalf of the Guardians of the Poor for a family who had presumably been local and then moved to Bradford for work in the worsted mills there.

Sometimes an accident caused a death, and there seems to be something of a gossipy nature to the diary entries. On 22 November 1819, 'Mr. Robson of Leyburn died. His death was occasioned by a fall from a gig about 3 weeks since, the wheel of which came off & he pitched upon his head. He was on his return from Richmond. Six children left without father or mother.' Three days later: 'I went to Leyburn to attend the funeral of poor Robson. He was buried at Wensley about half past one o'clock.' Leyburn did not then have a parish church, but lay within the much older parish of nearby Wensley. John Robson was a director of the Hutton family bank, and in charge of its Leyburn branch.

Newly-invented agricultural machinery caused accidents, especially to children. Tuesday 30 December 1823: 'A little boy of John Weighell's (my tenant at Clifton) had his arm caught in the thrashing machine. Mr. Campbell was under the necessity of taking the arm off above the elbow.' Guns were a frequent cause of accidents. Saturday 8 November 1828, 'Two pupils of Mr. Others of Middleham, Richard Bruere & Carbonell, were out shooting yesterday near Kirkby Fleetham, when the contents of Carbonell's gun were lodged in the chest of Bruere who died instantly.' Much later, on Sunday 2 March 1851, 'Buckle dined with us and was called away to Harry Webster's who had got a hand damaged with a gun. Mr. Buckle returned to tell us Webster's right hand was so much damaged it was necessary to remove it half up the arm.'

Timothy Hutton was well aware that the poor could not afford doctors' bills, and he often paid for a medical man to attend to one of his tenants. His brother Matthew's Hutton Charity provided dispensaries at Leyburn and Reeth, and for severe cases to be forwarded to hospitals in York, Leeds and Newcastle upon Tyne. Timothy's eldest brother John, by his Will of 1839, bequeathed £100 to William Ware of Leyburn, gentleman. William Ware had succeeded John Robson as the manager of the Leyburn branch of the family's Swaledale and Wensleydale bank.[97] No reason is given for

97 White, *op.cit.*, p.625.

John's generosity to him, but the explanation may be implicit in a reference in Timothy's diary for Friday 18 October 1842: 'Mr. Ware late of Leyburn died in the Asylum at York.' The York Lunatic Asylum, later Bootham Park Hospital, had been established in the 1770s. Presumably Ware had been taken there through the good offices of the Hutton Charity.

EDUCATION OF THE POOR

Although not of such an academic persuasion as his eldest brother John, education was, nevertheless, clearly important to Timothy Hutton. He had begun his own schooling when he was only about five years old, and later put to good use the education he received at Richmond Grammar School and Christ's College, Cambridge. In adult life he enjoyed the company of scholars such as James Tate and James Raine.

There are several examples of Timothy ensuring that those in a less fortunate position had educational opportunities. For example, his £100 bequest to John Robinson, the son of his coachman, mentions that he had already partly educated the boy, and wished him to be able to continue his education. Timothy also took a particularly close interest in the education of William Fisher, the third son and youngest of the four children of Revd John Fisher, rector of Marske, who had died before William had completed his schooling.

The Clifton Castle area had too scattered a population to warrant the founding of a school there. However, Timothy's older brothers, John and Matthew, were both involved in establishing new schools or augmenting the endowments of existing ones to provide for the education of village children. The charity established by Matthew's Will began from 1835 to fund the Hudswell schoolmaster to teach ten extra scholars, and the Marske headteacher an extra fifteen.

The school at Marske had been established about 1820 by John Hutton in an existing building there, and he had paid for the education of the children of his staff and tenants. Not long after the Marske estate came into Timothy's ownership on John's death in 1841, Timothy was overseeing the construction of a new, purpose-built village school. On Friday 3 May 1844 he, along with the Richmond surveyor Christopher Bradley, and Thomas Carter, the stalwart but crusty Marske steward, 'went to set out the place where the School is to be built in the Clints Close.' The building, now a house, is still there, next to the gate on the road which leads to Clints, with its iron-fenced former playground alongside. By the summer of 1856 Timothy had had to find two new schoolmasters for Marske in quick succession, having appointed one at Easter who died suddenly. He also helped provide further education by supporting Mechanics Institutes in Richmond and Masham.

Clifton Castle – stable clock and cupola. The clock was bought second-hand by Timothy Hutton, and still keeps perfect time.

Photo: Guy Carpenter.

Clifton Castle – cantilevered stone staircase. The form, of one flight branching into two, called an imperial staircase, demonstrates John Foss's skill as an architect.

Photo: Guy Carpenter.

Clifton Castle - from a 19th-century two-colour lithograph, showing the original very plain surround to the front door. The two small figures may represent Timothy and Elizabeth Hutton.

In a private collection.

Clifton Castle in September 2019. Note the change to the door surround, made after Timothy Hutton's lifetime.
Photo: Guy Carpenter.

Ruins of medieval Clifton Castle, watercolour over pencil, by George Cuit the elder, dated 1803.

At Clifton Castle. Photo: Guy Carpenter.

Clifton Castle under construction, next to ruins of old castle, watercolour over pencil, by George Cuit the elder, dated 1803.
At Clifton Castle. Photo: Guy Carpenter.

Distant view of Clifton Castle from the River Ure, signed by George Cuitt the younger, dated April 1833. At Clifton Castle. Photo: Guy Carpenter.

A sketch design, unexecuted, by George Cuitt the younger, for a gateway at Clifton Castle. At Clifton Castle. Photo: Guy Carpenter.

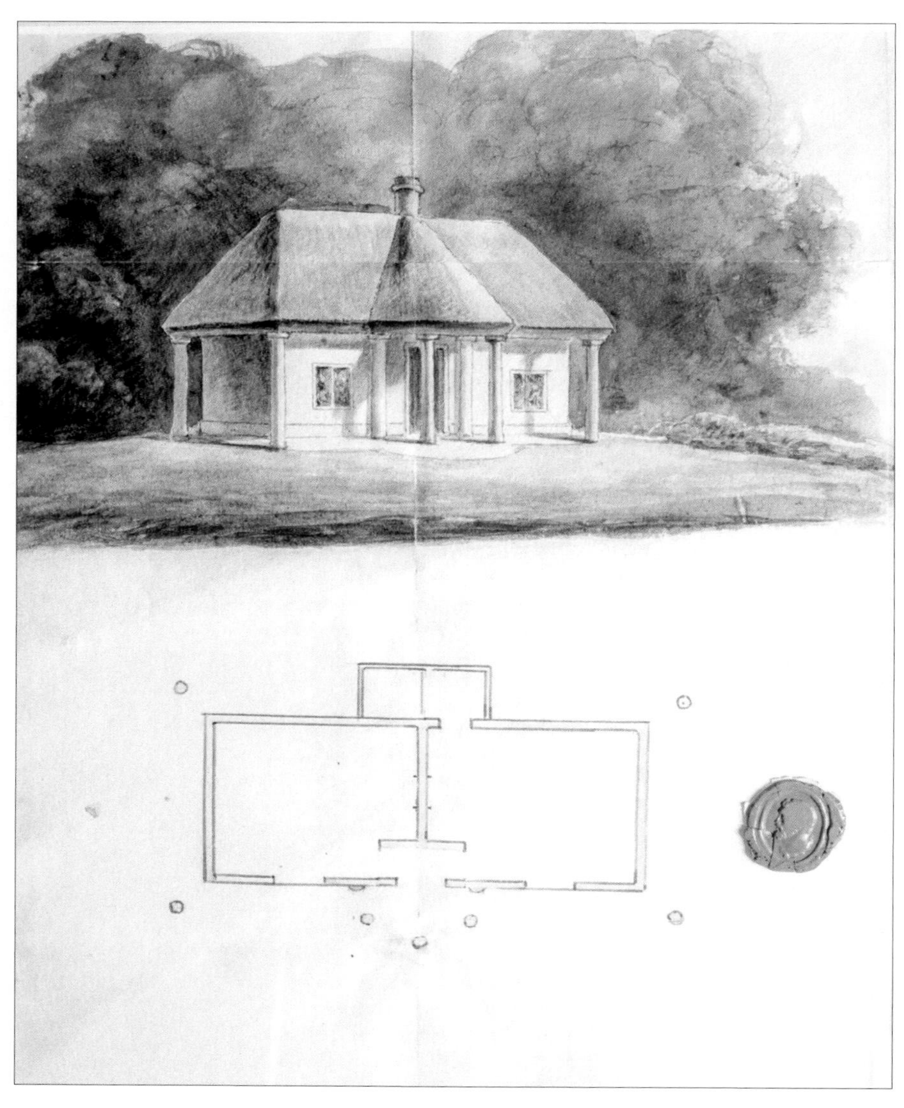

A sketch design, unexecuted, by George Cuitt the younger, for a gate lodge at Clifton Castle.
At Clifton Castle. Photo: Guy Carpenter.

Contemporary portrait of Matthew Hutton (c.1525-1606), who brought the Hutton family to Swaledale. The most distinguished of Timothy Hutton's ancestors, Matthew was Archbishop of York 1595-1606, and Lord President of the Council in the North 1596-99. This oil painting hangs in the palace of the Archbishop of York. The inscription in the bottom left-hand corner reads Matthw. Hutton A.BP.1594, presumably the date he was appointed, rather than when he took up the office.

Courtesy of the Office of the Archbishop of York.

The elaborate bed Timothy Hutton commissioned for Clifton Castle from a London cabinetmaker c.1825, now in the State Bedroom display at Temple Newsam House. The hangings were replaced in 1896.

Courtesy of Leeds Museums and Art Galleries.

Whitaker's History of Richmondshire, vol II, (1822), detail of spine of the copy which belonged to John Hutton. He has had it bound to match other books in his library at Marske Hall. Below the title is embossed the crest of the Hutton family's coat of arms.

In a private collection. Photo: Guy Carpenter.

Timothy and Elizabeth's Hutton's pew in Downholme Church, since moved from family chapel to rear of church.

Photo: Guy Carpenter.

Downholme Church, 1863 hatchment from Timothy Hutton's funeral, showing the Hutton coat of arms impaling that of the Chaytor family. The all-black background indicates that both he, and his wife Elizabeth, had died.

Photo: Guy Carpenter.

Downholme Church, 1874 hatchment from John Timothy D'Arcy Hutton I's funeral, showing the Hutton coat of arms impaling that of his wife, Emily Lamb. Her coat of arms includes lambs! Only the background on his side is black, indicating that Emily was still alive when he died.

Photo: Guy Carpenter.

Distant view of Halfpenny House. The building on the camera side of the road is the brewhouse built by Timothy Hutton in 1832.

Photo: Guy Carpenter.

Monument in St Mary's Church, Richmond to Sir Timothy Hutton d.1629 and his wife Elizabeth née Bowes d.1625. The couple are shown as kneeling portrait effigies. Below are their numerous offspring.
Photo: Guy Carpenter.

Distant view of Walburn Hall.
Photo: Guy Carpenter.

SPORTING ACTIVITIES

Typically of a country gentleman of his time, Timothy Hutton spent a lot of time watching or participating in sporting activities. Some, such as cricket and horse racing, are unexceptional today, others were acceptable at the time but seem to us even more barbaric than the view many people now hold about fox-hunting.

To start with those which are not controversial. The diaries make two references to cricket matches. On Thursday 1 July 1830, 'Mr. Peirse, Mr. Clarke & self rode [from Thimbleby] to see a cricket match betwixt Yarm & Thirsk, the latter won.' A somewhat grander event took place on Tuesday 29 September 1857, 'A Crickit match. Richmond against all England this day at Richmond.' Attendance at archery meetings is mentioned at Swinton on 5 August 1836, at Spennithorne on 19 July 1838, again at Swinton on 2 September 1840, at York on 25 June 1845, and at Bedale on 22 July 1852.

Timothy seems not to have kept racehorses himself, but there are references to him going to see horses being trained in Middleham. On five occasions between 1849 and 1851 Timothy, accompanied by various friends, went to see the horses being exercised on Middleham Moor, and once went on afterwards to visit the Spigot Lodge stables.

Two horse races are mentioned. One, probably the most celebrated contest ever in the history of British racing, took place on Tuesday 13 May 1851: 'The great match at York, the Flying Dutchman & Voltigeur, won by the Flying Dutchman. Three of my men went to see the Race.' The second was on Wednesday 17 September 1856: 'From York we went to Doncaster to see the St. Leger run for. Expected to see Ellington win & to my great disappointment he was not placed, he might be 5 or 6.' 'Ellington', sired by 'Flying Dutchman', and trained in Middleham by Thomas Dawson, was owned by Admiral Harcourt of Swinton Park. The horse had won The Derby earlier that year, admittedly on a very slow course that had defeated the other contestants, but that was why the expectations had been so high a few months later. The only other mention of horse racing is on 6 April 1853, when Timothy went to Wensley to see a steeplechase.

There are surprisingly few references to angling. The Clifton estate included riparian rights on the river Ure, and on several occasions Timothy allowed other people to enjoy his water, especially early in the trout-fishing season. For example, on Tuesday 13 April 1813 Timothy 'Got a note from the Duke of Leeds to ask permission to angle at Clifton, which I granted to his Grace & any of his friends.' Timothy's close friend the artist George Cuitt was a keen angler, and on Monday 21 April 1823 'Mr. Cuitt fished up to Clifton. He dined with us.' Much later, on Monday 27 May 1861, Timothy allowed Christopher Lonsdale Bradley, the son of his land agent, to fish, he 'caught some very fine trout.'

Timothy was party to what is now a much less forgivable river sport, the nineteenth-century pursuit of otter hunting with otter hounds. There are six references to the activity in the diaries, and fortunately, to modern eyes, all seem to have been unsuccessful.[98] Unsurprisingly there are several references to foxhounds and fox hunting, and various members of the local gentry are recorded as calling while hunting. Many such meetings were probably those of the Bedale Hunt, which had commissioned a picture of its members in 1840. Timothy did not keep a pack of foxhounds himself, but he allowed hunting on his land, particularly by Lord Darlington of Raby Castle, a fervent proponent of the sport[99] who hunted frequently.

Sometimes people came to grief while hunting, as on Friday 26 December 1823: 'Poor Marmaduke Theakston drown'd in the River Tees in attempting to follow the Hurworth Hounds. A similar accident happened on the same day to Peter Walburn in the river Ure in trying to follow Lord Darlington's hounds.' Marmaduke Theakston's body was eventually found, and taken from the River Tees, on 5 January 1824. A fatality also occured on Wednesday 23 January 1828, when Timothy's diary records: 'Col. Elsley fell dead from his horse when out hunting near Ripon.'

Another activity involving dogs was the coursing of hares using greyhounds. On Wednesday 18 February 1824, Timothy rode to Hornby Castle, the seat of his sporting friend the Duke of Leeds, to join a party for greyhound coursing there. He unexpectedly gained a bonus from the visit: 'Brought home some coal which was found in sinking a well in the stable yard at Hornby. The seam was about 18 inches thick.' Timothy's neighbour,

98 Friday 7 May 1841: 'The Duke of Leeds ...... went otter hunting. They found one but did not get him'; Tuesday 10 May 1842: 'Major Straubenzie [of Spennithorne] call'd: they had been after the otter hounds'; Tuesday 2 May 1843: 'The otter hounds were at Clifton'; Monday 19 April 1847: 'Mr. Lomax here with his otter dogs. They had an otter in the boat dub most of the day but did not kill him'; Wednesday 21 April 1847: 'The otter dogs passed to Masham and afterwards returned to try the River Cover'; Thursday 22 April 1847: 'The otter hounds passed down the river in the afternoon and I followed them to the Mill. They went no further than Masham, and came up the river again and gave over at Brigwath being unsuccessful all the day.'

99 oxforddnb.com, William Henry Vane.

William Danby of Swinton Park, also hosted hare coursing meetings. Like other such sporting events, a day in the field was often followed by a gentlemen's dinner.

The sport of greyhound racing developed from coursing and, by December 1829, Timothy had acquired a white greyhound bitch called 'Fly', which he 'tried' at Hornby, where there was an important greyhound breeding tradition. The following December, 'Fly' won the first race but lost the second. By Thursday 1 November 1832, Timothy was one of the two stewards for a coursing race at Leyburn, which was followed by a dinner at the King's Head Inn there, hosted by the publican Richard Coultman. The Leyburn Coursing Club's annual dinner in the first week of November became a regular fixture in Timothy's diary.

Another regular activity was shooting, and various birds were targeted. Grouse were then, as now, shot from the 'Glorious' 12th of August each year, but in Timothy's time the season only lasted until the end of that month. The number of birds shot was much smaller than today, as the heather moorlands of North Yorkshire were not 'keepered' until the mid-nineteenth century. Timothy records several 'bags' as consisting of just two birds, and '8½ brace before 10 o'clock' was clearly unusual. Nevertheless, the birds could be quite a size, and one of 26½ ounces is mentioned in 1833. Sometimes Timothy recorded the total number of birds bagged during the grouse-shooting season, the largest seems to have been 21½ brace in 1836.

At the time of Timothy's early diaries, it seems the tradition was for the gun party to dine out in the open, and sleep in a convenient barn, as they were too far away to return home at night. But later Timothy had more comfortable arrangements on his Walburn estate. What is now Boston Farm, on Ministry of Defence land, became a somewhat grander house, and the Huttons would go and stay there for the grouse-shooting season.

Timothy and Elizabeth took up residence by 11th August each year, the servants having gone ahead earlier in the month to get the house ready. James Tate, writing to Timothy in late July 1835, opens the letter with 'It is now sometime to the day which carries Mrs. Hutton & yourself to the rural retreat at Boston in Downholmshire.'[100] Sometimes Timothy's diaries record an incident from the shooting season which happened while at Walburn. For example, on 17 August 1837: 'Out shooting & got two brace. Had the bad luck to lose my watch on the Moor.'

By the 1850s Timothy's eyesight was deteriorating, which meant he no longer joined the shoot himself, and on 12 August 1852 recorded that his

100 Typescript of original letter in the author's possession.

keeper had killed eight brace. On 12 August 1856 his friend, Charles Carter, who had retired from service in the East India Company,[101] and was related by marriage to the Chaytor family and often stayed at Clifton Castle and Marske, 'shot 9 brace and a hare at Skelton' on the Marske estate. Carter had a son, also Charles, who was also involved in India, and on Tuesday 3 January 1843, Timothy 'Rode to Bedale and met Carter and his son Charles at the Bank where I made arrangement to advance £500 for Charles's outfit to India.'

Later in the autumn there was pheasant shooting, also woodcock (2 March 1805), duck, snipe and partridge. Occasionally there were accidents caused by guns. The diary entry for Sunday 30 December 1827 reads: 'Sent to Downholme to enquire if the report was true that Anty. Croft's son was shot which is too true. It was owing to a double barrelled gun he was shooting with & in getting over a fence one of his barrels had gone off.' Anthony Croft was one of Timothy's tenant farmers at Downholme, and young William was aged only sixteen.[102] The family would suffer further tragedies, for Anthony Croft and his wife Margaret also lost their daughter Mary at the age of seventeen in 1835, and their son Thomas in 1839 aged twenty-six. Anthony Croft survived his offspring until he died in 1850 at the age of eighty.[103]

Each year around 10 May there was rook shooting, to reduce the number of young birds, the species being a threat to arable crops. The tally was six or seven dozen. A regrettable entry was made on 9 February 1823, when there was heavy snow on the ground: 'Walk'd to the Lodge to see a wild swan shot. Mr. Edwd. Carter sent [it] to Clervaux. It was shot at Theakston by one of Mr. Carter's servants. Mr. Clervaux intends having the swan stuffed.' This Carter family were the squires of Theakston, a village to the east of Clifton near the modern A1(M) road. Clervaux Chaytor, brother to Elizabeth Hutton, and his family were living in Timothy's former home, Clifton Lodge. Clervaux's wife was Edward John Carter's sister.

101 So described when staying with Timothy at Clifton Castle the night of the 1861 census.

102 Downholme parish register, buried on 31 December 1827.

103 Tombstone inscription in Downholme churchyard.

FOOD AND LIQUOR

Timothy's diaries record his many attendances at formal dinners, and he clearly enjoyed such events. He took delight in noting the numbers present, and often the names of the people with whom he dined. From what can be inferred of his character, it is likely that he particularly valued the interesting company they provided, including perhaps the thought-provoking opinions of fellow diners, and news they brought from other locations. His weight inevitably reflected so many large meals, and he observed in July 1832, when he was fifty-two, that he weighed fifteen stones eleven pounds, and his brother John sixteen stones four pounds.

Presumably he enjoyed his food, though he hardly ever gives any information on what fare was provided, or what he thought of it. A rare exception occurred when he was in Liverpool in July 1841, for what he describes as the Great Agricultural Meeting. He attended the cattle show, and was unimpressed by the food: 'A very bad dinner, the meat was not sweet.' However, this is hardly surprising as he says nearly three thousand people were at the dinner!

There is also little information about the family's everyday food, he noting only special or seasonal delicacies. Some seem rather surprising. On Sunday 17 November 1822 he 'Wrote to Mr. George Wise in Devonshire to thank him for a box of apples.' Were Devonshire apples particularly prized? Conversely, something that would be very rare today is noted, as on Tuesday 30 April 1833: 'Kit [Wilson] & I crossed the river to look for morels [a rare and much sought-after type of mushroom], we only got 17.'

Other produce was from the countryside, as might to be expected. On Friday 16 May 1823, 'Mr. Marmaduke Theakston sent his servant over to Clifton with a fine Tees salmon.' Venison is mentioned a few times, such as on Saturday 23 October 1819, 'Had a haunch of venison to dinner', and on Tuesday 2 December 1845, 'C. Mudd shot a buck.' These deer were presumably from the family's own estates, as on 28 December 1860, when Timothy and Elizabeth were stuck at Clifton due to heavy snow, 'Sent Thomas to Leyburn for a Doe killed at Marske.'

Sometimes the venison came from further afield. On Monday 26 September 1842, while he was at Marske, 'His Grace the Duke of Leeds sent me a haunch of Red Deer venison which I had dressed for dinner.'

Even this may not have been from the duke's Hornby Castle estate, for on Thursday 26 September 1844, 'C. Mudd ...... brought a haunch of venison [to Marske] that arrived at Clifton from the Duke of Leeds from Scotland.' Again on Friday 6 October 1854, 'We had for dinner a haunch of venison the Duke of Leeds sent to me from Scotland which proved excellent & much liked by the party.'

Game birds seem to have been eaten regularly, but are implicit more in connection with their shooting than as food. However, Timothy was able to provide, for the Richmond Freemasons' dinner on 6 October 1837, grouse which had been shot on his Walburn estate. The birds would have been suitably well hung following their shooting that August.

The diaries contain far more references to liquor than to food, although Timothy clearly did not approve of those who could not hold their drink in a gentlemanly fashion. His diary entries are rarely critical of people, but on Monday 11 March 1805 he noted, 'Mr. Kirkby came at half past ten o'clock and very much in liquor, it destroy'd the pleasure of the evening.' Revd Thomas Barker Kirkby, an old boy of Richmond School, had been the perpetual curate of Downholme since 1803. Quite a young man on his appointment, it would seem his proclivity to drink affected his health, for he died in 1808.

There are many diary entries concerning wines and spirits, but Timothy doesn't tell us whether they were for regular consumption at Clifton Castle, or were for special occasions such as birthday parties. Sometimes he gives details of how they were to be stored, and in most cases he says from whom he bought them, and where the supplier was based. On 10 May 1814 he 'Got a pipe[104] of wine from Lancaster.' Lancaster was then an important river port, particularly for trade with the West Indies. Timothy spent most of the morning of 8 August 1815 in his cellar, bottling off a pipe of Madeira, and he spent a snowy morning on 9 November 1816 in the wine cellar arranging the wines and spirits.

'Some wine' costing £44 was collected from Mrs Lucas in Ripon by Dodsworth, the estate brewer, in June 1816. On Saturday 24 January 1818 Timothy 'Wrote to John Baines in London to send me half a Pipe of Port Wine from Mr. Soulby's', which arrived in bottles on 25 February. It didn't last long, unless he was laying it down: on 9 March 1818 he 'Gave Mr. Knowles (of Lancaster) an order for a pipe of port wine.'

104 A measure of wine which varied with the type of wine and where it had come from. It was a large quantity like a barrel.

On 18 March 1824 Timothy noted that 'Mr. James Wray of Leyburn call'd. I paid him for some brandy he sent me.' Wray was a businessman who traded in various commodities as well as spirits, and was also an investor in Swaledale lead mines. Timothy was to note in his diary on Tuesday 8 April 1845 that he had died.

The brandy was soon followed by some sherry, for on 16th June that year Timothy 'Wrote to John Spence of London. Sent a cheque for £41 6s 6d for 12 doz. of sherry he sent me.' On 16 December 1827 he wrote to Mr Miles of Yarm [then an important port on the River Tees] '& sent a draft for £37 6s for some wine he has procured for me at Frankford [*sic*] called Hockeimer' [a dry white wine, originally imported from Hochheim on the River Main in Germany]. This arrived, in a cask of continental measure called an auhm, in February the following year, but it took till 28 April for Timothy to get it bottled. For this task, the Richmond wine merchant George Smurthwaite travelled over to Clifton. Smurthwaite's skills must have impressed Timothy, for he would subsequently fulfil orders to supply wines and spirits, as in January 1833 when he was asked to supply Clifton Castle with a butt [a large cask] of sherry. Richmond, being a town of some sophistication, provided a market for discerning grocers and wine merchants, and also such ancillary occupations as cork cutters.

Professional bottling was clearly an expense additional to the purchase of wines and spirits. Occasionally Timothy bought such from a fellow landowner who had already seen to the bottling, such as in May 1832, when six dozen bottles of wine were bought at a sale at [Constable] Burton Hall.

Once Timothy had taken over the Marske estate after his brother's death, he needed to keep the cellars of Marske Hall stocked as well as those of Clifton Castle. Smurthwaite placed, first five dozen, and then twenty dozen, bottles of sherry in the Marske cellars in May 1853 and October 1854. Port continued to be ordered from further afield, a pipe from Mr Newbery of London in May 1845, and fifty dozen bottles from Mr Volans of York in October 1848, 'which I got packed' in the cellar.

Despite being unimpressed by the taste of whisky on his first Scottish tour in 1803, 'whiskey' found favour with Timothy for a few years from the late 1820s. On Saturday 17 May 1828, 'Mr. James Robson came & dined with me. I paid him for the whiskey Mr. Clarke & I got, 10 gallons each, £18 15s 0d.' On Thursday 17 June 1830, 'Got a letter from Newcastle to inform me the whiskey had arrived there (from Robert Aitken Esqr. of Glasgow) & to say that 1/- per gallon new duty would have to be paid on it. I rode to Bedale to request Henry Glaister [his old solicitor confidant] would send to his friend in Newcastle to pay the money.' The consignment arrived on 20 July, and, on 30 August, 'James Robson came early in the morning to assist in bottling the whiskey. The whiskey was short two gallons – 78'. Presumably there should have been eighty gallons.

There is only one reference to champagne. On Tuesday 15 October 1861, the day before Timothy's eighty-second birthday, 'Mr. G. Smurthwaite came & his man arrived with qu'r. pipe of port & some champagne.'

FREEMASONRY

Timothy Hutton was an active freemason, joining Richmond's Lennox Lodge shortly before he came of age in 1800. He served as master of the lodge in 1822, 1823, 1825 and 1830. His diaries record the events he attended, and also his progression to higher ranks. The first such entry is dated Thursday 27 December 1810: 'St. John's Day. Dined at Richmond with the Free Masons.' This was the feast day of St John the Apostle and Evangelist, and the Richmond lodge made it their main annual meeting and dinner, so it occurs many times in the diaries.

The present lodge in Newbiggin had not yet been built, and in Timothy's time the freemasons usually met in the King's Head Hotel, often referred to by him as Yarker's after the then landlord, Michael Yarker, himself a freemason. So we have on Monday 27 December 1819, 'Rode to Richmond. Dined at Yarkers with the Freemasons, 32 sat down to dinner.' Sometimes the business part of a lodge meeting was held in Richmond Town Hall.

A different sort of entry occured on Sunday 14 May 1820: 'At the Freemasons Lodge where I was made a Royal Arch Mason.' On St John's Day 1821 Timothy noted 'Mr. Foss & self rode to Richmond. Dined at the Free Masons Lodge – St. John – 32 dined there. Slept at my mother's in Frenchgate.' John Foss, the Richmond architect who had been working at Clifton, was also a freemason. Sometimes more detail is given about the events. In 1822, 'Dined at the King's Head, Richmond, the day of our annual feast – St. John – the Lennox Lodge of Freemasons. We got down to dinner at 3 & broke up at 10 or a little past.'

Some years something special happened. In 1824:

> 'The Festival of St. John. Went in procession with the Freemasons to church. We dined afterwards together at the King's Head, about 50 sat down to dinner. Lord Dundas honoured us with his company, he is Provincial Grand Master. I was requested to take the chair by the Master, William Richardson, when Lord Dundas left us.'

The presence of so prominent a local freemason had apparently increased the attendance. A visit to Richmond by a royal freemason also led to an unusual diary entry on Friday 26 October 1827:

> '[At] Richmond to attend a meeting of the Freemasons & afterwards joined the members of the lodge in procession to meet the Duke of Sussex our Grand Master. We return'd to the Lodge & there had the honour of receiving his Royal Highness & after I had welcomed His Royal Highness to the Lodge, Mr. Lockwood [the Rector of Richmond] read the address. I went afterwards to the Town Hall where I dined with the Mayor & Corporation &c &c.'

Another 'one-off' masonic event occurred on Thursday 15 July 1830: 'Went to Richmond to attend the Freemasons Lodge; being the day of the late King's funeral the brethren went in procession to church accompanied by the Mayor & Aldermen &c. The masons dined at the King's Head.'

The St John's Day event was occasionally re-scheduled: Monday 29 December 1833, 'Went to Richmond to dine with the Free Masons. Saturday was our anniversary but being the market day, the feast was heald [*sic*] this day.' One might expect that snow would often affect December meetings, but the only mention of this seems to have been for the St John's Day meeting in 1836: 'on account of the weather there was only a thin attendance of members.'

Not all the freemasony events Timothy attended took place in Richmond. On Thursday 21 October 1830, he 'Went to the Freemason's Lodge [at York] & there met Lord Dundas, the Provincial Grand Master for the North & East Ridings. Was there appointed Junr. Warden. We all dined at the Falcon Inn.' Another meeting attended further afield, when Timothy was rising up the masonic 'ladder', was on Thursday 22 October 1835 when he was in Hull: '[At] twelve o'clock went to the Free Mason's Lodge ----- I was appointed Deputy Provincial Grand Master by our Provincial Grand Master, the Hon. T. Dundas. We dined at the Humber Lodge at five o'clock.'

Several members of the Dundas family held senior office in freemasonry, including Lawrence who became the first Earl of Zetland in 1838, although he did not live long to enjoy that title. Timothy noted on Monday 11 March 1839 'Rode to Ask [*sic*] Hall to present an address from the Humber Lodge of Free Masons to the Earl of Zetland on the death of his father.' The second Earl was also a keen freemason. On Friday 27 December 1839, '[Dined at Richmond] at the Freemasons Lodge. Mr. George Smurthwaite Master, but Lord Zetland took the Chair.'

The enthusiasm for travelling hither and thither for masonic events eventually waned. Tuesday 15 September 1840: 'Answered a letter from the Earl of Zetland who had written to request that I would attend a

Provincial Grand Lodge at Beverley on the 22nd October which I declined on account of the distance.' Sometimes the Provincial Grand Lodge met more conveniently in Richmond, partly to accommodate Lord Zetland. On Friday 30 September 1842, 'To Richmond to the Provincial Grand Lodge of Masons where I dined.'

However, the coming of the railways put York within easier reach. Wednesday 27 September 1843, 'Left Clifton before six in the morning for Northallerton Station & got to York per railway at half past 8. Met Lord Zetland at the Savings Bank Room where we held a Provincial meeting of Freemasons. I left York & got home about nine o'clock [in the evening].' Of course, unseasonal weather could still disrupt plans, as on Wednesday 18 October 1848: 'Snow.... prevented me going to York to attend the provincial Grand Lodge.'

On Saturday 27 December 1845 Timothy particularly enjoyed Lennox Lodge's annual St John's Day dinner: 'To Richmond..... at the Free Masons Lodge, twenty five sat down to dinner. Lord Zetland in the chair being the Grand Master of England. Harland Master of the Lennox Lodge. The most agreeable party I ever met on the occasion.' John Harland from Swaledale was an old friend, and colleague in Timothy's lead-mining ventures.

Provincial Grand Lodge meetings could bring a larger number of people together. Tuesday 8 November 1849: 'Attended the lodge of Freemasons at the Town Hall [in Richmond] a provincial grand lodge. Dined with the brethren at the King's Head, about 80 sat down to dinner.' Not only were Timothy's friends John Foss and John Harland fellow freemasons, the records of Lennox Lodge show that John Clarke, the Clifton Castle coachman from 1806, joined in 1820. However, he was proposed, not by Timothy, but by Michael Yarker of the King's Head, for whom Clarke later worked.

MERCERS, GROCERS AND HABERDASHERS

Another Richmond institution of which Timothy Hutton was for a time an ardent member was the Company of Mercers, Grocers and Haberdashers. One of the thirteen ancient trade and craft guilds in the town, it was the one most closely associated with the merchant class. Its archives survive in an unbroken record from 1580. As the guild system in general declined in the early-nineteenth century, most of the Richmond companies of which records survive gradually wound down, until only the Mercers, Grocers and Haberdashers remained. Another guild, the Fellmongers, a marriage of skinners and glovers, was refounded in 1982.

'Timothy Hutton Esquire' was admitted to the Mercers, Grocers and Haberdashers on 4 January 1810. By this date there were few practising mercers, grocers or haberdashers joining, by having either served an apprenticeship, or by patrimony (being the eldest son of a member). So most new members were those from outside those trades, and were admitted by redemption (paying for the privilege). Timothy handed over the money for his redemption in the customary two sums – £1 6s 8d to become a member of the company, and 3s 4d to the mayor to become a freeman of the town.

The first time the company features in the diary is on Thursday 11 November 1813: 'Mrs. Hutton and I went in the carriage to Richmond. Dined at the King's Head with the Mercers, Grocers & Haberdashers Company.' Elizabeth must have had other activities to enjoy in Richmond, for the Mercers' company had, in effect, become a gentlemen's dining club. Timothy, of course, seems to have liked nothing better than dining clubs. He had a somewhat speedy rise up through the membership, recording on Thursday 8 January 1818 'I dined with the Mercers Company & was appointed Warden of the Company for this year.' The warden was the leading member for a year, and presided at the business, and dinners.

The membership of the company was fairly small at this time, not much more than a dozen, and on Thursday 4 January 1821 Timothy noted, 'The day fine. Walk'd to Richmond [from Marske]. Dined at Yarkers. A meeting of the Mercers Company. Ten of the Company sat down to dinner.' The timing of a Mercers' Dinner was different from those of the present day, being not in the evening. According to the diary entry for Thursday 4 November 1824: 'Dined at the King's Head at 4 o'clock with the Mercers

Company.' This timing meant that occasionally Timothy attended both the mercers and the freemasons on the same day. So, on Thursday 4 November 1830: 'Set off for Richmond at half past twelve o'clock. Dined with the Mercers' Company, Mr. G. Mitchell, warden. In the evening at the Freemasons Lodge.'

Membership of the company increased as the nineteenth century went on. On Thursday 14 November 1833 Timothy recorded, 'Went to Richmond & dined with the Mercers Company of which I am a member. 17 dined.' This is the last mention of the company in the diaries, and Timothy's name is not included among later lists of attendance. Timothy's eldest brother John was also admitted to the company. This was in 1838, so much later than his younger brother, and John took no part in its activities.

PART FOUR: INVESTMENTS

Roads and Railways

Lead Mining

Banking

ROADS AND RAILWAYS

Timothy Hutton's diary entries provide almost no information about his income, which must have been considerable to support not only his lifestyle but also his building programmes. Where he was involved in activities which had the potential to generate income, it is unclear whether this or a more philanthropic aim was primary. His regular attendance at meetings of the Highways Sessions, by which the Justices of the Peace maintained 'the king's highway' at county level, was certainly not profitable. As a local landowner he was concerned with the roads in his part of North Yorkshire, and most meetings were held in Bedale, usually in October.

Timothy was also involved with several turnpike road trusts, which, established by individual Acts of Parliament, greatly improved an existing road or created a new one. Such trusts were mainly administered by the landowners through whose land the route passed, and these had the potential to generate at least some income.

Improved roads meant that regular coach services could run more efficiently, and Timothy notes the start of new services, such as on Monday 15 May 1815: 'A coach from York to Lancaster by Masham started this day.' Lancaster was then an important port on the west coast, and was the destination of a turnpike road from Richmond begun in 1750, and of which he and John Hutton were later trustees.

Various sections of the Great North Road had been 'turnpiked', and Timothy attended trustees' meetings at Catterick Bridge where several schemes converged, including the northbound Piercebridge and southbound Boroughbridge sections. He gives the names of his fellow trustees present on Tuesday 3 December 1811: 'Sir R. Hildyard, Col. Crowe, Col. Strawbenzie, Major Cradock, Messrs. Alderson, Booth, Robson, Redshaw, Wycliffe, Gale, Stapleton, Blackburn, Leaf & self.'

Some interesting details of improvements, both implemented and aborted, for the Catterick Bridge area appear in the diaries. On Thursday 15 May 1821 the trustees met 'Mr. McAdam to receive his report of the road. We were all very much pleased with Mr. McAdam's frankness and candour.' A few years later there was even talk of constructing an early railway in the Catterick area. On Wednesday 23 March 1825, Timothy

'Got a letter from Mr. Wyvill respecting a meeting intended to be held at Catterick Bridge on ye 6 April to get a rail road to Catterick Bridge.'

On the day of the meeting Timothy recorded, 'Went to Catterick Bridge; took Mr. Pulleine with me from Crakehall. We attended a meeting of gentlemen in the neighbourhood respecting a rail road from Croft to Catterick Bridge. The first day of the Catterick Bridge races.' Doubtless the lure of the races ensured a good turnout! The gentlemen must have been sufficiently enthusiastic to form a committee, for on Thursday 4 August that year Timothy 'Rode in the gig [to Catterick Bridge] to attend a meeting of the committee of the Rail Road.' The idea did not, however, proceed.

There was also a Masham & Thirsk turnpike trust, the party of its directors that dined at Masham on Thursday 8 August 1816 being, 'Mr. Danby, Mr. Monson, Col. Pulleine, Col. Serjeantson, Mr. Milbanke, Mr. Clarke, Mr. Harrison, Mr. Wrather, Mr. H. Morton, Mr. Heslop, Mr. Ibbetson, Mr. Baines, Col. Dalton, Mr. W. Barnes, Mr. Brown & self.'

In the 1830s there was a scheme to make a turnpike road between Richmond and Reeth. The old route, via Marske, was steep and somewhat tortuous for wheeled traffic. This was one of the roads where an almost entirely new route had to be devised; it followed a relatively level valley-bottom path beside and newly crossing the River Swale. A spur back to Marske was also constructed. The old route remained in use by the caravans of packhorses bringing Swaledale lead down the dale.

The first meeting of the new trust was held in the King's Head Hotel in Richmond on Saturday 8 August 1835, with Sheldon Cradock of Hartforth in the chair. A month later another meeting was held in Leyburn, as another spur would connect the new road to Wensleydale by joining the Richmond to Lancaster turnpike road at Halfpenny House near Barden. Further meetings took place in the September, and by March 1836 there was a bill in Parliament. Officers of the trust were appointed in June, and by August, when at Boston for the grouse shooting, Timothy could ride to see construction work starting. The engineer for the Richmond to Reeth turnpike road was the Richmond land surveyor Thomas Bradley, who with his son Christopher would become a close friend of Timothy's. The clerk to the turnpike road trustees was Ottiwell Tomlin, then the town clerk of Richmond.

For the next few months, when he was over at Marske, Timothy, sometimes with John, went to see how work on the new road was progressing. On Saturday 7 October 1837 Timothy was able to walk from Richmond to see the new bridge to take the road across the river Swale under construction at Lownethwaite. By the summer of 1839 Timothy could return from Marske by the 'New Road.' Once the road was functioning, annual accounts had to be received, and the toll gates let.

On Tuesday 14 January 1845 he notes, 'Mr. John B. Langhorn [of Reeth] came to Marske to get my signature to a paper respecting an application to Parliament for an amended Act for the Reeth Road.' It is not clear whether this amendment was proceeded with. By this date the diaries are more concerned with proposals for railways, but there were still a few local roads and bridges to attend to.

The availability of bridges made a huge difference to the efficiency of roads. A poor or weak bridge could necessitate a lengthy detour, and a new bridge could considerably shorten journey times. Timothy was obviously very sympathetic towards the efforts of those trying to provide bridges. An unusual entry occurred in April 1829, when he noted that the trustees of the Bedale Savings Bank had decided to donate money, subscribed by the neighbourhood towards the bank's establishment, and which was no longer needed, towards building and finishing two bridges at Bedale and Crakehall.

More often it was his own money he contributed. On Saturday 22 August 1829, when Timothy was staying at Boston for his annual grouse shooting, he noted, 'Mr. Cockcroft of Middleham call'd to request that I would subscribe towards a bridge to be thrown across the Ure at Leyburn Wath. Engaged to give £10.'

This new bridge, designed by the architects Hansom and Welch, was a suspension bridge, following those built by the Scottish engineer Thomas Telford to great acclaim in Wales, over the Menai Straits and the River Conway. The Middleham example was not so successful, and failed shortly after completion when, it is said, somewhat surprisingly, a herd of cattle crossing the bridge 'fell into step'. Marching armies are always ordered to 'break step' on a bridge to avoid vibrations causing shock waves through the structure. The Middleham Bridge was patched up, but the deck was later replaced by a cast-iron carriageway, although the idiosyncratic castellated pylons remain. It was still in its original form when, on Friday 25 October 1839, Timothy noted that he had been to Wensley and returned home by the 'Suspension Bridge.'

A further £10 was donated towards another new bridge in Wensleydale, at Constable Burton, in May 1830, and Timothy was able to visit it on 4 April 1831. After Timothy had succeeded his brother as squire of Marske, he built a new road up the valley of the Marske Beck to the hamlet of Skelton.

Thomas Bradley's son Christopher was the surveyor for this project, which was planned in 1845. The road, and a bridge over a steep little gill, were constructed in the autumn of 1846, and on his sixty-seventh birthday on 16 October that year, Timothy obviously visited the works, and was pleased to note in his diary, 'The masons got the arch for the bridge turned.'

The later years of Timothy's diaries concern various railway lines, some only projected, others completed, many of which he did invest in. The first entry mentioning this innovative method of travel, other than the aborted idea for Catterick Bridge, was Saturday 26 January 1833: 'Left Manchester at 8 o'clock by the Railway and arrived in Liverpool before ten [o'clock]. 32 miles, we went at the rate of 25 miles in the hour.' This noteworthy speed was exceeded the following day on their return to Manchester 'on one part we went at 30 miles.' The return journey to Leeds the next day by stage coach seemed very slow by comparison! On Monday 28th, he and his man caught the 5.30a.m. 'Telegraph' coach in Leeds, which dropped them at Leeming Bar on the Great North Road, and they walked the rest of the way home, arriving at one o'clock.

The Liverpool and Manchester Railway, the first railway to be double-tracked along its entire thirty-five-miles length and to use steam power exclusively, had only opened in 1830. Timothy was so intrigued by this novel adventure that he recorded in detail the fares: 'From Bedale to Ripon, one in & one outside [the coach] 7s; Ripon to Leeds 14s 6d; To Manchester £1 5s; Liverpool by the Railway 11s; To Leeming Bar £1 8s 6d; 6d each to & from the Railway.'

In another entry Timothy records an early, more local, railway. With his brother John he set off from Marske early in the morning of Friday 3 June 1836, for Darlington. From there they travelled 'in one of the Railway Coaches to Stockton.' The Stockton to Darlington railway was the first to provide a passenger service hauled by steam locomotive in 1825.

Railway lines gradually came closer to Clifton, the main line from London to York opening in 1840, and soon pushing further north. By July 1841 Timothy was able to travel to and from meetings in York by trains from and to Northallerton. Returning home, he was able to catch a coach from Northallerton to Bedale, where the young footman Joseph Simpson met him with the gig.

On Thursday 15 July that year Timothy left Clifton at 5a.m., got to Northallerton Station at 7a.m., and to York an hour-and-a-half later. He attended the Conservative meeting at the George Inn in Coney Street, dined at York Station [the old station, now offices of York City Council, not the present railway station], left at 3.30p.m., and got back to Clifton before 7p.m.

The first time Timothy travelled to London by train was Monday 2 May 1842, when he again left Clifton at 5a.m., and arrived at the Tavistock Hotel about 8p.m. By Tuesday 22 October 1844 he commented on improving journey times: 'I arrived [back at Clifton] at 9pm, coming by the fast train we were only ten hours from our start to our arrival at Northallerton Station.'

Before long there was talk of a railway line from Northallerton running through Bedale and on up Wensleydale. During the summer and autumn of 1845 there were numerous meetings in Leyburn about it, and at the end of 1852, when the line had reached Bedale, there was discussion of the route to Leyburn. This affected Timothy directly as it just passed through some of his land, and in May 1854 some of his trees were taken down for it.

After the line from Darlington to Richmond opened in 1846, it became much easier to travel north or south from Marske. Timothy's diary for 15 August 1850 noted, 'Pulleine leaves Marske for Newcastle', and on Monday 30 September 1850 he himself 'Left Marske before six o'clock for the Richmond Station' on his way to London.

This was the era of railway companies being set up, making money and amalgamating or failing at a rapid rate, and Timothy refers to several companies whose names would keep changing, as happened during the construction of the Richmond line. Several railway companies were based in York, and there he mentions meeting George Hudson, the 'Railway King', who was Lord Mayor of that city in 1846, although Hudson would soon afterwards spectacularly fall from grace. Other companies were based in London, and Timothy travelled there for meetings, by train of course, before retiring from these in 1847. One of the last diary entries concerning railways was transferring capital into the North Eastern Railway, because it would produce interest at 4%. This is the most specific mention of investment income throughout the diaries.

LEAD MINING

As a landowner in the Yorkshire dales, Timothy was obviously well aware that investing in mining lead could be profitable, and his in-laws, the Chaytor family, had long been doing so. The income lead generated was clearly important to the Chaytors' finances, for straight away after his father-in-law died in 1819, Timothy appointed an agent to act for his mother-in-law 'for £55 a year for the mines, the sale of lead &c., & agent for the land.' Lead mining would become one of the ventures that Timothy's diaries leave us in no doubt that he was investing in.

Timothy's brother John's estate at Marske was close to extensive lead workings. It would seem the two brothers had earlier been discussing such activity for, on Tuesday 28 August 1810, Timothy notes, 'My brother & self went to see the mines in Arkengarthdale & in Swaledale.' However, there are no references to Timothy investing in such until the 1830s. In July 1833, while staying at Marske, he rode into Arkengarthdale and saw the famous 'Octagon' smelting mill there, and then crossed over the hills into Swaledale to visit the Old Gang complex. The following month he visited the lesser-known smelting mill on Stainton Moor, near his Walburn estate.

Timothy seems to have cogitated further before actually becoming involved with lead mining, but on Monday 27 June 1836, again while staying at Marske, Timothy met up in Reeth with his three Richmond-based partners. They were Ottiwell Tomlin, the town clerk of Richmond and clerk to the Richmond to Reeth turnpike road, Thomas Bradley, the land surveyor responsible for that road, and his son Christopher Lonsdale Bradley, who had followed in his father's footsteps as a land surveyor. Timothy noted: 'We rode to the mines we have engaged to work. We returned to Reeth to dinner & afterwards appointed agents &c &c for the workings.'

This enterprise was based at the house of mine agent John Lawes at Strands, a small hamlet between Gunnerside and Isles Bridge near the River Swale. The four investors met there regularly for the 'lead pay' or return on their capital. On Wednesday 20 November 1839 Timothy noted in his diary 'To the pay at Strands...... went to the mines & had the pleasure to see a great quantity of lead smelted & unsmelted.' He does not record the amount of the 'pay' or return on the investment.

Timothy also invested in lead mines in other areas. On Friday 24 March 1837 he 'Wrote to Chris'r. Bradley and sent a cheque for two hundred pounds having purchased of Mr. Tomlin an 1/8 of the Blakethwaite mines. The partners have now equal shares one 1/4 each, £155 12s 3½d for Mr. Tomlin the balance to go to the mining acct. at the bank to pay expenses.'

The workings at Blakethwaite, at the head of Gunnerside Gill, were particularly lucrative and proved a good investment, sufficient to justify the expense of investing in modern equipment such as steam engines for pumping water out of the workings. On Wednesday 16 February 1842 Timothy rode up to Blakethwaite, 'Went up the Mine and saw the new engine set to work for the first time.' Later that year, on 20 July, 'Mr. C. Bradley call'd at Marske in the evening on his way to Richmond to report to me the state of our mines which was very favourable particularly the working at Watersike. The men have cut to the vein & the prospect is good.'

Timothy also invested in lead mines on Grinton Moor, the pay-outs for which took place at the smelt mill there. Following the pay-out on Wednesday 17 July 1839, the investors dined with Edmund Alderson Knowles, who as well as being an investor in lead mines, was a wealthy hosier who owned the knitting manufactory at Paradise in Low Row. 'After dinner some plate was presented by Mr. Knowles to Mr. Harland at the request of Mr. Morley, Mr. J. Wray, Mr. White being conjoint with Mr. Knowles for the great attention he had paid to the mines which are now exceedingly productive and long may they continue so is my earnest wish for all their sakes.'

John Harland was a gentleman who lived at Marrick, where there were also rich veins of lead. On Monday 19 August that year, Timothy went 'To Marrick to dine with Harland who gave a dinner to his partners in the Grinton Moor mines in consequence of their having presented to him some plate the day we dined with Mr. Knowles.'

In 1851, Timothy was taken by the two Bradleys to see the mining field at Stonesdale, high up Swaledale, but he seems not to have followed this up with investment. The Barker family were involved with lead mining in Swaledale for many generations, and on Wednesday 14 November 1855 Timothy noted 'Mr. C. Bradley went with me to Healaugh to attend the funeral of my friend John Barker of Grinton.'

A reference to another mineral occurred on Thursday 13 June 1839. 'Frank Morley came and rode with me [from Marske] to Cordilleras and Feldom [on the Marske estate], from thence we went to see the place where copper is got in Buddle House Farm.' The name of Buddle House Farm, near Kirby Hill, comes from the process of 'buddling' or washing out the dross to leave the stones containing copper ore.

Frank Morley of Marrick Park was part of Timothy Hutton's extended family, as in 1836 Morley had married Charlotte, the eldest child of John Clervaux Chaytor, the younger brother of Timothy's wife Elizabeth. Timothy and Elizabeth were very fond of Frank Morley, and he makes a few appearances in Timothy's diaries: Monday 7 May 1838 'Frank Morley went to hunt at Hackfall', and on Wednesday 4 January 1843 'Morley went out hunting to meet Prince George of Cambridge.' So this outing to Buddle House Farm was probably a mixture of social activity and potential business, although no investment seems to have been made in copper mining.

Frank and Charlotte Morley had a son, also called Francis. Timothy notes the elder Frank Morley's return to Marrick Park after an (unexplained) absence of five-and-a-half years on 10 March 1854. Perhaps he had returned because his health was failing, although he was only in his early-forties. On 4 August 1854 Timothy records, 'Got a letter from Frank Morley Jr. to announce the death of his poor father, which took place yesterday at Marrick from inflammation of the lungs.' On Thursday 10 August 1854 Timothy 'Went to Marrick Park to attend the funeral of our much lamented friend Morley.'

Timothy remained in contact with the younger Frank Morley, and noted on Monday 11 June 1855, 'Frank Morley left Clifton early in the morning for Scarborough to take leave of his Mother &c &c previous to his joining the 2 Regt. of Buffs.' Perhaps his mother, Charlotte, had gone to Scarborough to take the waters there, for she certainly lived on for many years after her husband's death, and was buried at Marrick at the age of eighty on 24 April 1891.[105] By this time her son, still lord of the manor of Marrick, had risen to become Colonel Francis Morley, and Marrick Park had become a tenanted farmhouse.[106]

105 There is a monument on the south wall of Marrick Church commemorating Francis Morley of Marrick Park and his wife Charlotte Chaytor.

106 Bulmer *op.cit.*, p.490.

BANKING

Swaledale and Wensleydale Banking Company, £10 note.
Courtesy of Richmondshire Museum.

Timothy Hutton was involved in banking as a shareholder in the family bank, and also in his role as a gentleman who engaged in philanthropic activities. Into this latter category fell his link with the Bedale Savings Bank, an offshoot of the Bedale Book Society, a local group which met every three months, and held a sale of books twice a year.

On Wednesday 21 January 1818 he recorded 'Dined at Bedale, the meeting of the Book Society. The members of the Book Society that attended at Bedale entered into agreement to try to establish a Savings Bank at Bedale.' This noble aim was clearly realised, and promptly, for on Tuesday 10 March 1818 he was able to note: 'Rode to Bedale. The Savings Bank opened, we received upwards of £392.' Tuesday is still Bedale's market day. He went again on Tuesday 13 July 1819: 'Rode to Bedale. Attended at the Savings Bank, being my turn to attend as one of the trustees.'

As a trustee of the Bedale Savings Bank, Timothy was able to recommend that money, surplus to that needed to set it up, and which had been subscribed from amongst the neighbourhood, should be donated towards the building and completing of two bridges in Bedale and Crakehall in April 1829. Later in his life, after inheriting the Marske estate, Timothy also helped set up a Savings Bank in Reeth in 1844. This, however, was less successful, and got into difficulties in 1847. Timothy organised a subscription to repay the unfortunate depositors.

The bank established in Richmond by Timothy's eldest brother John in 1806, of which Timothy was a shareholder, must have been a source of income to him, particularly in the latter part of his life, although he does not directly refer to receiving any dividends from it in his diaries. The bank prospered, particularly following, only a few years after its establishment, its appointment as Deputy Receivers of Taxes for the North Riding of Yorkshire.[107] Soon after its establishment in Richmond, a branch of the bank was opened in Leyburn, and in December 1811, after the Clifton tenants had paid their annual rent, Timothy noted that 'Mrs. Hutton took £1,000 to the Bank at Leyburn.'

This was the era when the landed gentry, particularly those focussed on their locality, set up many banks which later came to be seen as county banks.[108] In Richmond the Hutton bank was known as the 'New Bank', because there was already an 'Old Bank'. This had been established by Sir John Lawson of Brough Hall, near Catterick, and Miles Stapleton, and was the bank which gave its name to Bank Yard off the high row of Richmond Market Place. On Tuesday 28 February 1826 Timothy noted in his diary, 'Attended a meeting of the Trustees of the Bedale Savings Bank to take into consideration a letter receiv'd from Mr. Stapleton [of] the Old Bank [at] Richmond.' Timothy does not elaborate on the contents of the letter.

Much of the credit for the early success of the Hutton Bank may lie in the banking expertise of one of its founders, William Ellis (1758-1816). He forsook London in 1806 to join the bank as a partner, settling in Richmond and becoming much involved with the town. He was admitted into the Company of Mercers, Grocers and Haberdashers by redemption in 1807, serving as Warden of the Company in 1813.[109] An elegaic poem, written on his death at the age of fifty-eight on 4 December 1816, was retained among the papers of John Hutton.[110] William Ellis was buried on 9 December 1816 in St Mary's Parish Church, Richmond, where there is a monument to him on the north tower wall, erected by his surviving partners John Hutton,

107 Clarkson, *op.cit.*, p.136.

108 Cannadine, *op.cit.* p.44.

109 Waggett, Ralph, 'A Transcript of the Archives of the Company of Mercers, Grocers and Haberdashers of Richmond, Yorkshire 1580-1980', (unpublished typescript).

110 Waggett, Ralph, *A History of the Company of Mercers, Grocers and Haberdashers of Richmond*, PBK Publishing Ltd, (2002), p.202, quoting NYCRO ZAZ 82, "written by Thomas Leeming, 'An old man of 70 years of age and educated under that worthy tutor Mr. Temple.'"

John Rider Wood, Thomas Other, John Robson and Thomas Simpson, describing him as 'A truly honest able and Benevolent Man.'

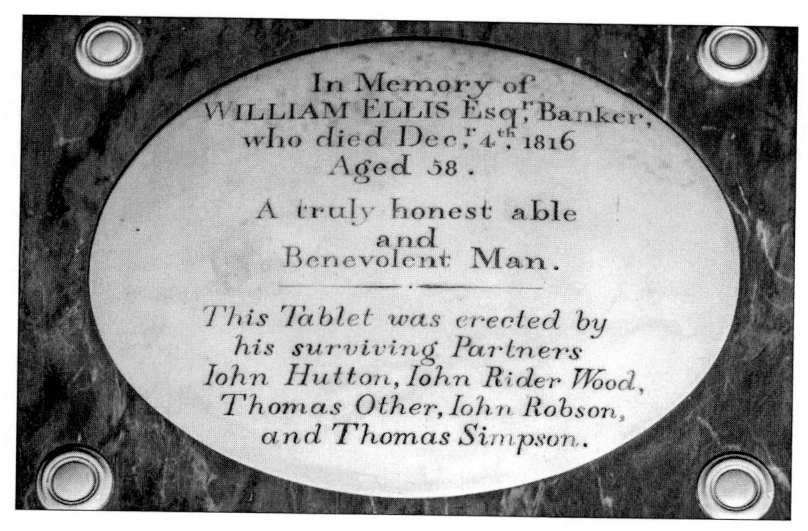

Monument below the tower of St Mary's Church, Richmond commemorating banker William Ellis, put up by his fellow partners in the Hutton Bank. Photo: Guy Carpenter.

The above Thomas Simpson (1791-1832) makes one brief entry in Timothy Hutton's diary. On Monday 23 June 1817, 'Mr. Simpson of the firm of Hutton Wood & Co was married this morning at Richmond to Miss Macknally his cousin.' Elizabeth MacNally was the younger daughter of Frances I'Anson, 'The Lass of Richmond Hill', and her husband the Irish playwright and barrister Leonard MacNally.

Thomas Simpson's later life was to give rise to unhappy reports, and he must have been a very different character from the esteemed William Ellis. Henry Wood, a Richmond botanist (and unrelated to the above banker John Rider Wood) who corresponded at length in a very gossipy manner with some of his friends, reported in September 1831 that Thomas Simpson was at Redcar and so ill from the effects of drink that it was thought he was unlikely to return to Richmond.[111] A few months later Wood had heard that Thomas Simpson had been expelled from the bank, and went on to say 'I understand that Fisher is to live in the house.'[112] The phrase 'the house'

111 Hendra, Leslie Anne (ed.), *A Voice from Richmond Yorkshire, The Letters of Henry Wood 1825-1832*, (privately published 2012), p.134.

112 *Ibid.* p.141.

refers to the Richmond building used as the bank, as it was the custom for a partner or senior member of staff to live at each branch.

The Hutton family must also have suffered some embarrassment concerning a member of its Richmond banking staff a few years before Thomas Simpson's fall from grace. The Richmond parish registers record the baptism, on 1 June 1827, of Margaret Mary, the daughter of Elizabeth Blades of Richmond, 'singlewoman', noting that the reputed father was William Kirby of Richmond, 'clerk at Mr. Hutton's bank'.

As the bank had become well established, John Hutton had not felt the need to appoint another expert outsider after the death of William Ellis. Instead he brought in a local man of some standing, Thomas Other (*c*.1779-1834), who came from Elm House in Redmire in Wensleydale. Other had married Jane Lister (*c*.1780-1829) , the eldest daughter of Edward Lister, owner of the Coverham Abbey estate near Middleham. He was sufficiently influential for the name of the bank to be changed to Hutton and Other.

A succession of early-nineteenth century acts of Parliament encouraged private banks to become 'joint stock' concerns, and Hutton and Other in 1836 became the Swaledale and Wensleydale Bank, reflecting Hutton's Swaledale connections and those of Other with Wensleydale. After the death of Thomas Other in 1834[113] he was succeeded as a partner by his son Christopher (1809-96),[114] and Christopher's son Thomas (*c*.1845-82) also went into the bank.

The bank continued to prosper steadily, and to the Richmond and Leyburn branches were added others at Bedale and Hawes, and eventually also Masham and Reeth. The Bedale branch was the closest to Clifton Castle, but Timothy seems to have used it rarely, although he went there on Saturday 4 October 1862, noting 'For the Lancashire Sufferers paid by the Bank at Bedale £5.'

One of Timothy's few other references to a specific financial transaction actually involved a London bank, not that of his brother. On Wednesday 21 March 1827, he 'Wrote to my bankers in London & sent a power of attorney to sell out stock to the amount of £9000 to pay for the land I bought of Mr. Stapleton at Burrill.' It was only later that Timothy became closely involved with the family bank.

113 Memorial in Redmire Church.

114 Timothy went to Elm House on Wednesday 28 August 1861 for the wedding of Ann Agnes, the eldest daughter of Christopher Other and his first wife Ann Stackhouse. Christopher Other's second wife was Eliza Ann Lamb of Middleham, whose sister Emily had married into the Hutton family.

Immediately after John Hutton's death on 14 August 1841, Timothy was invited to become a director. This he seems to have accepted with sadness and fortitude along with the other obligations he inherited, although it presumably brought him increased income. He made two similar entries in his diaries: Tuesday 31 August 1841, 'To Bedale.... attended at the Bank to meet Mr. Forster, Mr. Anderson[115] and Mr. Other, three of the directors, they requested that I would become a director'; and on Friday 3 September 1841, 'Went to Leyburn to meet some of the directors & shareholders, they requesting me to become a director and trustee in the place of my late brother.'

From then onwards, the bank featured regularly in Timothy's diary entries, starting on Friday 15 October 1841: 'In Leyburn I had to attend a meeting of the Bank Directors and some of the shareholders.' The Leyburn meetings were always on a Friday, market day in Leyburn, and occurred at least quarterly, though sometimes more often if there was a more urgent need to replace a director, or a senior member of staff, who had died. Some meetings were held in Richmond, as on Tuesday 16 November 1841: 'To Richmond, call'd ..... at the Low Bank', the Swaledale and Wensleydale premises being lower down the Market Place than the Old Bank.

Sometimes the diary entries recorded which directors attended the meetings, and occasionally a director is referred to who had not been attending. For example, on Friday 4 February 1842: 'Attended a meeting of the Bank Directors. Mr. Forster, Mr. Anderson and Mr. Other were at the meeting.' On Friday 19 August 1842, Timothy 'Left Marske..... at Leyburn to attend a meeting of the Directors of the Bank to take into consideration the appointment of a Director in the place of the late Mr. Jaques', and on Saturday 27 August 1842, 'Went to Richmond to elect a director. Mr. Rd. Jaques elected.' Richard Machell Jaques, of Easby Abbey near Richmond, a noted breeder of racehorses as well as a significant contributor to agricultural improvement, had succeeded his father, Robert Jaques.

Although it would seem the elder Jaques had not been a diligent attender at directors' meetings, his son certainly was. Wednesday 25 January 1843: 'Attended a meeting at the Bank [at Richmond]. Mr. Other, Mr. Anderson, Mr Jaques and self as directors. We afterwards went to the King's Head and attended the meeting of Shareholders to declare the dividend. A party of us (of 15 shareholders) dined at the Inn.'

Occasionally notes of apparently regular routine business are enlived by something different, as that for Saturday 18 March 1843: 'To Richmond

115 William John Anderson, the landowner of Swinithwaite, near West Witton.

to attend a meeting of the Bank Directors. Mr. Anderson & Mr. Jaques were there, but Mr. Other being detained in York as a witness on the man that broke into the bank at Hawes, we adjourned the meeting to Friday next at Leyburn.'

Another mention of a staff member occurred on Friday 6 October 1843: '..... went to Leyburn, a meeting there at the Bank, to appoint a clerk in the place of Horsley.' Two new directors were required in 1845. Friday 14 May, 'Went to Leyburn to attend a meeting of the Bank shareholders to appoint two new Directors – Mr. G. Robinson & Mr. I. Fisher appointed.' Isaac Fisher, appointed to run the Richmond branch following Thomas Simpson's expulsion in 1831, was now being promoted to the board.

Timothy was assiduous in attending bank meetings. On Thursday 24 December 1846, when there was thick snow on the ground, he recorded 'Went to Leyburn to attend a meeting at the Bank.' Those meetings which involved shareholders as well as directors were often followed by a meal, and Timothy would note the numbers dining, presumably because this was at the bank's expense: Wednesday 24 January 1844: 'I went to Leyburn to attend a meeting of the Bank Directors and shareholders. Dined at Leyburn, 19 sat down to dinner', and on Wednesday 27 January 1847, 'Went to Leyburn to attend the Bank meeting. Dined at the Bolton Arms with the Directors and some of the shareholders.' In January 1851, sixteen sat down to dinner, a year later it was twenty-two.

The details continued to be noted, as on Friday 17 December 1847, 'Attended a meeting at the Bank at Leyburn. Mr. Other, Capt. Wyvill, Mr. Anderson & Mr. G. Robinson were there.' Sometimes more details are given, as for Wednesday 25 January 1849: 'Went to Leyburn to attend the annual general meeting of the shareholders of the banking company. Mr. Other, Mr. Robinson, Mr. George Robinson, Mr. H. Robinson, Mr. Jaques, Mr. Fisher, Mr. Ward, Adjt. Carter, Revd. Mr. Bounty, Mr. Grime, Mr. Thos. Topham, Mr. Heslop and self dined at the Bolton Arms Inn.' Grime is described as clerk in the Leyburn bank when he witnessed Timothy's signature on legal documents in the early 1850s.

As time passed, more of the partners died. On Sunday 27 August 1854 Timothy noted 'Mr. Other and I attended the funeral of Mr. Isaac Fisher before breakfast.' Christopher Other was now the most senior partner, so it fell to him to accompany Timothy to the funeral in Marske. The following month a meeting was held in Leyburn to replace not only Isaac Fisher but also another recently deceased board member. Monday 25 September

1854, 'Attended a meeting at Leyburn & elected Mr. Robinson & Mr. Thos. Smurthwaite directors.'

Thomas Smurthwaite had worked his way up the bank's hierarchy having started work at the Richmond bank as a young clerk. Also showing considerable talent as an amateur actor and singer,[116] Smurthwaite would, sadly, after Timothy Hutton's death become involved in a London court case of 1869 concerning fraudulent investments in railway companies.[117]

On Timothy's death in 1863 his shares in the Swaledale and Wensleydale Bank were bequeathed, along with the Clifton Castle estate, to James Pulleine. In 1899 the Swaledale and Wensleydale Bank was taken over by the recently formed Barclay and Co. Ltd. The Richmond site of the Hutton bank is still in use [in March 2019] as Barclays Bank, despite the recent closure of branches of many banks.

116 Hendra, *op.cit.* p.6.

117 Chris Lloyd, 'Looking Back', *Darlington and Stockton Times*, March 1, 2019.

PART FIVE:
FRIENDS, NEIGHBOURS AND RELATIONS

Julius Caesar Ibbetson, George Cuitt and other Artists

James Tate, Scholar and Headmaster

Revd John Fisher and his Family

John Foss, Stonemason and Architect

Bradley Family

Swinton Park

Thorp Perrow

Chaytors of Spennithorne

Dodsworths of Thornton Watlass

Pulleines of Crakehall

JULIUS CAESAR IBBETSON, GEORGE CUITT AND OTHER ARTISTS

Throughout his life Timothy Hutton was friendly with several artists. Some who became his particular friends shared much of his life at Clifton Castle, and he collected examples of their work. He also acquired many pictures by other artists who were not part of his intimate circle.

The most distinguished artist of his close circle was Julius Caesar Ibbetson (1759-1817). Yorkshire born, Ibbetson spent much of his working life in the Lake District, but in 1804 moved to Masham, under the affable patronage of William Danby of Swinton Park. Ibbetson remained in Masham until he died, and thus for over a decade was a neighbour of Timothy's. Ibbetson had a large family, and his eldest son, also called Julius Caesar Ibbetson (1783-1825), later worked as a drawing master in Richmond.

Timothy's diaries record several occasions when he walked into Masham to visit the elder Ibbetson. On 22 March 1805 he and his eldest brother John 'had a glass of brandy & water with Ibbetson & bought a book of him.' In March 1811 Timothy walked into Masham and saw Ibbetson's latest pictures. He must have liked one he saw in progress on the easel, for a few days later he went back to see it finished. In 1812 he bought Ibbetson's picture of Roslyn Castle, near Edinburgh, for thirty guineas, and later that year bought another, of unspecified subject.

Timothy was away from home when, in October 1817, he heard that the elder Julius Caesar Ibbetson had died on 13th. Being unable to attend the funeral two days later, he noted in his diary when back at Clifton Castle on the following Sunday, 'Went in the carriage to Masham Church. Mrs. Ibbetson having sent me gloves & Hatband was the cause of my going to Masham Church & not being at home to attend the funeral of poor Ibbetson on Wednesday last.'

One of Timothy's mentors in his youth, and possibly the person who first cultivated his interest in art, was the elder George Cuit. In adult life Timothy remained close to George, and also to Cuit's beloved wife Jane. Thursday 8 January 1818 was to be a momentous, if sad, day in Timothy's life. He was in Richmond for the annual dinner of the Company of Mercers, Grocers and Haberdashers, and was to take office as the Company's

Warden for that year. But beforehand Timothy visited the couple at their Frenchgate home in Richmond.

It was to be the last time he saw either of them alive, for he found both George and Jane gravely ill. Indeed, Jane died two days later, aged sixty-two. Four weeks later Timothy's diary records: 'My poor old friend Cuit died at Richmond aged 74', followed on Saturday 7 February 1818 by 'My brother and me set off [from Clifton] for Richmond at 9 o'clock to attend the funeral of my poor old friend Cuit.' The Richmond upholsterer James Arrowsmith recorded[118] that Timothy and John Hutton, and Revd James Tate, and he himself, acted as pallbearers at Cuit's funeral. George Cuit's son, who always styled himself George Cuitt, a few days later gave Timothy and Elizabeth two of his father's pictures as a remembrance of him, and they were hung in the drawing room at Clifton Castle.

Timothy's relationship with the younger Cuitt was even closer, for they were exact contemporaries, even sharing the same birthday, 16 October 1779. The two young bachelors had visited Scotland together in 1803, and Cuitt had visited Timothy and his brother John in Marske in early January 1817.

George Cuitt had left Richmond and settled in Chester, probably through his links with his father's school friend the architect Thomas Harrison, who had moved there from Lancaster in the 1790s. Timothy visited George Cuitt and his wife Catharine in Chester in October 1817, and it was while he was there with them on that stay that he heard that Julius Caesar Ibbetson had died on 13th October. The three-some had had a happier day earlier in the visit, on Friday 10th, when they had gone to see the famous actress Eliza O'Neill perform the part of Belvidera in the play *Venice Preserved*.

Cuitt enjoyed considerable success while working in Chester, earning money from teaching in various schools, and also by producing several volumes of his etchings. He was particularly highly regarded in this art form, having been able closely to study a collection of works by Giovanni Battista Piranesi (1720-78), which his father had brought back with him from his Grand Tour. As well as his technical expertise in etching, Cuitt was also shrewd at marketing his volumes by subscription. Many of the subscribers were not only from the Chester area and among the newly-prosperous mercantile class in Liverpool, but also from his friends and contacts in the Richmond circle of Timothy Hutton.

By the early 1820s, not long after his father had died, George Cuitt was able to return to his Yorkshire roots, settling in Masham where he

118 Arrowsmith.

presumably also benefited, like Ibbetson, from the support of the local squire, William Danby of Swinton Park, as well as that of his friend and neighbour at Clifton Castle. Cuitt built himself a villa-style house in Masham, which he called Bellevue, and much enjoyed planting its garden.

Now that the two friends were living close by, Timothy and Cuitt were able to pursue artistic interests together. In December 1823 Cuitt wrote on Timothy's behalf to a London dealer in prints, with whom he was well acquainted, asking if he had in stock any engraved portraits of a long list of various illustrious Yorkshire families, both ancient and recently established.[119] These were presumably intended to decorate the walls of Clifton Castle.

Timothy continued to purchase Cuitt's pictures, and frequently had him prepare, for hanging in the house, pictures he had bought by other artists. On Saturday 17 January 1824, Timothy noted 'Mr. Danby gave me a picture of Sir Conyers D'Arcy which I sent for this morning', followed on 20th by the note that Cuitt had arrived at Clifton to varnish it. A prominent courtier, and long-serving MP for Richmond, Sir Conyers D'Arcy (*c.*1685-1758) had been on the list of illustrious subjects Cuitt had asked the London print dealer about.

Cuitt made three drawings of Timothy's Walburn Hall in November 1824, and after Timothy returned from his continental tour in the summer of 1826, Cuitt seems to have spent some time with the Huttons. On Tuesday 29 August 1826, when they had all spent a few days at Boston for the grouse shooting: 'Mrs. Hutton, Mr. Cuitt and self went in the carriage to Marske, we spent the day there. Mr. Cuitt cleaned and varnished some of the pictures for the Dining Room.' These seem from later evidence to have been family portraits.[120] Cuitt seems to have had to 'sing for his supper' again later in the year: Tuesday 21 November 1826 'Mr. Cuitt was engaged most of the day drawing a design for a gateway.'

The completed house at Clifton was painted in oils at least twice by George Cuitt. One canvas was inscribed on the back 'To Elizabeth from her sincere friend G.C. Clifton the Seat of Timothy Hutton Esq're. Morning Painted by G. Cuitt 1831.' Another was signed and dated by him April 1833. Sometimes Timothy and George went to look at pictures that other local friends had purchased. In 1840 they went to see, and were impressed by, a painting of the Bedale Hunt which Timothy says an artist called Martain was painting.[121]

119 Information from Peter Boughton.

120 Late-nineteenth century notebook "Inventory of the contents of Marske Hall".

121 Anson A. Martin produced a painting, later engraved, of the subject, dedicated to Mark Milbanke Esq. of Thorp Perrow.

The Cuitts and the Huttons saw much more of each other after the Cuitts moved to Masham, the foursome attending plays and other entertainments. The two men went fishing together, Cuitt later confessing how passionately fond of angling he had been in his youth.[122] They also shared an interest in architecture, visiting new buildings together, such as Holy Trinity Church in Ripon in 1827, Lownethwaite Bridge being built on the Richmond to Reeth turnpike road in 1831, the new vicarage at Masham in 1834, and the new church at Healey under construction in 1847.

George Cuitt, then aged 71, and his wife Catharine, aged 65, were recorded as staying with the Huttons at Clifton Castle on the evening of 30 March 1851, when the census was taken. Catharine Cuitt, née Ayrton, who gave her place of birth as Ripon, came from a musical family which produced many cathedral organists. On Saturday 15 July 1854 Timothy heard that Cuitt was dying, and then that he had died: 'Mr. Cuitt died at one o'clock, poor George. I am grieved to lose him, we have known each other near 65 years.' This confirms that the two had known each other from the age of about five, as well as having been at Richmond Grammar School together. Timothy's brother-in-law Clervaux Chaytor 'went with me to Masham to attend the funeral of my old and valued friend Cuitt' on Wednesday 19th July. Timothy called on Catharine the next day, with a lawyer, as they were executors of Cuitt's Will.

Throughout the diaries there are many references to other artists. On Saturday 23 July 1813, dining with Captain Horn at Thornton Steward, he notes, 'Met Fryer the artist there.' While on holiday in Liverpool on Tuesday 7 October 1817, he records, 'Paid Mr. Winstanley for the 10 pictures I bought at the sale yesterday, the amount £71 9s. 1d. We were at the Blind Asylum.' It is not clear whether the Blind Asylum was linked with the pictures, or if it was a separate event on the same day. The pictures arrived at Clifton Castle on 20 October, 'tolerably safe; a little damage to one or some of frames injured which I got repaired by Wm. Wright who afterwards fixed them up for me in the rooms.' William Wright was the local carpenter in Thornton Watlass who had made many of the new fittings for Clifton Castle. In April 1819 Timothy visited London, and bought more pictures, which he was putting up at Clifton on 5 May. On 10 June that year he records 'Mr. Buick, an artist, came ..... to sleep at Clifton.' This may have been Thomas Bewick (1753-1828), the Northumberland artist best known for his woodcuts.

Timothy also attended house sales with a view to purchasing pictures. In early September 1819 he was in Lancaster and noted 'Attended the

122 Information from Peter Boughton.

sale of the late Duke of Hamilton's pictures. Did not purchase any. They sold at so very high [a price], the best being bought in by the Duchess of Somerset.' However, in October 1823, he did acquire some pictures from a sale at Wycliffe-on-Tees, and a few days later George Cuitt cleaned and varnished them.

Timothy also visited private art collections. In October 1823 he and his friend Thomas Robson, who had been staying at Studley Royal near Ripon, rode to Newby Hall to see William Weddell's famous collection of classical statuary and his Gobelins tapestries: Thursday 9 October 1823, 'Robson & me rode to see Newby Hall, well worth seeing, the statues grand, the tapestry beautiful.'

In 1836 Timothy had his portrait painted by James Lonsdale. He had come across this artist early in the year, as he noted on Saturday 29 April, 'Drove Mr. Cuitt to Newton to see Mr. Forster's picture by Lonsdale.' Forster, whose death would be noted by Timothy in 1852, lived at Newton-le-Willows near Bedale, but no further details of him are given. Strangely we learn from Timothy slightly more about Mr Forster's servant, who became the landlord of the Bruce Arms at West Tanfield, as Timothy attended his house-warming there on Thursday 9 July 1840.

James Lonsdale (1777-1839) was a Lancashire-born but London-based professional painter who specialised in portraiture, often returning north to paint northern sitters, such as the recorder of Lancaster and mayor of Liverpool.[123] These paintings were among the many that Lonsdale exhibited at the Royal Academy. It will be seen that Lonsdale was a near contemporary of Timothy Hutton's, being just two years older. However, Lonsdale, who perhaps had an average life-span for the period, was getting towards the end of his life, whereas Timothy would live for well over twenty more years.

Lonsdale arrived at Clifton Castle on the morning of Friday 15 July 1836, and the sittings began that afternoon, continuing all day on the Saturday, Monday, and Tuesday morning. The portrait was finished on Saturday 23rd, and Timothy paid Lonsdale, the amount unspecified, on Monday 25th. Three months later, two of Lonsdale's assistants arrived: 'They varnished my portrait.' It is not known where this oil painting of Timothy Hutton is now. However, there is something of an irony in this, for

123 oxforddnb.com. I am grateful to my friend Richard Green, formerly Curator of the City of York Art Gallery, for help in identifying this artist. Lonsdale's portrait of Forster was exhibited at the Society of British Artists in 1835 as ' -- Foster, Esq.'

among Lonsdale's sitters was Arthur Bluncell Sandys Trumbull Hill, third Marquess of Downshire and later Earl of Hillsborough, whose descendants have subsequently owned Clifton Castle. The present location of this latter portrait too is unknown.

JAMES TATE, SCHOLAR AND HEADMASTER

The story of James Tate (1771-1843) is an extraordinary one, and it has been told in detail elsewhere.[124] What is remarkable is the friendship that developed between James Tate and Timothy Hutton. By birth, class and economic position, as well as how their lives panned out, the two men were far apart, yet for both it was one of the most significant relationships that either enjoyed.

James Tate, the eldest son of Thomas Tate and his wife Dinah, was born in Bank Yard, off Richmond Market Place, on 11 June 1771. Thomas Tate was an itinerant maltster, though well-read and with strongly-held radical political views. Despite their humble circumstances, Thomas and Dinah became convinced of their firstborn's intellectual potential. And so, after the prerequisite elementary education, they approached Anthony Temple, the long-established Master of Richmond Grammar School. As a local lad, James Tate was eligible for one of the free places provided there for the bright sons of Richmond artisans. Temple admitted him to the school in 1778.

At Richmond School, James Tate was, of course, a day boy. During his years there, he would get to know all the Hutton brothers, paid-for scholars from a gentry family, who boarded in the Master's home, Oglethorpe House. Despite such contrasting circumstances, Tate forged a close bond with Timothy, and his elder brother John, which lasted throughout their lives.

Unexpectedly, one might think, their paths on leaving Richmond School were contiguous, for all three went up to Cambridge, a measure of Anthony Temple's ability as a classical scholar. The Hutton brothers, of course, went to university as part of a family tradition, and followed in their late father's footsteps by entering Christ's College. In Tate's case, however, it was testimony to his determination to excel in Greek and Latin studies. In his case, the academic environment of Sidney College [later Sidney Sussex College] was to be very different from all he had known till then.

Tate must have been very grateful, on a snowy November day in 1790, when he travelled on the coach to start his first term, to be accompanied

124 Wenham, *James Tate.*

The family of Revd James Tate

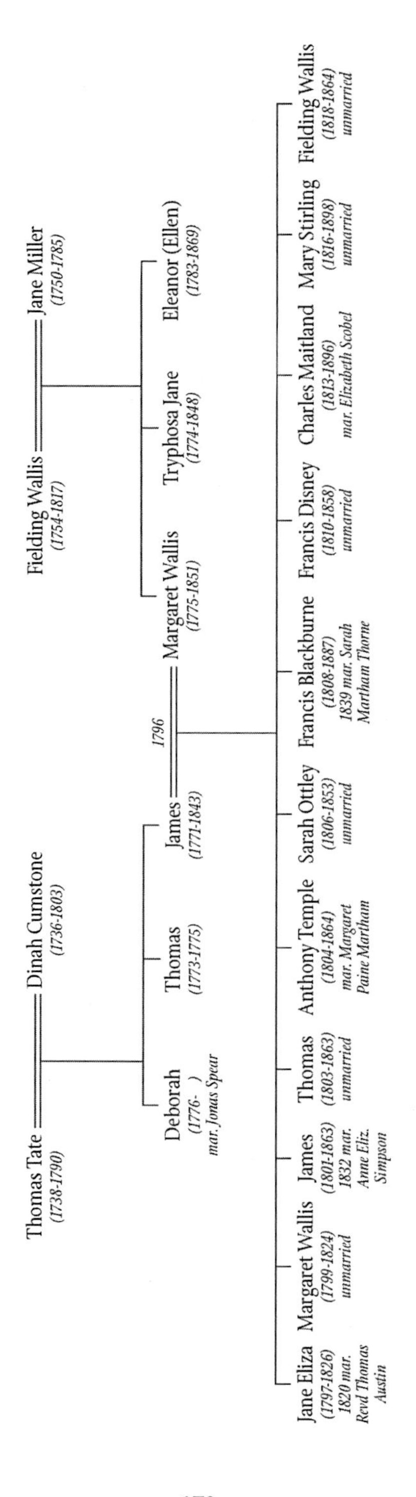

═══ *marriage with date if known*

mar. = married

by two Richmond old boys who were heading back to Cambridge. One was William Wragg, a West Riding boy who was returning to Sidney, the other was another ex-boarder, William Chaytor of Spennithorne, who was returning to Trinity Hall. Chaytor would later become Timothy Hutton's brother-in-law.

The Hutton brothers would both leave Cambridge without a degree. They did not need such to return to their lives in North Yorkshire as well-educated and cultured gentlemen with country estates. It was Tate who graduated, was elected a Fellow of Sidney, and was ordained. Following a long and complicated saga,[125] he was appointed Master of Richmond School in 1796, in succession to Anthony Temple who had died in 1795.

Once Tate had taken up his post at Richmond School, he married. Margaret Wallis was one of the daughters of Fielding Wallis, a leading actor in Samuel Butler's company of players, and her older sister Jane was the famous actress 'Miss Wallis of Bath'. Tate's marriage strengthened his lifelong interest, not only in the Butler company, but also in the theatre in general, an interest he shared with Timothy Hutton.

Margaret Tate was obviously a highly intelligent and educated lady and, like her husband, an engaging companion. Timothy and Elizabeth were clearly very fond of her, as they were of James. A great deal of information about the Tates' relationship is provided not only by Timothy Hutton's diaries, but also by surviving letters written to him by Tate.[126]

James and Margaret Tate had eleven children between 1797 and 1818. The Tate children were named, not only after their parents, James and Margaret, and their grandfathers, Thomas Tate and Fielding Wallis, but also after several of Tate's mentors, such as Anthony Temple and Francis Blackburne.[127] The mastership of Richmond School did not bring with it a high salary and Tate, like other masters before and after him, supplemented his income with fees earned from taking in outside pupils who boarded in his family home, Swale House. To help with the housekeeping work involved with this, as well as that of the large Tate family, another Wallis sister, Eleanor, known in the family as Ellen, came to live with them. Tate paid her a weekly wage of 10s 6d for this.[128]

125 Detailed in Wenham, *James Tate.*

126 These survived in the library of Clifton Castle in 1944-5 and were copied out by Peter Wenham by kind permission of Lady Curzon-Howe; these copies are now in the author's possession.

127 Wenham, *James Tate*, p.428.

128 Wenham, *James Tate, ibid.*

The friendship with Timothy Hutton was to provide some assistance to Tate's precarious financial position. In 1802 Timothy Hutton offered Tate the curacy of the chapel of ease at Bellerby, not a very lucrative position, but better than nothing. Tate held it until the incumbent of Downholme, Thomas Barker Kirkby, died in June 1808. Kirkby, a slightly younger man than Tate himself, who had also been a pupil of Richmond School under Anthony Temple and studied at Sidney College, Cambridge, had only held the living of Downholme since 1803. Timothy was now able to appoint Tate perpetual curate at Downholme, at which point Tate resigned from Bellerby.

It was only a few weeks later, in September 1808, that John Fisher, the rector of Marske died, and John Hutton appointed Tate to that living also. Tate employed a curate to help with parochial duties, but was conscientious in taking as many services as he could at both churches, regularly driving out from Richmond to do so.[129]

James Tate came to be dubbed in the literary world 'the Scholar of the North', and the essayist and wit Sydney Smith would later describe him as 'a man dripping Greek'. Richmond School under Tate's mastership became the leading classical school in the north of England, famed for its teaching not only of Latin, but particularly of Greek. Families from far and wide sought to get their sons accepted as boarders, and Tate could afford to be choosy, selecting those best able to benefit from the high standard of his teaching. Many Richmond School pupils went to the largest and most influential of the Cambridge colleges, Trinity, and there won so many academic prizes that they became known as 'Tate's Invincibles'. Tate was assiduous in keeping up with his old pupils, and Timothy's diaries show that he too was often in their company.

Tate was also known as an excellent preacher, and Timothy clearly relished hearing him, supporting him by attending services in both Downholme and Marske churches. On Sunday 20 January 1811: 'Went to Downholme Church [from Marske] in the morning. Heard an excellent sermon by Mr. Tate'; on Sunday 12 January 1812: 'At Marske Church & heard Mr. Tate preach. Mr. Tate & Mr. Jackson[130] of Kirkby Hill dined at Marske'; and on Sunday 30 June 1816: 'Went to Marske Church. Mr. Brass[131]

129 Wenham, *James Tate,* p.185.

130 Thomas Jackson had been the usher, or assistant master, at Richmond School under Anthony Temple. He was a rival candidate for the post of Master when Tate was appointed. He later became the Master of Kirkby Hill Grammar School at Kirkby Ravensworth.

131 John Brass, one of Tate's 'Invincibles', later Vicar of Aysgarth.

did the duty. Mr. Tate, Mr. Sheepshanks,[132] Mr. Ward, Mr. G. Smurthwaite, Mr. G. Cuitt, Mr. Brass & self dined with my brother.' The conversation around the dinner table that day must have been stimulating to say the least.

Some of Tate's ex-pupils visited Timothy at Clifton Castle, as on Saturday 23 August 1817: 'Mr. George Macfarlan came to breakfast. He was on his way to Cambridge.' George Macfarlan was an 'Invincible' who attained many academic prizes, and was later Vicar of Gainford on the river Tees. Timothy sometimes hosted visits from pupils who were still at the school, as on Saturday 11 June 1825: 'Three of Mr. Tate's boys came to see Clifton. They stopped and dined with us.... Croft, Philips & Walker the names of the lads from Richmond.' As the day was James Tate's birthday, presumably he was there too.

Much detail of James Tate's close friendship with the Hutton brothers is documented in the letters Tate wrote to John. Many of these have survived because they were carefully filed by the Marske librarian Michael Fryer, and over eighty such letters have been published.[133] Tate's letters to John were long and were sent frequently, and John must have written back in similar vein, although these have not survived. A letter Tate wrote to John on 20 March 1820 begins: 'My dear 'Squire, A thousand thanks for your most entertaining Letter.'[134] Tate's letters show that they all shared private jokes, and were sufficiently close for him sometimes to chide John, or give him advice. Timothy, it seems, was not quite such an enthusiastic correspondent as John. Tate sometimes complained that he had to rely on John's letters to get news of Timothy.

Timothy's diary does, however, provide many intimate insights into Tate family life, such as on Wednesday 17 May 1820: 'Wrote to Mr. Tate to congratulate him upon his daughter Jane's marriage to Mr. Austin. They were married this day at Richmond & set off for Scotland afterwards. Margaret Tate accompanied them.' Was it common in Regency times for the bride's mother to accompany a couple on their honeymoon? Or did Timothy record it because it raised an eyebrow?

Jane Eliza was the Tates' first-born child, and she was marrying the newly-ordained Revd Thomas Austin, one of Tate's 'Invincibles'. Austin would shortly afterwards be appointed curate at Spennithorne Church,

132 Richard Sheepshanks, another 'Invincible', later a Fellow of Trinity College and an astronomer of note.

133 Wenham, *Letters of James Tate.*

134 Unpublished letter from James Tate to John Hutton.

Elizabeth Hutton's home parish, before moving to Haughton-le-Skerne near Darlington. Jane and Thomas Austin had four children before she sadly died in her late-twenties in 1826, and was buried in Richmond churchyard. Timothy felt for James Tate so much at having lost his eldest child, that he noted on Tuesday 18 April 1826: 'Sent a letter of condolence to Mr. Tate.' Tate subsequently felt partly responsible for helping educate his Austin grandchildren, a burden which added to the demands on his finances.

In 1826 the Mastership of Rugby School fell vacant, and several of Tate's friends thought he should apply for the post in the light of his glowing reputation at Richmond. A wide range of people were involved in canvassing for him, including Timothy, who refers on Sunday 29 September 1827 to circulating a list of the governors of Rugby School to a friend in the hope that he would know some of them to put in a good word for Tate. Tate did not, though, get the job, as the appointment went in 1828 to Thomas Arnold, who would in due course become famous as 'Arnold of Rugby'. Arnold's views on education featured in Thomas Hughes's *Tom Brown's Schooldays* published in 1857.

A few years later, however, a more advantageous opportunity arose, one through which Tate would increase his personal prestige considerably, and potentially also improve his financial situation. He was unexpectedly offered a Canon Residentiaryship at St Paul's Cathedral in London. The invitation came from the Prime Minister, Charles, second Earl Grey, the first Whig Prime Minister for many years, who had finally, after a long struggle, succeeded in getting passed the Act to Reform Parliament. Grey knew Tate as a prominent Whig and supporter of Reform; indeed the town of Richmond itself had strongly supported the campaign. Furthermore Grey, who had a very large family, had, like several other prominent Whig politicians, sent some of his sons to Richmond School, starting in 1819 with Henry George Grey, Viscount Howick (1802-94), who would become the third Earl Grey in 1845.

No time was wasted, and Tate was collated at the beginning of February 1833, before he had even had time to resign from Richmond School. Three canons, plus the Dean, formed the chapter of St Paul's, and they were in those days each housed in Amen Corner, just north-west of the cathedral. Nowadays members of the St Paul's chapter live round the corner in Amen Court, but Amen Corner is the address Tate used on his letters.

One of Tate's fellow canons was Sydney Smith. Each canon did a month of duty in residence by rotation (Tate's first such spell was in the June), and when not so committed could spend time on other activities, an arrangement which suited Tate extremely well. Both Timothy and John were generous in allowing the new Canon Tate to settle in London for a few months before resigning the livings of Downholme and Marske. He was succeeded in both posts by Revd William Kendall.

Tate's friendship with the Hutton brothers continued, despite the distance now between them. Tate wrote many letters which contained gossip about the people he met in his new life, and described details such as the music played in St Paul's on a Sunday when he preached there. When prints were made of the portrait painted of Tate soon after his arrival in London, the first two copies were despatched up north to John and Timothy. This followed the pattern established when Tate's book *Horatius Restitutus* had been published in 1832, for the first two copies had been despatched to Marske and Clifton,

Tate found London life very agreeable, but he was no businessman, and he soon discovered that, far from being much better off financially, as he had anticipated, he had considerable expenses in living there. Fortunately he was able to take in plurality other church livings linked with St Paul's Cathedral. The first of these was at Hutton [the name of which generated many punning references in correspondence with John and Timothy Hutton] near Brentwood, and later at Edmonton. He employed his son Thomas Tate, who had also taken holy orders, as his curate to undertake many of the duties at these. Timothy Hutton made a point of visiting James Tate at Edmonton when he was in London in May 1842.

Timothy knew all the Tate children well. As we have seen, Timothy had shared with James the latter's sorrows over them, and of course Timothy had also shared the joys, not only in letters but doubtless in conversation with his friend. Some of Tate's younger sons had had youthful bouts of being somewhat wild. Timothy had been particularly kind to Anthony Temple Tate when, having something of a bad spell while a young man in his early-twenties, he had him to stay at Clifton for a few days in early October 1826. Timothy Hutton had also tried find him work: 'Thurday 25 March 1830 Ant'y. Tate took breakfast at Clifton. Wrote in his behalf to Mr. Danby to get him appointed Clarke [*sic*] of the Masham and Thirsk road.' Timothy was a trustee of that turnpike road.

Thus Timothy must have shared James Tate's great relief when the excellent news arrived that Anthony Temple Tate had started studying to become a solicitor. Tate's long letter of May 1838, sent from Hutton Rectory, included 'By the bye, my Son Anthony (now steadiness in all points: God be thanked for it!) is settled as Solicitor at Brentwood. Something like <u>bread</u>

comes in at present: addition of butter may come by and by.' This last remark is very typical of James Tate's sense of humour, shared with his intimate circle.

After John Hutton died in 1841, Timothy discussed with Tate the fulsome wording he wanted on the monument he was having erected to John in Marske church. On Wednesday 15 February 1843, Timothy noted in his diary: 'Wrote to Mr. Tate respecting the inscription for the monument of my late brother.' The monument arrived a few months later, Timothy recording on Thursday 30 August 1843: 'Smith the sculptor came [to Marske] to put up the monument which arrived in the evening from the railway.' As the railway had not yet reached Richmond, this presumably involved transport by cart from Darlington.

The monument was erected on the north chancel wall of the chancel on 5 September: 'Smith the sculptor finished the monument and I paid the account.' The monument is signed *T. Smith, SC, 5 Savoy, London*. Thomas Smith was an eminent artistic, as well as monumental sculptor, exhibiting at the Royal Academy from 1827 to 1852.[135] Presumably Tate had forged the connection between him and Timothy. However, by the time the monument actually arrived, James Tate himself had died, on 2 September 1843, still in office as a canon of St Paul's Cathedral, and so was duly buried in the crypt there.

As well as keeping up his friendship with James and Margaret Tate after they moved to London, Timothy also remained in touch with their offspring, particularly their eldest son, also James, who was appointed to succeed his father as Master of Richmond School. Timothy noted in his diary hosting several of the younger Tates on Tuesday 26 July 1842: 'Mr. [James junior] & two Miss Tates came to dinner, likewise Mr. J. Robson.' Much later Timothy entertained a number of the Tate family at Marske: Tuesday 20 August 1861, 'Mr. & Mrs. Anthony Tate [and] the Rev. Thos. Tate call'd & lunched here.'

The younger James Tate continued living with his family and boarding pupils in Swale House, and remained as head of the school until his death in 1863. A few years into his mastership, a scheme was proposed by some of his father's most devoted former pupils to replace the old school, which was still operating in its original Elizabethan building in Richmond churchyard, with a 'Tate Testimonial'. Timothy noted on Wednesday 4 October 1848: 'Attended a meeting at Richmond respecting the School to be built.'

135 Gunnis, Rupert, *Dictionary of British Sculptors 1660-1851*, Odhams, (1953), p.359.

Two years later he recorded, on Friday 27 September 1850, 'The New School opened at Richmond.' The 'Tate Testimonial', extended over the years, remained the seat of Richmond Boys' Grammar School until in 1971 it merged with two other secondary schools to become Richmond Comprehensive School. The building's use as a school ceased in 2011.

Reverend John Fisher and his family

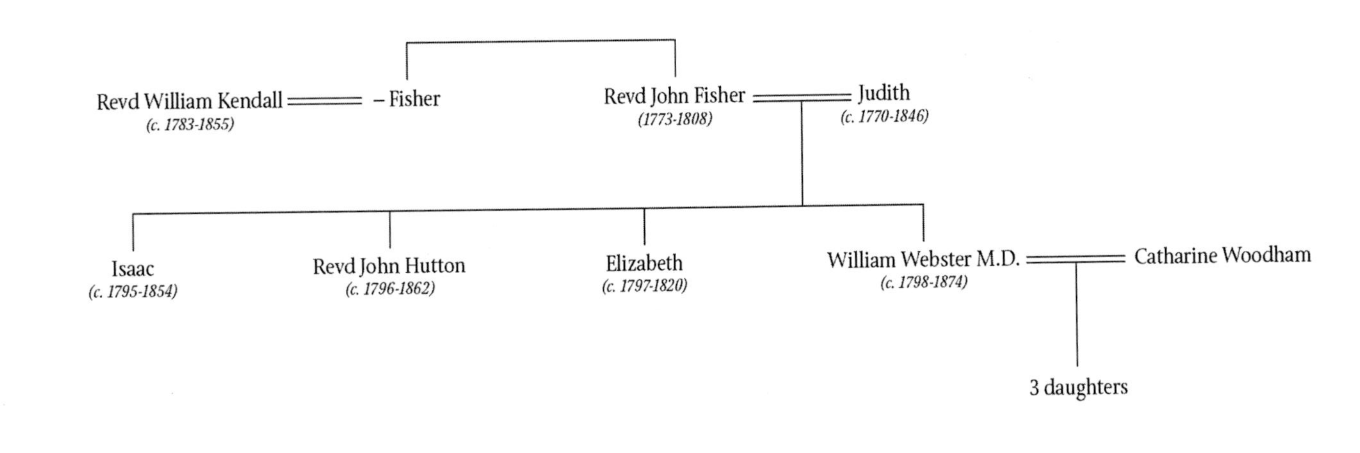

REVD JOHN FISHER AND HIS FAMILY

Timothy Hutton's relationship with the Fisher family was less intense than that with James Tate. However, it has a place here for several reasons. All the Fisher family members played a part in Timothy's story, their lives straddling the period of Timothy's life. They were typical of those in Timothy's circle in having members who overcame the family's adversity to progress to national significance. Above all the Fishers demonstrate the benevolence shown by John and Timothy Hutton to those less fortunate than themselves.

When James Tate was presented by John Hutton to the rectory of Marske, he was following in the distinguished footsteps of many previous rectors who had been appointed and generously supported by the Hutton family. Revd Richard Horne, rector 1747-1803, has already been mentioned as a mentor of the young Hutton brothers. He was succeeded in 1803 by John Fisher (1773-1808), a Westmorland man who had been a contemporary of John Hutton's at Christ's College, Cambridge, and who was to be James Tate's immediate predecessor.

Sadly, Revd John Fisher's incumbency was cut short when he was thrown from his horse while travelling over the moors, breaking his leg, an accident from the effects of which he died on 12 September 1808,[136] aged only thirty-eight. Both Tate and the Hutton brothers continued to be involved in the Fisher family's well-being, and John Hutton would, when he made his Will in 1839,[137] make bequests to the three surviving offspring of Revd John Fisher.

Indeed, when Tate was offered the post of rector of Marske, for which he as Master of Richmond School could not be resident, he particularly requested John Hutton to allow John Fisher's widow Judith, and daughter Eliza, still living at home, to remain in the rectory house, and to enjoy its glebe, without rent.[138] The request was, of course, acceded to.

John Fisher's elder two sons were sent to board with James Tate at Richmond School. The eldest son, Isaac, has already been referred to as later residing at the Richmond headquarters of the Hutton and Other Bank.

---

136 Raine, *Marske* p.13.

137 National Archives, PRO PROB 11/1956/196.

138 Wenham, *Letters of James Tate*, p.20.

He lived the life of a gentleman in Richmond, and was a member of the corporation, serving as mayor in 1848. He also became an accomplished archer,[139] and additionally served as Secretary of the Richmond Scientific Society.[140] Timothy's diary records for Friday 13 September 1839, having had a tooth out in the morning, 'Went to Marske after and met at dinner at three o'clock, Mr. Cooke the Mayor of Richmond, Isaac and William Fisher.' Despite his seeming prosperity, 'Isaac Fisher Gentleman' was left £100 in John Hutton's Will.

The second son was named John Hutton Fisher after his father's friend from his Christ's College days, the children all being born in Westmorland, before they moved to Marske under John Hutton's patronage. John Hutton Fisher (*c.*1796-1862) was clearly very bright and became one of Tate's 'Invincibles', going up to Trinity College, Cambridge. Timothy Hutton recorded in his diary for Wednesday 18 October 1815: 'Hutton Fisher set off for Cambridge'.

The boy duly had a distinguished academic career, not only winning various prizes as a student at Trinity, but being elected a Fellow there from 1820 to 1831. Becoming ordained, he was appointed Vicar of Kirkby Lonsdale in Westmorland, a living in Trinity's giving, which he held from 1831 to 1860. Revd Hutton Fisher was bequeathed the small freehold property in Maulds Meaburn, Crosby Ravensworth in the County of Westmorland, which John Hutton had inherited from his mother. Revd Hutton Fisher seems to have spent the end of his life in Cambridge and was buried there on 15 March 1862 in the large churchyard of St Benedict's Church, usually known as St Bene't's, Cambridge's oldest church with an Anglo-Saxon tower.

Timothy took Hutton Fisher and his younger brother William on a tour of France, Germany and Italy in the summer of 1826. William Webster Fisher was the family's fourth child, and being born only *c.*1798 was still a little boy when their father died in 1808. Presumably there was not enough family income for him to go to school in Richmond, as his two older brothers had done. It would seem that Timothy Hutton, who was possibly his godfather, took responsibility for his education.

The boy makes several appearances in the diaries. On Monday 4 February 1811, 'William Fisher & I left Clifton after breakfast, got to Borobridge at 1 o'clock, where we dined. Left Borobridge at 3 & got to Thorp Arch at ½ past 5 where we stoped [*sic*] all night.' The following day, 'After breakfast

139 Clarkson, *op.cit.* p.303.

140 Wenham, *James Tate* p.423.

went with W. Fisher to the School where I placed him under the care of the Revd. J. Peers.' Revd John Peers ran a school at Thorp Arch near Wetherby, as confirmed by Timothy's entry for Tuesday 30 July 1811: 'Mrs. Hutton & I took William Fisher to Thorp Arch.'

Timothy and Elizabeth's choice of school seems to have worked well, for William Webster Fisher (*c.*1798-1874) was to become a distinguished medical man. A Fellow of Downing College, Cambridge from 1834 to 1844, and Downing Professor of Medicine 1841 to 1874,[141] he was a physician at Addenbrooke's Hospital and had a large practice in Cambridge.

John Hutton, who made his Will shortly before William Fisher became so famous, bequeathed £100 to 'William Fisher of Cambridge, brother of the said Isaac Fisher.' William had married Catharine Woodham in 1854, and they had three small daughters before she died, leaving him a widower living in Downing College at the time of the 1861 census. William Fisher himself died at the East Lodge of Downing College in 1874.

While a Fellow of Downing College, he was able to accommodate other members of his family there, and Isaac clearly went to stay with him. Timothy notes on Wednesday 23 August 1854, 'Mr. Thos. Smurthwaite call'd to show me a letter he had received informing him of the death of Mr. Isaac Fisher at his brother's in Downing College, Cambridge.' Thomas Smurthwaite, who was about to become one of the directors of the Hutton and Other Bank, would have received that information in his official capacity through the bank at Richmond.

The following day, Timothy was himself given the news: 'Got a letter from Professor Fisher M.D. Downing Col. Cambridge, which I answered.' Isaac's body was brought up to Marske for burial there on Sunday 27th: 'Mr. Other and I attended the funeral of Mr. Isaac Fisher before breakfast', Christopher Other being the senior partner in the Hutton bank.

John Fisher's third child was a daughter, Elizabeth, known as Eliza, born *c.*1797. She seems to have had a rather delicate constitution, and died early in 1820 at the age of just twenty-three. Timothy Hutton noted on Sunday 23 January 1820, 'Eliza Fisher died at Richmond; the daughter of the late Rev. J. Fisher of Marske.' It is amazing how quickly Timothy could be apprised of such sad news, which travelled from Richmond to Clifton the same day, despite there being heavy snow on the ground. James Tate wrote the following day to his son James, 'Poor Eliza Fisher died yesterday betwixt *xi* and *xii* in the day. And had I not turned back soon enough from our

141 Venn *Alumni*.

attempt to reach Marske for the Sunday morning duty there, it might have been my fate to perish from the storm and drift of the preceding night.'[142] Despite the bad weather, Eliza was buried at Marske on 26th January.[143]

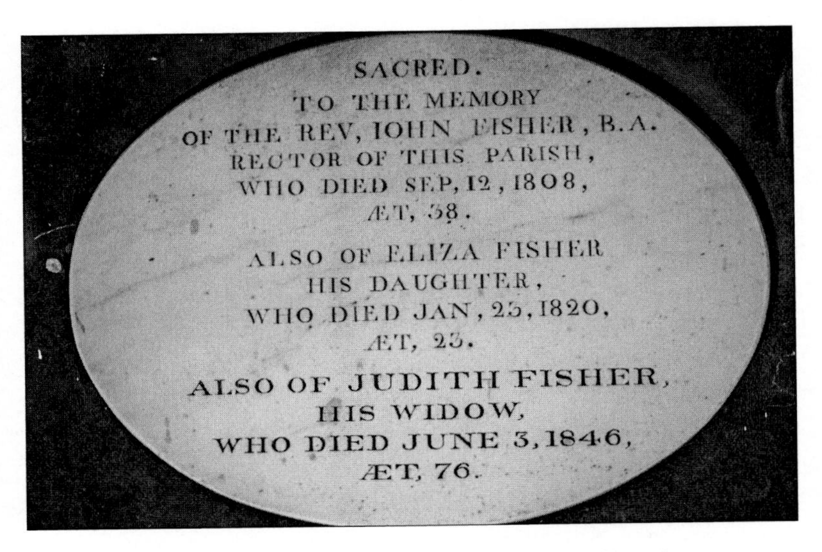

Wall monument to Fisher family in Marske Church.
Photo: Guy Carpenter

On the north chancel wall of Marske church, close to the Hutton family chapel, is a monument signed by Richmond stonemason William Foss (son of John, the architect of Clifton Castle) and dated 1821. The inscription commemorates Revd John Fisher BA, his daughter Eliza, and his widow Judith, who died 3 June 1846 aged 76. Clearly from its position it was put up by John Hutton, although the Hutton family themselves did not then have any such wall monuments.

When James Tate left Richmond for London in 1833, William Kendal, who had been his curate at Marske, was appointed to the livings of both Marske and Downholme. Kendal had married a sister of Tate's predecessor John Fisher.[144] Timothy, who had just set off for Scotland at the time of the wedding, recorded in his diary on Monday 29 June 1812: 'Mr. Kendal and Miss Fisher were married this morning at Penrith.'

142 Wenham, *James Tate*, p.279.

143 National Burial Index.

144 Raine, *Marske*, p.15.

William Kendal died in 1855 aged seventy-two. His cousin took over at Downholme, but at Marske he was succeeded by Revd Thomas William Robson, the stipendiary curate at Hudswell,[145] and the eldest son of Timothy's friend Thomas Robson. Timothy, as squire of Marske, recorded in his diary for Saturday 8 September 1855, only six days after William Kendall had died: 'At Richmond. Met Robson there & gave the living of Marske to his son Thomas.'

Thomas Robson of Holtby Hall, in the small hamlet of Holtby a short distance north-east of Crakehall, was an old friend and near-contemporary of Timothy Hutton, and was to feature twice more in Timothy's diaries: Tuesday 18 March 1856: 'To Bedale, met Robson – it being the anniversary of his marriage, 50 years this day'; and Wednesday 14 May 1856, 'To dine at Holtby being Mr. Robson's birthday 73.' Timothy became very interested in longevity, and although at seventy-three Thomas Robson was a few years younger than himself, 'golden weddings' must have been relatively rare in the mid-nineteenth century.

145 *Ibid.* and clergydatabase.org.uk.

John Foss and his family

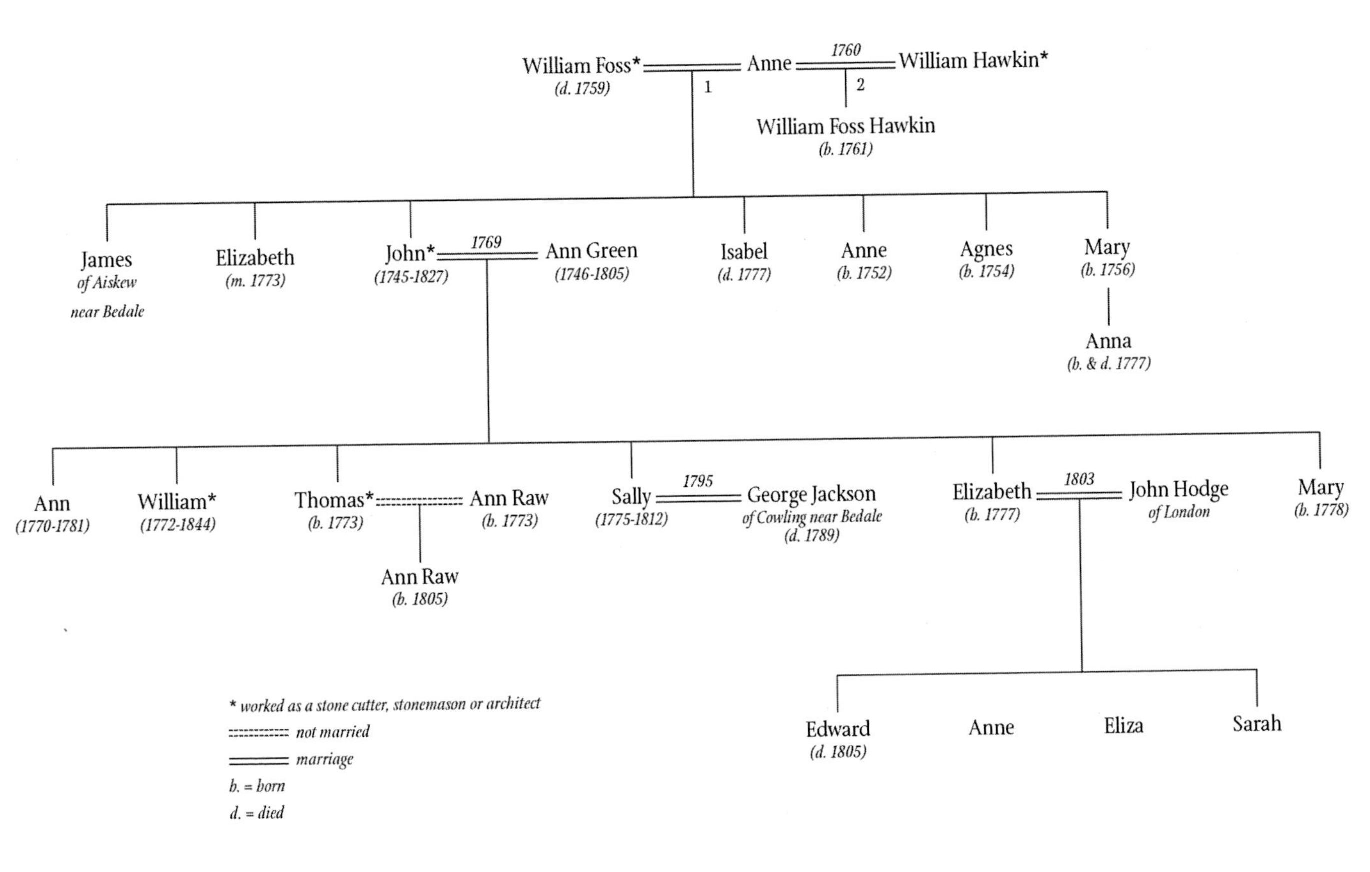

JOHN FOSS, STONEMASON AND ARCHITECT

The Richmond stonemason-cum-architect John Foss (1745-1827) was a member of Timothy Hutton's close circle. It is not very clear how they first became acquainted as they came from very different backgrounds, but doubtless most people prominent in Richmond society, like Timothy, would know Foss. He was an alderman of the town, known to be a local 'character', and he had already produced a variety of buildings for many local landowners.

Foss was a very talented craftsman in stone, but he had additionally acquired architectural expertise as a designer, a skill which he must have obtained by experience rather than by education. For whatever specific reasons, Timothy Hutton chose him as the architect of Clifton Castle and its estate, and the house would prove to be Foss's masterpiece.

John's father William was a stone-cutter who died in 1759, leaving a number of young children, including John then a boy in his teens. John's mother Anne got married again, to another stonemason, William Hawkin, who seems to have continued the family business, in which young John initially learnt his trade. John Foss was to become very skilled, particularly in selecting suitably high quality stone from quarries, as well as working it with expertise. He had had little formal schooling, but acquired design knowledge from working as clerk of works for the local commissions of several high-ranking architects, notably John Carr of York,[146] and also James Wyatt.

Foss carried out work at many of the country seats neighbouring Clifton Castle, notably Swinton Park and Thorp Perrow.[147] He was clearly good company, and a frequent and welcome guest at the dinner tables of many local landowners in and around Wensleydale[148], which was probably one reason why he received so many commissions from them. He also found time to serve twice as mayor of Richmond, in 1811 and 1822, a situation which put him in a good position to get work from the town.

146 Wenham, Peter, "John Foss of Richmond", *York Georgian Society Annual Report for 1976*, pp 27-35.

147 Wenham, Peter & Hatcher, Jane, "The Buildings of John Foss", *York Georgian Society Annual Report for 1977*, pp 32-44.

148 Arrowsmith.

From losing his father in his early youth, John Foss's private life continued to contain much sorrow. His wife Ann, and at least two of their daughters, predeceased him, although their son, William, lived on until 1844 and continued in business as a stonemason. Timothy's diary for Wednesday 13 March 1805 records: 'Mrs. Foss of Richmond died'. Typically, Timothy heard the sad news on the very day that it occured, as borne out by the inscription on the Foss family's tombstone in St Mary's Parish Church in Richmond.

Another sad loss followed swiftly afterwards, for on Tuesday 2 April 1805 Timothy noted: 'Mr. Foss came to Clifton. Went with him down to the house. Mr. Foss was very unwell having lost his grandson the day before.' Clifton Castle was at this time in the early stages of its construction, a situation which would be placing great pressure on Foss.

Work on Clifton Castle and its estate continued for many years. On Thursday 1 February 1810 Timothy notes: 'Mr. Foss & I at Clifton setting out the new road up to the house.' Sometimes there were tasks elsewhere on Timothy's behalf, such as checking on developments planned by other local owners which might have a bearing on the Clifton estate, including the proposed erection of a weir on the river Ure. Although it is not known how much Timothy Hutton paid John Foss overall, the figure of £441 10s has been suggested.[149] The only relevant diary entry is dated Saturday 11 May 1815: 'Paid Mr. Foss twenty five pounds for attending as architect.' This can only have been an interim payment, for building work would continue for several more years. The stable block was only finished in the summer of 1824, for Timothy made the diary entry on Friday 11 June of that year, 'Mr. Foss measured off the stable, the stonework, roofing and slating.' This was just three weeks after William Terry had fixed the stable clock.

Foss was not only Timothy's architect and stonemason, but they obviously became good friends. Furthermore, Timothy and Elizabeth were particularly kind to him during his long widowerhood, frequently having him to stay at Clifton, even before the new house was finished, and later seemingly at Christmas. Timothy's diaries record many convivial times shared with John Foss. The two were among the thirty-two men who attending the Freemasons' Dinner in Richmond on 27 December 1821, and they dined with the mayor William Thompson (senior) on 21 October 1819. On 29 January 1822 Timothy attended Foss's own mayoral dinner: 'We had an excellent entertainment. About 40 sat down to dinner.'

149 Worsley, *op.cit.*, quoting a memorandum book compiled by a later owner of Clifton Castle, John Cowell.

Timothy recorded on Friday 20 July 1827: 'Poor old Foss was buried this day.' Foss had, according to his tombstone, died on the 18th, aged 82. Arrowsmith says of his latter years

'.... when he was advanced in years and when many of his patrons were either dead or had withdrawn from active life.....a few really staunch friends stood by him, the chief of whom were Mr. Timothy Hutton and his brother Mr. John Hutton of Marske and Mr. Danby of Swinton, into the residences of all these gentlemen he was received right up to the time of his death with a hearty welcome. In particular he was indebted to Mrs. Timothy Hutton for many kindnesses and attentions which made his latter days less unhappy.'[150]

John Foss's Will, made on 18 February 1824, included amongst its bequests, 'I give my picture of Swinton with the frame to John Hutton Esquire and I give my picture of Richmond and my case of drawing implements which case is marked with my name "Jno. Foss Richmond" to Timothy Hutton Esquire which trifling legacies I beg these gentlemen to accept as trifling tokens of my remembrance of the many acts of kindness and friendship shewn to me by them.'[151] It is unclear what happened to the case of drawing implements, but the only known portrait of Foss, by the Richmond artist William Ripley Robinson, remained in the hands of Mrs Joan Curzon-Howe-Herrick of Thornton Watlass in 1976. She was the widow of the last owner of Clifton Castle by indirect descent from Timothy Hutton's family.

150 Wenham, "John Foss of Richmond", p.34.

151 Wenham & Hatcher, "The Buildings of John Foss", p.32.

Thomas Bradley and his family

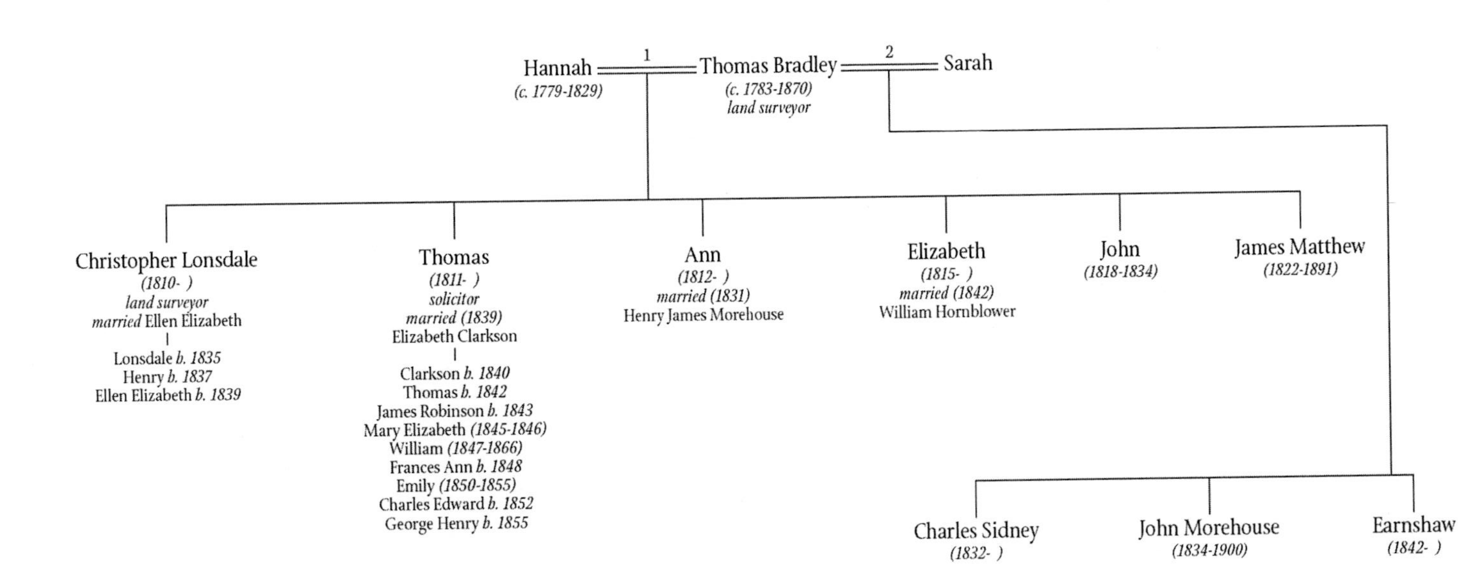

══ *marriage*

b. = *born*

THE BRADLEY FAMILY

Two generations of Bradleys acted as land agents for Timothy Hutton. Their work for him included land sales and purchases, tithe commutation, lead mining, estate roads and bridges, and also surveying turnpike roads. Several members of the extended Bradley family occur in Timothy Hutton's diaries, and it is sometimes hard to know which one of them is being referred to. Disentangling them is complex, as they used the same forenames in successive generations, and one of them married twice and later had young children contemporary with his own grandchildren. Timothy's diaries show how he extended his friendship to the family, who neither shared his own gentry background, nor went back to his childhood, like the Tates or the Cuitts, but had built up his respect through another working relationship.

The link with Timothy Hutton starts with Thomas Bradley, a land surveyor who lived in Frenchgate in Richmond, just below Church Wynd, next door to the architect John Foss. Bradley, like many others in Timothy's circle, was a member of Richmond Corporation, serving as mayor in 1831. Thomas and his first wife Hannah had six children: the eldest, Christopher Lonsdale Bradley (born 1810), also became a land surveyor, and the second son, Thomas junior (born 1811), became a solicitor. Christopher Lonsdale Bradley had three children with his wife Ellen Elizabeth, including a son called Lonsdale Bradley. Thomas Bradley junior and his wife Elizabeth Clarkson had nine children

There were two more sons, and two daughters. Ann married Henry James Morehouse, a surgeon of Kirkburton in West Yorkshire, at Richmond parish church on 19 October 1831; Elizabeth's marriage is noted in Timothy's diary for 28 September 1842: 'Miss Bradley married this day to Mr. Hornblower.' William Hornblower was of Huddersfield, also in West Yorkshire. .

After Hannah, the first wife of the senior Thomas Bradley, died aged fifty in 1829, he and his second wife Sarah had three sons, all of whom enter Timothy Hutton's diaries. The eldest, Charles Sidney (born 1832), is mentioned as entering an archery competition in Bedale in 1852. The second, John Morehouse (born 1834), for whom Elizabeth Hutton was godmother, 'came to see me before he went to Cambridge' on 12 October 1853. The boy had been admitted as pensioner to Corpus Christi College in the April of that year.[152] The third son received an enigmatic entry in Timothy's diary on Monday 25 September 1848: 'I went to Richmond to dine with the Bradleys Sen'r. it being the christening of their son Earnshaw, 6 years old. 17 dined.'

The elder Thomas Bradley (*c.*1781-1870) began his association with the Hutton family on 28 January 1817, when James Tate wrote to John Hutton, whose land agent 'Mr. Wright' had recently died, recommending Bradley to him for his 'friendly qualities, my belief of his talents & integrity, & my liking for his chearful [*sic*] modesty & unoffending frankness ...... Mr. B. is in London, & knows not one syllable of this matter.' John Hutton presumably followed Tate's advice, and shortly afterwards conveyed the information to Timothy, for Bradley was appointed as land agent for the Clifton estate on Saturday 1 March that year.

Timothy was keen to acquire additional land, and Bradley acted as valuer for such negotiations. So on Tuesday 2 November 1819:

> 'Mr. Bradley & self went in my carriage to Bedale to attend the sale of Col. Hildyard's estate at Newton-in-the-Willows. Bid for Lot 6 (Jackson's Farm) but did not buy it. It was bought by Atkinsons. It was the only lot I bid for. Mr. Elsley [of Patrick Brompton] bought James's farm for one thousand pounds. Less than I would have given for it, but I did not like to bid against Mr. Elsley. Had Col. Hildyard offered the estate to me (which I requested of him) he would have got more for it than he has done by selling it by auction. At Mr. Bradley's valuation it would have come to near one thousand pounds more.'

Another abortive attempt to buy land was launched on Monday 25 November 1833: 'John Hodgson came to Richmond. Mr. Bradley tried to bargain with him for some of his land at Hunton now on sale which they could not agree for..... the quantity of land was only 30 acres, which Hodgson valued at £70 acre.' Bradley represented Timothy concerning the Enclosure of Crakehall Ings in 1835, and the Tithe Commutations at Thornton Watlass in 1836/7 and Burton-upon-Ure in 1837/8. On Tuesday 24 May 1842, after John Hutton's death, 'Mr. Bradley and me went to Clints [near Marske] to take possession of the property purchased of Mr. Errington.' John Hutton had been in the process of buying the neighbouring estate when he died, and Timothy completed the transaction on his behalf.

---

152 Venn *Alumni.*

The rents paid by tenants for their property formed a major part of the income needed to support a country estate. It was thus important for this regular task to be carried out as efficiently as possible and, as we have seen, in the earlier part of his adult life, Timothy carried it out himself, standing the tenants a dinner as both a thank-you and an incentive. However, later on, he delegated this, partly, perhaps, because he was busier with his other activities, and also because he probably felt more prosperous. Whatever the reasons, from 1837 Thomas Bradley collected the Clifton estate rents twice a year. Later, his son, Christopher Lonsdale Bradley, took over this task, and added to it the collection of the Marske rents after John Hutton's death.

Both Bradleys were involved in many of the ventures with which Timothy Hutton was involved, such as being partners in his lead-mining investments. Thomas Bradley was the surveyor for the Richmond to Reeth turnpike road, and its spur to Marske, in which Timothy was a key player. Christopher Lonsdale Bradley undertook several projects for the Marske estate after John Hutton's death, designing for Timothy the new village school in 1844, and the new road through Skelton up to Telfit (1845/8). He also in 1852/3 supervised land drainage works using clay tiles made at Marske by 'Smith the tile-maker'.

The Bradleys father and son were sufficiently favoured by Timothy to be allowed to shoot grouse at Walburn. After Timothy's death, James Pulleine continued to use the Bradleys as his land agent at Clifton, until Thomas Bradley fell from grace in some unspecified way and had to move away.[153] Yet he was back in Richmond when he died in 1870 at the age of eighty-eight.

153 NYCRO, introduction to calendar of ZAW archive.

The Danby family of Swinton Park

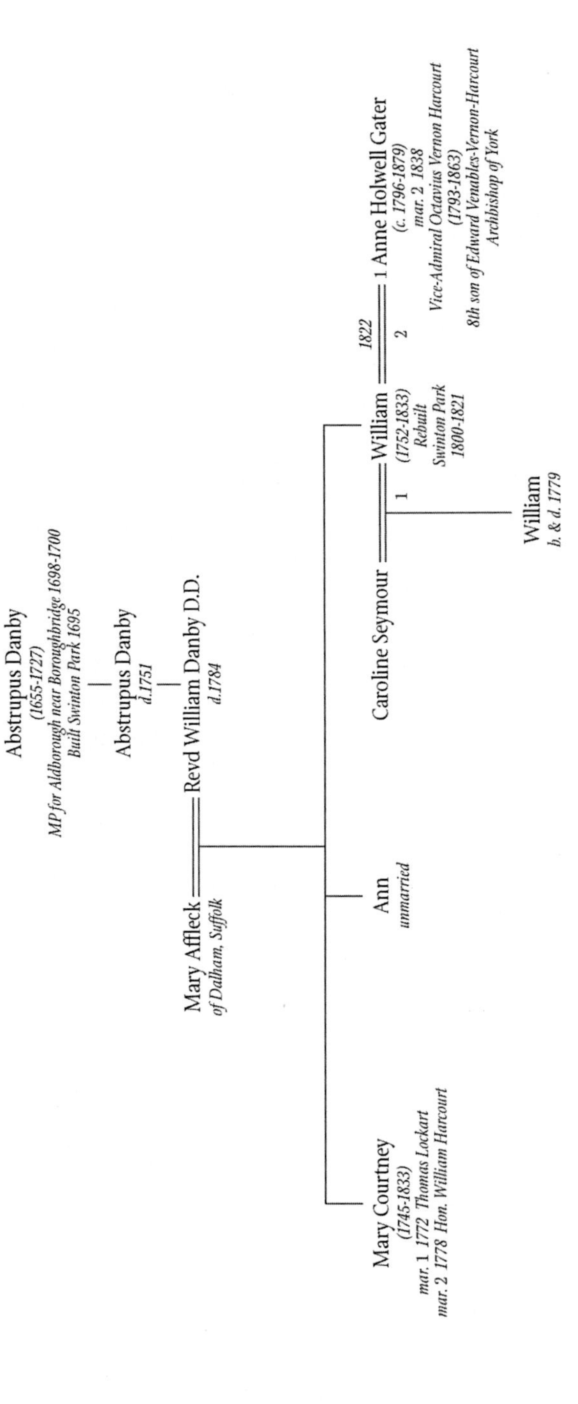

═══ marriage with date if known
mar. = married
b. = born
d. = died

SWINTON PARK

Swinton Park lies just south of Masham, about three miles from Clifton Castle. The house, generally known as Swinton Castle, was greatly enlarged in the early-nineteenth century, but in contrast to the classicism of Clifton Castle it is in castellated Gothick fashion. Work can be attributed to several architects, including James Wyatt (1746-1813), but much of it was done by John Foss of Richmond. On Sunday 17 October 1813 Timothy noted in his diary, 'Mr. Foss and my brother rode to Swinton to see Mr. Danby's improvements.'

'Mr. Danby' was William Danby (1752-1833), who not only greatly altered and extended the mansion he inherited, but also elaborately landscaped the estate, including the creation of a chain of lakes. Although a generation older than Timothy, and much wealthier, he was very much a kindred spirit.

William Danby, a highly-cultured gentleman, the son of a doctor of divinity, had been privately tutored at Eton, and then became a fellow-commoner at Christ's College, Cambridge. After enjoying a Grand Tour, he returned to become, not a politician, but mainly a writer, also a genial host and a philanthropist.

It was through his patronage that the artists Julius Caesar Ibbetson and George Cuitt settled in Masham, the nearby small market town to which he extended his improving zeal. The poet Robert Southey, visiting Masham in 1829, remarked: 'The most interesting person whom I saw during this expedition was Mr. Danby of Swinton Park, a man of very large fortune, and now very old.'[154]

Danby was fortunate in discovering a thin seam of coal on his estate, which helped him fund his good works, for which he was complimented by the agricultural commentator Arthur Young. During the various phases of the Napoleonic wars, when many soldiers were recruited and then dismissed, causing great hardship, he employed a large army of labourers to create his outdoor works. These included the construction of a 'Druid's Temple', a miniature monument loosely based on Stonehenge, which Timothy and his wife, and her younger brother Clervaux and his wife,

154 Wikepedia.

visited on Friday 25 May 1810. Many years later Timothy noted, on Sunday 20 May 1860, 'In the afternoon rode to the Druids. Pleased with the growth of the larch, they were planted about 60 [years] ago.'

William Danby married twice. His first wife, Caroline née Seymour, died on 5 March 1821 at the age of sixty-six. As, according to the memorial to her in Masham church, she died at Bristol Hot Wells, it took over a week in those pre-railway days to bring her back home for burial. Timothy noted on Thursday 13 March 1821, 'Mr. Cuitt, Mr. Knowles & self walk'd to Masham. We were in the church & saw the vault making for poor Mrs. Danby.' The family vault was at the east end of the south aisle of Masham church. William and Caroline had had a son William, but he had died as an infant in 1779.

The following year, 1822, William Danby remarried, this time to a lady less than half his age, he being by now in his mid-seventies. However, he and his new wife, Anne Holwell Gater, continued to mix in the same circles as Timothy and Elizabeth. For example, they all met up at the consecration of the new Sharow church near Ripon on Wednesday 28 September 1825.

William Danby's home continued to be known as a place where interesting and unusual people were entertained. His generosity extended in some cases to accommodating people of some celebrity on a more permanent basis in Swinton Castle. An extraordinary encounter there was recorded by Richmond upholsterer James Arrowsmith, who was at Swinton on business one day in 1823:

> 'Present was Miss Ridsdale, a celebrated dwarf only 31½ inches high. She was patronised by the Danby family and was a frequent visitor to Swinton. After completing my business I was sitting with Miss Ridsdale and the housekeeper when Mr. Foss arrived. He was in such spirits as to make him most amusing and entertaining. Later in the evening in high good humour he proposed building a cottage for Miss Ridsdale in Harrogate.'

Arrowsmith then goes on to describe how John Foss, who was known for rarely making architectural drawings, proceeded to make a sketch-plan for the intended cottage with a dining room, drawing room, colonnaded portico and gardens with a hot-house, greenhouse and fruit trees.

It would seem that this luxurious cottage was never built, for Timothy Hutton noted in his diary on Wednesday 2 January 1828: 'Miss Ridsdale the dwarf was found dead in her bed at Swinton.' She was buried in the churchyard at Hampsthwaite near Harrogate, a new church only built in 1821, and her tombstone records 'In memory of Jane Ridsdale, daughter of George and Isabella Ridsdale, who died at Swinton Hall in the parish of Masham on the 2nd day of January 1828, in the 59th year of her age, being in stature only 31½ inches high.'

William Danby continued improving Swinton Park right up to the end of his life, and on Friday 29 July 1831 Timothy noted: 'Went to Swinton, rode with Mr. Danby in the Park to where he is building a house to feed the deer in.' His demise came two and a half years later. On Wednesday 4 December 1833 Timothy regretted: 'Mr. Danby died at Swinton. He was to me a sincere friend and excellent neighbour, and though upwards of 80 years of age, I cannot but deplore the loss of so good, and truly benevolent man, as he was.' Such a fulsome tribute is echoed in the lengthy wording of the large memorial to him on the south wall of Masham church, carved by the leading monumental sculptor Robert William Sievier of London.

On Friday 13 December Timothy rode to Swinton for the funeral. 'The tenantry on horseback in threes, to the number of 80 before the hearse, and 6 horses followed the mourning coaches. Gentlemen's carriages of the neighbourhood 19, the labourers 60 on foot. The day was favourable and the whole passed off as well as could possibly be wished.' Shortly afterwards, on Thursday 27 February 1834, Timothy noted: 'Mrs. Danby sent me a superb mourning ring.'

Anne was able to afford high quality, for mourning rings as well as her husband's memorial, for she was now a wealthy widow. She had not had any children by William Danby, and there were no surviving children from his first marriage. She was still quite a young woman, and before long she would marry again, and Swinton Park would thus have a new owner. In the meantime, she continued to enjoy a full social life, throwing parties and balls, some of which were attended by Timothy and Elizabeth Hutton.

William Danby's sister Mary had in 1778 married as her second husband William Harcourt, and members of that family had visited him at Swinton. Timothy had enjoyed the Earl of Harcourt's art collection at Nuneham Courteney, near Oxford, when in the area in March 1810. Timothy's diary includes an entry for Saturday 19 September 1829: 'Dined at Swinton to meet Lord & Lady Harcourt', and then on Friday 25 June 1830, 'Receiv'd a very kind letter from my friend Mr. Danby dated at St. Leonard's Hill, Windsor, informing me of the death of his brother-in-law Lord Harcourt.' This was the third Earl of Harcourt, who had died without heirs, and his relatives, the Vernon family, in 1831 assumed the additional surname of Harcourt to inherit his properties. Timothy's diary for Wednesday 23 September 1835 contains the somewhat enigmatic entry: 'Mrs. Danby brought the Marquise D'Harcourt to see Clifton.' This may be a rare example of Timothy's acerbity.

On Thursday 22 February 1838 Timothy entered in his diary: 'Mrs. Danby to be married this day to Capt. Harcourt R.N.', to whom her late husband had been distantly related as an in-law. The marriage took place by special licence at Stanton Harcourt church on the picturesque estate and model village of the earls of Harcourt. Octavius Vernon Harcourt, recently retired from the Royal Navy, was the eighth son of Edward Venables Vernon Harcourt, Archbishop of York. Having had a distinguished naval career, Octavius was in retirement promoted to rear-admiral and then vice-admiral. Thus he is referred to later in Timothy's diaries as Admiral Harcourt, and as such was the owner of the Swinton estate.

Octavius and his new wife continued the Danby tradition of socialising with their landed neighbours. Timothy noted on Thursday 14 February 1856: 'Adm'l. & Mrs. Harcourt lunched here', and on Saturday 15 March 1856, 'At Masham in the afternoon, met Adm'l. & Mrs. Harcourt there, the former laid the corner stone of the Mechanics Institute Building or the Riddell Memorial.' The establishment of mechanics institutes, to encourage adult education, was a cause close to Timothy's heart, and that in Masham commemorated the late vicar, Thomas Riddell.

Anne and Octavius Harcourt continued William Danby's reputation for benevolence in the Masham area. In the late-1840s Harcourt built an imposing new church at Healey, a village on the Swinton estate not far from Masham, and after the success of his horse 'Ellington' winning The Derby in 1856, used some of the proceeds to add to the church a vicarage. In 1858 he built the Danby Vernon Harcourt Almshouses in Masham, which have since had their name shortened to the Harcourt Almshouses.[155]

Octavius Harcourt died at Swinton in August 1863, a few months after Timothy Hutton's death, and was buried at Masham, where there is a wall memorial to him. Anne outlived him too, being buried, also at Masham, in 1879 as Anne Holwell Danby Vernon Harcourt aged eighty-three. Swinton Castle now continues the spirit of William Danby's hospitality as a country house hotel.

155 Eight cottages for retired people, now managed by Anchor Hanover Housing.

THORP PERROW

The Thorp Perrow estate lies rather less than three miles north-north-east of Clifton Castle as the crow flies. It was the seat of a branch of the Milbanke family, who also had estates at Barningham, and Halnaby near Croft. In the time of Timothy Hutton's early diaries, Thorp Perrow had a young squire, Mark Milbanke (1795-1881), who had inherited it as a boy in 1802 when his father William died. He was very different from William Danby. Far from having cultural interests he concentrated on having a good time in his youth, and later entered politics. But he too in his way was close to Timothy as a neighbour.

The young Mark had the house at Thorp Perrow improved, on somewhat austere classical lines, by John Foss of Richmond, so as to create large rooms for the balls and parties that were his youthful enthusiasm. However, the considerably older Huttons clearly much enjoyed being entertained there by their younger neighbour. On Monday 1 January 1810 they went to a New Year's Day ball there, not returning home until 5a.m. the next day.

At the end of that year, on Saturday 29 December, Timothy noted: 'Mrs. Hutton & I dined with Mr. Milbank & Mrs. Clarke at Thorpe. Of the party, Mr., Mrs. & Mr. Edward Carter, Col. Coore, Mr. G. Ellesley, Capt. Taylor, Maj'r. Brooke, Mr. & Mrs. Wise, Miss Brooke.' Mrs Clarke, helping out as hostess, was the wife of the rector of Thornton Watlass, Revd George Foord Clarke, and they lived at The Hermitage in Thornton Watlass. The other guests were either local landowners or officers in the North York Militia, or both, like Timothy. Colonel Henry Coore was the squire of Scruton, and Gregory Elsley that of Patrick Brompton. The squire of Theakston's son Edward was soon to marry Elizabeth Hutton's sister, and as a result made a Will on Thursday 18 February 1813: 'Mrs. Hutton, Miss Heseltine & self witnessed the signing of Mr. Edwd. Carter's Will.' Miss Heseltine seems to have been a close associate of Elizabeth Hutton's, for she is only mentioned in her company. The deferential way Timothy refers to her suggests she was not an employee.

On Thursday 2 May 1816, Mark Milbanke came of age, an excuse for several lavish parties. Timothy's diary for that day suggests a very festive tone: 'Rode to Thorpe & spent the day. Mr. Milbanke 21 years old this day,

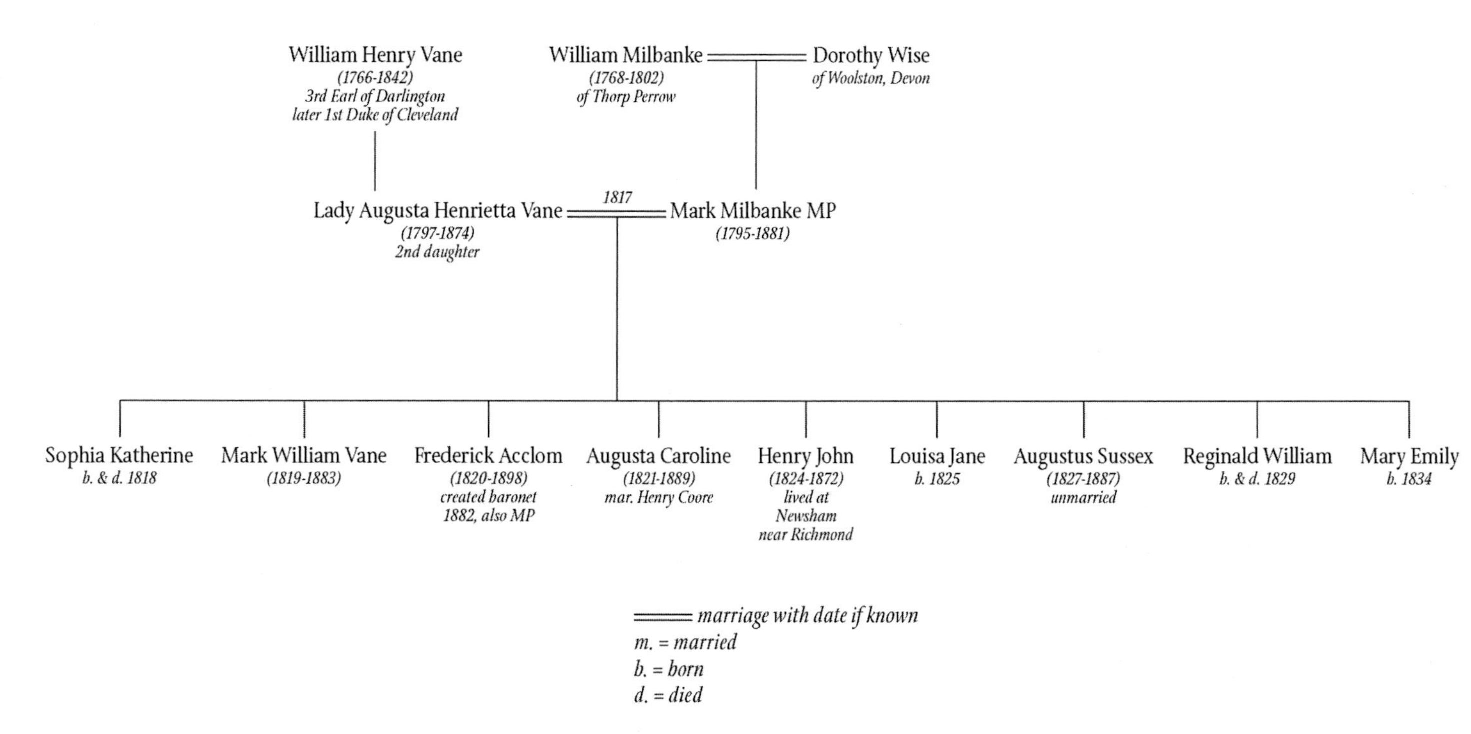
THE MILBANKE FAMILY OF THORP PERROW
William Henry Vane
(1766-1842)
3rd Earl of Darlington
later 1st Duke of Cleveland
William Milbanke
(1768-1802)
of Thorp Perrow
Dorothy Wise
of Woolston, Devon
Lady Augusta Henrietta Vane
(1797-1874)
2nd daughter
1817
Mark Milbanke MP
(1795-1881)
Sophia Katherine
b. & d. 1818
Mark William Vane
(1819-1883)
Frederick Acclom
(1820-1898)
created baronet
1882, also MP
Augusta Caroline
(1821-1889)
mar. Henry Coore
Henry John
(1824-1872)
lived at
Newsham
near Richmond
Louisa Jane
b. 1825
Augustus Sussex
(1827-1887)
unmarried
Reginald William
b. & d. 1829
Mary Emily
b. 1834
marriage with date if known
m. = married
b. = born
d. = died

there were races at Thorpe & fireworks in the evening.' A fortnight later, there was a celebration for the estate: 'To Thorpe in the evening to a dance, & never spent a pleasanter night in my life. The dance was given to his tenants & their families. About one hundred & fifty were there.' Timothy admitted, 'Got from Thorpe at a quarter past five this morning' on the Friday.

Clearly young Mark Milbanke needed a wife to share his jollifications, and he married well. Monday 2 June 1817: 'Mark Millbanke of Thorpe was this day married at St. James's Church, London to Lady Augusta Vane, 2nd daughter to Lord Darlington.' She was Lady Augusta Henrietta Vane, and her father, William Henry Vane, the third Earl of Darlington.[156] Needless to say, this event justified another celebration. So when the couple returned from honeymoon, on Wednesday 27 August 1817, Timothy, and presumably Elizabeth also, went 'to a Ball at Thorpe. Upwards of one hundred & forty sat down to supper. Mr. & Lady Augusta Milbanke paid the greatest attention to all the Company.'

Straight on cue, Timothy recorded, on Tuesday 17 March 1818, 'Lady Augusta Milbanke brought to bed of a daughter this afternoon.' Sadly, Sophia Katherine did not survive, but Lady Augusta went on to have many more babies, including sons Mark, born in 1819, and Frederick Acclom, born in 1820, who each in turn would succeed their father as owners of Thorp Perrow. The latter also stood as an MP towards the end of Timothy's life.

From the 1820s, Mark Milbanke spent less time at Thorp Perrow, becoming a Whig MP through the influence of his father-in-law. He then makes fewer appearances in Timothy's diaries, except, for example, when he joined a hunting party using Clifton land. He did, however, serve as High Sheriff of Yorkshire in 1837, and called Timothy Hutton to do duty on the Grand Jury in York that year.

Lady Augusta, presumably busy bringing up her increasing young family and looking after the estate in her husband's absences, only gets one later mention. On Thursday 25 October 1827, the day before a big freemasons' gathering in Richmond: 'The Duke of Sussex, Sir John Beresford [of Bedale], Lady Augusta Milbank & Mrs. Dundas called.' The next Milbanke baby was named Augustus Sussex after George III's sixth son. Lady Augusta's legacy to the Thorp Perrow estate included the planting of a pinetum, which is the origin of the present arboretum there.

156 *History of Parliament.*

THE CHAYTOR FAMILY OF SPENNITHORNE

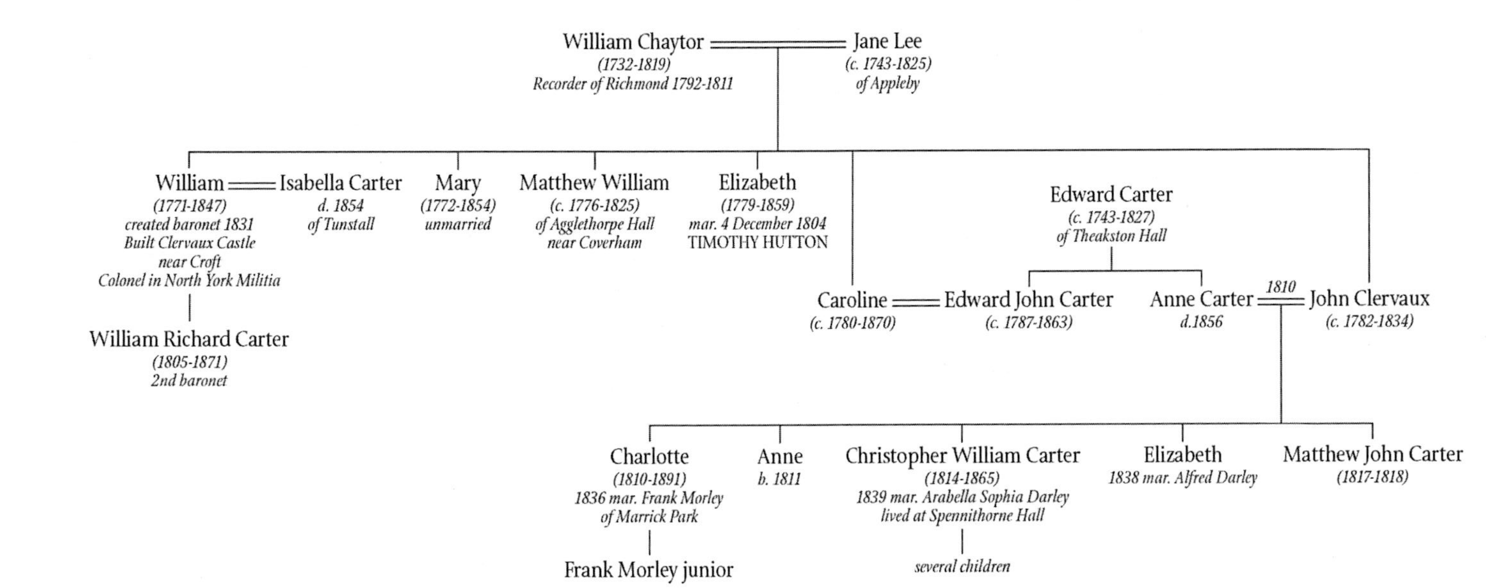

═══ *marriage with date if known*
mar. = married
b. = born
d. = died

THE CHAYTORS OF SPENNITHORNE

On 4 December 1804 Timothy married Elizabeth, daughter of William Chaytor of Spennithorne[157] near Leyburn in Wensleydale. The main line of the Chaytor family was, and is, based at Croft-on-Tees, but had a Wensleydale branch from 1730 when Henry Chaytor, nephew of the Croft squire, married Jane Smales. She was the daughter and heiress of Matthew Smales of Gilling West, into whose ownership had passed Spennithorne. The Wensleydale branch of the Chaytors prospered, and successively remodelled Spennithorne Hall, close to the parish church of St Michael and All Angels, into a large Georgian country house. Some of the improvements were overseen by Timothy's architect friend John Foss of Richmond.

By the time Timothy Hutton was born, the owner of Spennithorne Hall was William Chaytor (1733-1819), a lawyer who held the prestigious post of Recorder of Richmond from 1792 to 1811. This specifically meant that he was the officer in charge of the town's Court of Record, a jurisdiction granted by the charter of Queen Elizabeth I in 1576 for cases up to £100. In practise he was also the Corporation's legal adviser, who had to be a barrister at law.

William Chaytor was a man so highly regarded by the Borough of Richmond that twice he was presented with a piece of silver plate as a token of their gratitude and affection for him. In 1805 a large silver bowl[158] to the value of eighty guineas was engraved with the Richmond coat of arms and the inscription:

> 'To William Chaytor, Esq. of Spennithorn, Recorder of Richmond, this Bowl was presented by the Corporation of that Borough in grateful testimony of his able and faithful services as their legal advisor, and especially of his late successful efforts in investigating and maintaining their many valuable rights and privileges, now finally secured to them. Thomas Simpson, Mayor, A.D. 1805.'

The inscription refers to the lengthy and contentious process of enclosing the open fields and other lands of the town, a controversy which had

157 Formerly often spelled without the 'e' at the end.

158 Clarkson, *op.cit.*, p.223.

been ongoing since the 1760s. On 18 March 1811[159] the Corporation finally accepted the resignation as Recorder of the, by now, elderly William Chaytor. This time the presentation was of a silver cup. He had resigned on 9th March because the Corporation failed to take his advice on the interpretation of the town's Elizabethan charter. An unknown author wrote on Chaytor's death:[160]

'Illustrious Chaytor! Thy distinguished name
Will shine recorded in the book of fame
Till mem'ry fail, a name like thine so dear,
Must ever claim the tribute of a tear.'

Something more of William Chaytor's illustrious and varied career is told in the lengthy inscription on the wall monument to him, in the chancel of Spennithorne church:

> 'Vice-Lieutenant of the North Riding, a Bencher of the Inner Temple, a Justice of the Peace for over 60 years, once a Member of Parliament for Penryn and Hedon, Recorder of Appleby and Richmond, and a Captain in the North York Militia in 1759.'

William Chaytor's household at Spennithorne Hall included many staff, and he paid tax for three male servants there in 1780.[161] In the churchyard at Spennithorne is the tombstone, erected by William Chaytor, to Paul Greathead, his faithful manservant for fifty years, who was buried on 5 February 1816 aged sixty-five. What a loss this must have been for a man in his eighties.

Timothy Hutton had known William Chaytor all his life. After all, Chaytor had been one of the trustees appointed to look after the interests of the Hutton brothers by Timothy's father's Will. The two families also had an unlikely factor in common. The three older Hutton brothers had all been born before their parents married, and William Chaytor's eldest son, William, had also been born ahead of his parents' marriage. This younger William Chaytor went up to Trinity Hall College, Cambridge in 1788, and was one of the companions who travelled in the same coach when

159 Richmond 'Coucher' [or Corporation Minutes] book as transcribed by R W Waggett, p.168.

160 Waggett, *A History of the Company of Mercers etc*, p.202.

161 "Tax on Male Servants 1780", p.68.

Timothy's boyhood friend James Tate began his studies at Sidney College, Cambridge in November 1790.

Doubtless William Chaytor senior had mentored his young Hutton charges with some knowledge of the law, but it is highly likely that he had also passed on to them something of his business acumen. Chaytor was a particularly successful speculator in the mining of both lead and copper in the area. So wealthy had William Chaytor become that, when his daughter Elizabeth married Timothy Hutton, he was able generously to endow the union with a large fortune. James Tate, writing to his sister Deborah five days before the marriage, signed off by regaling her with the titbit that Timothy Hutton had spent the day and had eaten 'beefstake' with the Tate family, and had given them the exciting news that he 'is to be married next week to one of Mr Chaytor's daughters, with fifteen thousand pounds fortune.'[162]

James Tate was sufficiently familiar with Timothy and Elizabeth Hutton to pen her a little doggerel poem[163] following her first birthday as Timothy's wife. It would seem to allude to the dowry that his boyhood chum was now enjoying. It is dated 1 May 1805 [Tate was a few days late, as it had been Elizabeth's birthday on 17 April]. This is the first verse :

> 'Lady, for whose natal day
> That rogue of Marske once filch'd the lay,
> And proud of borrow'd feathers shone
> As if the plumes were all his own.
> May I present the tribute due
> From truth & honesty to you.'

Timothy clearly had a deep affection, not only for Elizabeth – referred to throughout his diaries, as was then the custom, as Mrs Hutton – but also for many of her family. On Wednesday 10 October 1810, Timothy took a party of Chaytor ladies to Richmond races: 'Mrs. Hutton, the two Miss Chaytors & Self went to the [Grand]stand'. The group went on to enjoy together the assembly that followed the races that evening. The 'two Miss Chaytors' were Mary, Elizabeth's oldest sister, and her younger sister Caroline, who would shortly become Mrs Edward John Carter.

The Chaytor womenfolk were all very close, and enjoyed many expeditions together. On 24 September 1811, Timothy noted that 'Mrs. &

162 Wenham, *James Tate*, p.248.

163 *Ibid.*, p.404.

Miss Chaytor & Mrs. Hutton set off after breakfast for Redcar', the east coast seaside resort very fashionable in Georgian times for its fine sandy beach. 'Mrs. Chaytor' was Timothy's mother-in-law, and 'Miss Chaytor' was her eldest daughter Mary, so described according to the convention of the times.

Mary Chaytor remained single, and she holidayed with the Huttons on several future occasions. Although continuing to live mainly in her family home at Spennithorne, she spent a lot of time at Clifton Castle, which lies only about six miles away to the south-east, as the crow flies. She was such a familiar figure at Clifton that much later, on 11 February 1844, Timothy particularly recorded the death of her servant, James Anderson.

Later still, on Monday 29 March 1852 Timothy noted, 'Miss Chaytor spent the day with us. Miss Chaytor's birthday, 80 this day.' He sadly recorded on Monday 18 December 1854, 'Miss Chaytor died at 9am.' This was followed, on Saturday 23 December 1854, by 'Attended the funeral of Miss Chaytor to Spennithorne.' The burial register gives her age as eighty-three.

Timothy was very fond of his father-in-law William Chaytor. In the latter's later years, Timothy made a point of attending his birthday celebrations each 22 January. On that day in 1811 'Mr Chaytor's birthday, aged 79', and in 1814, travelling from Marske, he struggled to reach Spennithorne due to heavy snow, but 'got there for dinner.'

The entry for Wednesday 22 January 1817 was fuller:

> 'Set off for Spennithorne & arrived there at 2 o'clock. Mr. Chaytor's birthday, aged 84. He was born at Gilling in Yorkshire in the year 1732/3 Jan'y. At that period they did not begin the year in the register until the latter part of March or the beginning of April, consequently Mr. Chaytor was born in 1733 beginning the year in Jan'y.'

This comment refers to the change from Julian to Gregorian calendars in 1752, the new year having previously begun at Lady Day, or 25 March. Timothy did not mention William Chaytor's next two birthdays, so perhaps he was in poor health, but he noted for Saturday 15 May 1819: 'Poor Mr Chaytor expired at ½ past 10 – by the Spennithorne clocks it was 11.' This reference to the clocks at Spennithorne being kept at a different time is not explained.[164]

164 King Edward VII created 'Sandringham Time' to make the most of the winter daylight for shooting by advancing the clocks all over his Norfolk estate by half an hour [*Yorkshire Post*, Friday December 21 2018 p.2] Did William Chaytor do something similar?

On Wednesday 19th, Timothy was at Spennithorne helping make the funerary arrangements: 'Wrote to Messrs. Bundall & Co. for patterns of mourning rings.' The funeral was on Thursday 20th: 'Mr. Chaytor was buried in Spennithorne Church at a little past six in the evening. Miss Chaytor, Mr. Clervaux, Mr. Matthew, Mrs. Hutton & Self attended the funeral.' Caroline Carter was not present, perhaps due to a confinement.

On Wednesday 26th Timothy wrote to Bundall & Co, returning the sample mourning rings and placing an order for ten to give to family and close friends. 'At the request of Mrs. Chaytor ordered rings for the following persons:- Mrs. Chaytor, Mrs. William Chaytor, Mrs. Carter, Mrs. Clervaux Chaytor, Mrs. T. Hutton, Miss Chaytor, Mr. M. Chaytor & Mr. Hutton. Likewise ordered one for Mr. Clervaux on his own account & one for Mrs. Hutton to present to Mr. Baines.'

All were either members of, or married into, the Chaytor family except for 'Mr. Baines', who was an old family friend. Timothy's diary for 1 February 1820 records: 'Mr. Baines of Tanfield (father of Mr. Baines of Masham) was buried this day. He died at his son's house at Tanfield on Sunday last. He was in his 96th year, having lived in the reigns of George the 1st, 2nd, 3rd & 4th.' Revd John Baines was buried in the churchyard at Well. His son, also John, the Masham surgeon, did not outlive his father for long, and died at the age of sixty-one. Timothy noted his death on Saturday 5 May 1821, and Timothy and Clervaux Chaytor attended the funeral in Masham three days later of 'our much lamented friend Mr. Baines.' There is a memorial to him and his wife Henrietta on the south chancel wall of Masham church, paying him a fulsome tribute to his many sterling qualities.

Timothy's mother-in-law Jane, formerly Jane Lee of Appleby, lived on after William Chaytor's death for nearly six years, and during her widowhood Timothy was able to do many acts of kindness for her, perhaps seeking to repay what her late husband had done for him. On 20 January 1825 Timothy sadly recorded, 'Mrs. Chaytor died this morning at her house at Spennithorne', and on the 26th, 'The funeral of poor Mrs. Chaytor.' She too was buried at Spennithorne.

Elizabeth Hutton also had three brothers who feature, to a greater or lesser extent, in the diaries. The eldest, William (1771-1847), has already been mentioned as going up to Cambridge. He married Isabella Carter, who was a member of the Carter family of Tunstall near Richmond. William Chaytor became a colonel in the North York Militia, was created baronet in 1831, and served as Whig MP for Sunderland from 1832 to 1835. He inherited the Croft estate, but rather than live in the ancient hall there, he built over the period 1839 to 1844 a Victorian Gothic mansion, Clervaux Castle, since demolished.

This William Chaytor first appears in Timothy Hutton's diaries on Wednesday 4 July 1810, 'Mrs. Hutton & I went to Croft to the christening of Col. Chaytor's daughter.' The baby was Elizabeth, named after her godmother Elizabeth Hutton, and Timothy and his wife took a particularly fond interest in this niece. On Friday 19 December 1823 Timothy noted in his diary, 'Mrs. Hutton and Miss Heseltine went to Richmond to fetch Elizabeth Chaytor from School.' The thirteen-year-old was presumably returning home for Christmas from a girls' boarding school in Richmond.

Colonel William and Isabella Chaytor's eldest son, William Richard Carter Chaytor (1805-71), who became the second baronet, was also an MP for Durham. This second baronet married twice. The death of his first wife is entered in Timothy's diary on Friday 15 September 1837: 'Anne the wife of William Chaytor jun'r. died this evening at Hagg Cottage in Swaledale. She gave birth to a son on Sunday last.' On Tuesday 19th Timothy 'Attended the funeral of Mrs. W. Chaytor in Spennithorne Church.' The burial records say she was twenty-four years old.

The first Baronet's death is also noted by Timothy, on Saturday 30 January 1847: 'Got a letter from Henry Chaytor [a younger son] to inform me of his father's death.' And on Tuesday 2 February 1847, 'Attended the funeral of Sir W. Chaytor at Croft. Dined at Clervaux Castle.' Lady Isabella lived on until 23 December 1854.

Elizabeth Hutton's next sibling, Matthew William Chaytor, lived at Agglethorpe Hall near Coverham. He is first mentioned by Timothy on Sunday 14 December 1817: 'Mr. Mat. Chaytor came to the Lodge and brought the half year's interest for Mrs. Hutton and myself of the thousand pounds from Mr. Chaytor.' This presumably related to the handsome dowry which Elizabeth had had from her father. Matthew died just a few months after his mother at the age of forty-nine, on Sunday 28 August 1825: 'Mr. Matthew Chaytor died about half past 12 o'clock in the morning.' On Thursday 1 September, Timothy 'Went to Spennithorne. Smith & I went forward to Agglethorpe to attend Matthew Chaytor's funeral.'

Elizabeth's youngest brother was John Clervaux Chaytor, his middle name taken from the family who had brought the Croft estate into the Chaytor family in the early-fifteenth century. Known as Clervaux, he was clearly a popular figure with both Timothy and Elizabeth, and they were very fond of him. An early diary entry notes that when Clervaux married Anne Carter, [sister to his brother-in-law, Edward John Carter of

Theakston], at Thornton Watlass Church on Thursday 16 January 1810, Timothy acted as 'father of the bride', giving Anne away. He was a trustee of their marriage settlement, her father having already died.[165]

The happy occasion obviously brought the whole household much pleasure. Timothy records that his coachman, John Clarke, took the couple to catch the London coach for their honeymoon, and afterwards 'The servants had a dance in the kitchen at night.' Seemingly as a thank-you, the groom sent Timothy from London a barrel of oysters which arrived on 6 February!

The young couple returned north and initially stayed with Timothy and Elizabeth in Clifton Castle, into which they had just moved, but shortly afterwards Clervaux and Anne moved into Clifton Lodge, recently vacated by Timothy and Elizabeth. On 30 May Timothy recorded, 'Mr. and Mrs. J. C. Chaytor left us & went to sleep at the Lodge for the first time.'

Anne was probably pregnant when she and Clervaux married, for Timothy records on 4 September 1810 the birth of their first child, Charlotte. Their second daughter, Ann, was born on 12 December 1811. Elizabeth was closely involved with the young family, and Timothy also was very aware of their domestic arrangements. It must have been a serious inconvenience to Clervaux and Anne when a key member of their staff had suddenly to be replaced. Timothy noted on Friday 19 February 1813: 'Beatrice Blades, the nurse at Mr. J.C. Chaytor's, died this morning at The Lodge.' Neverthless, a few weeks later, Clervaux could get back to joining Timothy on social outings, for on Wednesday 9 April 1813, 'Mr. J.C. Chaytor went with me in the carriage to dine at the Book Club' [in Bedale].

There was doubtless great rejoicing when a son, Christopher William Carter Chaytor, arrived on 21 February 1814. A second son, Matthew John Carter Chaytor, followed on Saturday 13 December 1817: 'Mrs. Clervaux Chaytor was brought to bed this morning at 1 o'clock of a boy.' This baby was buried at Spennithorne at the age of three months on 2 April 1818.

Clervaux and Anne remained close to Timothy and Elizabeth Hutton, and after Clervaux's death on 14 August 1834, at the age of fifty-two, Anne continued to receive their support. Christopher Chaytor came of age early in 1835, shortly after his father's death, and therefore before the period of formal mourning had elapsed. Timothy helped out with suitable celebrations by providing punch for the servants to drink with the birthday cake they were sent. The eldest child, Charlotte, married Frank Morley of

165 NYCRO ZAW 194, Microfilm 1780.

Marrick in 1836, and Timothy was also a trustee of this marriage settlement, in lieu of her father.[166]

After her children left home, Clervaux's widow Anne moved into Clifton Castle. On the 1851 census she was described there as a 71-year old Richmond-born 'annuitant'.[167] When 'Mrs. Clervaux Chaytor' died at the end of 1856, Timothy attended the funeral with one of her sons-in-law, Alfred Darley, who had married another daughter, Elizabeth, on 3 July 1838.

Another connection with the Darley family had been made when Christopher Chaytor married, on Tuesday 26 November 1839, Arrabella Sophia Darley of Bedale. Christopher and Arrabella moved to the Chaytor family home in Spennithorne.[168] They had a daughter, Adelina Sophia, in June 1841, who sadly died the following February, but six more children followed, and the family lived in some style with a number of staff, including a butler, cook and governess. Timothy regularly called on Christopher's family at Spennithorne Hall. Christopher Chaytor was buried at Spennithorne on 20 December 1865.

Another Spennithorne family is mentioned in Timothy's diaries. The Straubenzies were of Dutch origin, and sometimes called Van Straubenzie. Several generations used the first name Turner after one of them married into the wealthy Turner family of Kirkleatham in Cleveland. Timothy's first diary reference to the family was on Saturday 25 April 1812, 'Miss Anderson of Swinithwaite set off with Mr. Terry (the surgeon at Leyburn) for Scotland.' Was her companion the cause of some gossip? Or did she have poor health and require ongoing medical assistance?

Timothy's next mention of the family is the funeral on Saturday 14 March 1818 of Henrietta Maria Straubenzie, who had 'died in Cornwall where she had been staying for the benefit of her health.' She was the twenty-six-year old daughter of the then squire, Turner Straubenzie, a lieutenant-colonel in the North York Militia, with whom in that capacity Timothy had many dealings.

Turner Straubenzie died in April 1823, at the age of seventy-six, and his son, Thomas, who became a major in the Militia, was keen on otter hunting. Timothy noted his death too, in February 1843. Another sad note was written in the diary on Monday 21 March 1853: 'Mr. Straubenzie's house at

166 NYCRO ZAW 197, Microfilm 1765.

167 It also describes her as Timothy's wife's sister, but it should have said sister-in-law.

168 White, *op.cit.*, p.619.

Spennithorn burnt down.' The family rebuilt their abode and have, like the Chaytors, remained as owners of property in the village.

On Thursday 23 March 1843, Timothy had gone with Henry Straubenzie, the younger brother of Thomas who had just died, and William John Anderson, the landowner of Swinithwaite, near West Witton, to see the preceptory of the Knights Templars. Its foundations had been recently excavated, having been found, on Anderson's land, on the lower slopes of Penhill. This visit was at a time when Timothy was starting to be interested in such antiquarian matters.

Timothy was to be concerned for the Anderson family when they later suffered a grievous loss. On Saturday 4 November 1854 he noted: 'Rode to Bedale, call'd upon the Andersons to condole [*sic*] with them on the death of their son William in India.'

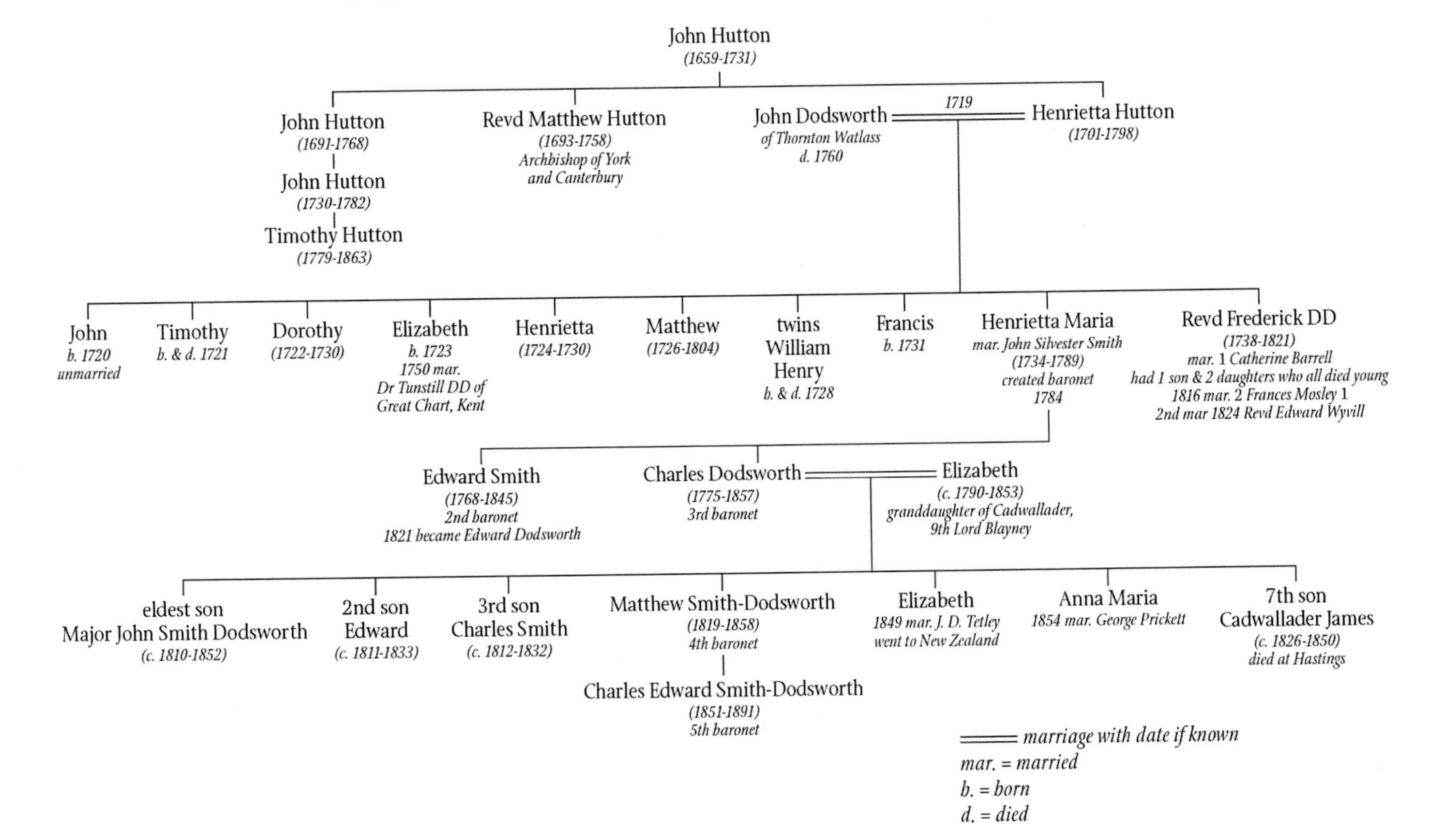

The Dodsworth family of Thornton Watlass
John Hutton
(1659-1731)
John Hutton
(1691-1768)
John Hutton
(1730-1782)
Timothy Hutton
(1779-1863)
Revd Matthew Hutton
(1693-1758)
Archbishop of York
and Canterbury
John Dodsworth
of Thornton Watlass
d. 1760
1719
Henrietta Hutton
(1701-1798)
John
b. 1720
unmarried
Timothy
b. & d. 1721
Dorothy
(1722-1730)
Elizabeth
b. 1723
1750 mar.
Dr Tunstill DD of
Great Chart, Kent
Henrietta
(1724-1730)
Matthew
(1726-1804)
twins
William
Henry
b. & d. 1728
Francis
b. 1731
Henrietta Maria
mar. John Silvester Smith
(1734-1789)
created baronet
1784
Revd Frederick DD
(1738-1821)
mar. 1 Catherine Barrell
had 1 son & 2 daughters who all died young
1816 mar. 2 Frances Mosley 1
2nd mar 1824 Revd Edward Wyvill
Edward Smith
(1768-1845)
2nd baronet
1821 became Edward Dodsworth
Charles Dodsworth
(1775-1857)
3rd baronet
Elizabeth
(c. 1790-1853)
granddaughter of Cadwallader,
9th Lord Blayney
eldest son
Major John Smith Dodsworth
(c. 1810-1852)
2nd son
Edward
(c. 1811-1833)
3rd son
Charles Smith
(c. 1812-1832)
Matthew Smith-Dodsworth
(1819-1858)
4th baronet
Charles Edward Smith-Dodsworth
(1851-1891)
5th baronet
Elizabeth
1849 mar. J. D. Tetley
went to New Zealand
Anna Maria
1854 mar. George Prickett
7th son
Cadwallader James
(c. 1826-1850)
died at Hastings
marriage with date if known
mar. = married
b. = born
d. = died

THE DODSWORTHS OF THORNTON WATLASS

Clifton Castle lies within the ecclesiastical parish of Thornton Watlass. The squires of Thornton Watlass were the Dodsworth family, living in the large old manor house there, and thus another of Timothy Hutton's neighbouring gentry families. Their relationship seems from the diaries to have been somewhat different from that with the elderly and compatible William Danby, or the fun-loving young Mark Milbanke.

Perhaps this was partly because the Dodsworths were not merely neighbours, but were distantly related to Timothy. His long-lived great-aunt Henrietta (1701-1798), a younger daughter of the first John Hutton (1659-1731), had in 1719 married John Dodsworth. Henrietta's portrait, in an oval frame, still hung in the Morning Room of Marske Hall in the late-nineteenth century. She was described as a tall and handsome woman, dressed in white and blue.[169] The armorial hatchment from her funeral still hangs in Thornton Watlass church.

Great-aunt Henrietta was only in her teens when she married, and was to bear her husband eleven children between 1720 and 1738. The youngest, Frederick, was still living, and the squire of Thornton Watlass, when Timothy's diaries start. Frederick Dodsworth (1738-1821), a Christ's College, Cambridge man, became a Doctor of Divinity in 1784, a senior canon of Windsor, and was rector of Spennithorne from 1778 until 1821, through which appointment he also had a link with the Chaytor family.

Dr Dodsworth married twice. His first wife was Catherine Barrell of Rochester in Kent, and they had one son and two daughters but all had died young. Timothy attended his second marriage on Wednesday 12 June 1816. Timothy's diaries note his attendance at many weddings; he was clearly a popular [and probably generous] wedding guest. However, he recorded this one in particular detail, for reasons which will become clear:

> 'To Aldborough to attend the ceremony of Doctor Dodsworth & Miss Frances Mosley's marriage at St. John's, Stanwick. Having been engaged to give away Miss F. Mosley & being appointed one of the trustees to the marriage settlement, was the cause of my attending so very soon at the very church where my good old aunt was so recently interred.'

169 Raine, James, "Marske in Swaledale", *Yorkshire Archaeological Journal*, vol. 6, (1881).

The circumstances surrounding this wedding were exceptional, in more ways than one. Only two days previously, Timothy had been at Stanwick church for his aunt Elizabeth Pulleine's funeral, and he was clearly somewhat embarrassed to be returning there for a happy occasion so soon after a very sad one. The loss of Elizabeth Pulleine would have been quite profound for Timothy, their relationship had been a close one, as will be seen later. Furthermore, although he may not yet have realised it, her branch of the family would eventually provide his heirs!

There was another, somewhat ironic, coincidence, in that it was one of Elizabeth Pulleine's granddaughters who was marrying Dr Dodsworth! Thus the bride was also distantly related to Timothy, although she had grown up in Burley-in-Wharfedale. This was why he was not only giving her away, but was also a trustee of her marriage settlement, another task for which he was frequently chosen. There was yet another strange circumstance about this marriage, and it is one on which he tactfully does not comment! Frances was about twenty-five years old, and Dr Dodsworth some fifty years her senior.

Rather less than five years later, Timothy heard on Saturday 31 March 1821: 'Dr. Dodsworth died this morning at a few minutes past eight.' He was buried in the family vault at Thornton Watlass Church on Monday 9 April 1821. Timothy 'Went to attend the funeral of Dr. Dodsworth. We, the trustees, remained in the church after the funeral to see the vault closed.' Timothy and his cousin Henry Pulleine were Frederick Dodsworth's executors.[170]

The morning after Frederick Dodsworth's funeral, Timothy 'Met Mr. Monson & Col. Pulleine at Thornton Hall at 10 o'clock to examine the papers & collect the money in the house. We found in notes & cash to the amount of £2,167 8s. 0d.' Even today, having over £2000 in cash in a house would be unusual, but in 1821 it must have been very exceptional. Perhaps the old divine did not approve of banks?

On 13 May, Timothy wrote to the jeweller Hamlet of London, sending his finger size for a mourning ring for Frederick Dodsworth, 'at the request of Sir Edwd. Smith.' Dr Dodsworth and Frances did not have any children, and with none surviving from his first marriage, the Thornton Watlass estate was to pass through a number of relatives in quick succession.

Frederick Dodsworth's sister Henrietta had married John Silvester Smith (1734-89), created baronet in 1784. Their son, the second baronet, as Sir Edward, now changed his name to Dodsworth to assume the Thornton

170 NYCRO ZAW 201, Microfilm 1780, Will of Dr. F. Dodsworth.

Watlass estate, and the family would later become Smith-Dodsworth. Sir Edward obviously believed in doing things well, and had gone to a top London firm from which to buy the mourning rings, then a fashionable item of funereal accoutrements. The firm of Thomas Hamlet of No. 1 Princes Street, Leicester Square, advertised that it was the silversmith and jeweller to their Royal Highnesses the Princesses Augusta, Elizabeth, Mary and Sophia.[171]

It was not long before Dr Dodsworth's young widow Frances, remarried, and Timothy notes on Wednesday 13 October 1824: 'Mr. Edwd. Wyvill & Mrs. Dodsworth were married this morning at Bedale.' She was marrying Revd Edward Wyvill, the rector of Finghall in Wensleydale, a living in the patronage of his family, the Wyvills of Constable Burton Hall. Other members of the Wyvill family mentioned in Timothy's diaries include Revd Thomas Monson (1764-1843), the fifth son of the second Baron Monson.[172] He and his son, Revd John Joseph Thomas Monson, both married two Wyvill sisters, daughters of Revd Christopher Wyvill. First the son married Elizabeth Anne in 1813, then the father married as his second wife Sarah, in 1843.

Edward, the rector of Finghall, and Frances Wyvill were to have a daughter, Fanny, who died in infancy in 1829, and Frances sadly died not long afterwards. Timothy's diary for Tuesday 29 March 1831 notes: 'After breakfast Mrs. Hutton & I set off for Fingall [*sic*] to attend the funeral of Mrs. Edw'd. Wyvill (she died 21 March 1831).' Frances was still only in her late-thirties.

Timothy made a later diary entry concerning Edward Wyvill on Wednesday 4 February 1852: 'Mr. Edw'd. Wyvill call'd & ..... brought me a picture of his painting of Kilder Castle, Northumberland.' Edward was to live on until September 1869, when he died in his mid-seventies. Other references to the Wyvills were on Tuesday 16 September 1856, 'Mrs. Wyvill died at Burton [Constable Burton]', and Friday 14 December 1860, 'Mr. Frank Wyvill called & lunched. He lately returned from New Zealand.'

Timothy notes the deaths of several other members of the Dodsworth family[173] and two more weddings. On Thursday 15 February 1849: 'Mr.

171 Bill-head in British Museum, Banks Collection, D.2.1782.

172 Venn *Alumni*.

173 Tuesday 19 March 1850, 'Mr Cadwallader Dodsworth died this morning'; Thursday 11 May 1852, 'Received an account of the death of Major Dodsworth. He died at Hastings at half past two o'clock. The account came to Thornton Hall by Telegraph'; Monday 13 June 1853, 'Lady Dodsworth died in the night'; Tuesday 28 July 1857, 'Sir Charles Dodsworth died about 2 o'clock, near 82 yrs, would have been had he lived to 22nd August'.

J.D. Tetley & Miss Elizabeth Dodsworth married at Watlass Church. I went to the wedding and a large party met at Thornton Hall at the breakfast or luncheon.' The Tetley family were based at Kilgram on the River Ure near Jervaulx Abbey. The bridegroom's father Joseph had died on board the *Tumar* in 1807 during the Napoleonic wars. Timothy was to note in his diary on Monday 7 September 1857: 'Went to Kilgram Bridge to see Tetley, he was to leave the neighbourhood for New Zealand tomorrow.' The second wedding Timothy attended was more unusual. Tuesday 1 August 1854: 'Miss Anna Maria Dodsworth and Mr. [George] Pricket married first at the Catholick Chapel at Leyburn & afterwards at Watlass where I met the party at church.'

There are two further diary entries concerning the Dodsworth family, both of which imply matters which are not explained. The second baronet was succeeded by his younger brother, Charles, who thus became the third baronet. On Friday 6 March 1857, a few months before the death of Sir Charles, Timothy visited him: 'Went to Thornton Hall to try to settle a little difference in the family there.' From what we know of Timothy Hutton, one can imagine that he would have skills as a peacemaker, but we are left wondering what the dispute was about.

Perhaps Timothy was making a further attempt at patching up grievances, when he visited the dowager Lady Dodsworth on Tuesday 7 December 1858: 'On my way to Bedale call'd upon Lady Dodsworth & gave her a Bible that formerly belonged to Mrs. Dodsworth my great aunt.' It was the long-lived Henrietta Hutton (1701-1798) who had connected the two families in 1718 by marrying John Dodsworth. As it was her older brother Matthew who had become Archbishop of Canterbury in 1757, perhaps her Bible was considered to be a particular family treasure.

Engraving of c.1838 by Nathaniel Whittock (1791-1860) entitled 'Marsk & Clints, The Seats of J. Hutton & M. Errington Esq'r's.' Behind Marske Hall, the stable block can just be seen to the extreme left in the trees, and Marske Church is just visible to the extreme right. The now-demolished Clints Hall, shown in the valley beyond Marske Hall, below the cliff-face which gave it the Norse place-name Clints, was purchased by the Huttons 1840-42. The engraving also shows the spur road to Marske from the Richmond to Reeth turnpike road being constructed.

In a private collection.

Etching by Timothy Hutton's friend the younger George Cuitt 'The Remains of a Chapel at High Burton near Masham, Yorks'. Timothy bought High Burton Farm in 1837.

In a private collection.

St Edmund's Church, Marske, early-mid 20th century postcard produced by Raphael Tuck & Sons, Ltd.

Courtesy of Richmondshire Museum.

Marske Hall, an early- 20th century winter view, showing many of the fine trees planted by John and Timothy Hutton. The Venetian window above the doorway marks one end of the Elizabethan long gallery, where portraits of the family were displayed.

Courtesy of Richmondshire Museum.

Matthew Hutton's hilltop monument, photographed by the author with access permission in 1975.

Large barn in Gothick style built by John Hutton on the hillside above Marske Hall, photographed by the author with access permission in 1987.

To Timothy Hutton of Clifton,
my very kind patron & friend,
I have sincere pleasure
in presenting this book;
and thus gratefully record it.
4 May. James Tate,
1832. Perp. Curate of Downholme.

Dedication to Timothy Hutton, written on 4 May 1832, by James Tate inside his recently-published book Horatius Restitutus.

In a private collection. Photo: Guy Carpenter.

Silver-gilt standing cup with cover, hallmarked 1589, given by Queen Elizabeth I to her goddaughter Elizabeth Bowes when she married Sir Timothy Hutton (d.1629) in 1592. Sold by the executor of the late John Timothy D'Arcy Hutton III in 1957.

Courtesy of Christies, London.

John Foss, portrait which belonged to Timothy Hutton, painted by the Richmond artist William Ripley Robinson (c1777-1845). Photographed by the author with permission in 1976.

Monument in Marske Church to John Hutton IV (d.1841), by the London sculptor Thomas Smith in 1843. The lengthy eulogistic inscription was composed by James Tate.

Photo: Guy Carpenter.

Portrait bust of John Hutton IV, showing a well-built elderly man with a thoughtful expression, a bald head fringed below with curls. Note the familial similarity with the portrait of Timothy Hutton reproduced as the frontispiece.

Photo: Guy Carpenter.

THE PULLEINES OF CRAKEHALL

As Timothy and Elizabeth Hutton did not have any children, he had to select which of his many distant relatives would, in due course, benefit from his estate. Two of his cousins-once-removed, brothers James and Robert Pulleine, were to be significant beneficiaries. The diary references to them therefore have some significance. How the family was related to Timothy is thus covered here in rather more detail than it might otherwise merit.

Timothy's aunt Elizabeth Hutton (1734-1816), the youngest surviving daughter of the second John Hutton (1691-1768), had in 1764 married Henry Pulleine (1734-1803). Henry's grandfather, Thomas Pulleine, who played a minor role in national history when he was appointed studmaster to King William III in 1689[174], had in the same year purchased Carlton Hall near Aldbrough St John, in the parish of Stanwick. Henry Pulleine's grandmother was Thomas's second wife, Dorothy Smithson. She was related to the dukes of Northumberland, among whose seats was Stanwick Hall, and Henry had been buried in the Northumberland vault in Stanwick Church. We have seen how Timothy's aunt Elizabeth had also been buried there when she died in 1816.

As a child, Timothy would have seen a lot of his aunt Elizabeth and uncle Henry, for Henry Pulleine was one of the family members who had helped to run the Marske estate until Timothy's eldest brother John came of age. Doubtless Timothy had also often seen their children, who were his first cousins. The eldest Pulleine cousin, Ann Babington, married Thomas Pulleyn Mosley, and their daughter Frances has already been mentioned as becoming the second wife of old Dr Dodsworth of Thornton Watlass.

Timothy's cousin Henry Percy Pulleine (1770-1833), played a large part in his life. Following the sale of Carlton Hall in 1810, Henry Percy in 1814 bought the manor of Crakehall, and with his wife, the former Elizabeth Askew, and their large family, moved into Crakehall Hall, an attractive house on the green. Aunt Elizabeth spent the last few years of her life with them there, until she died in 1839.

Henry Percy Pulleine was a military man, and, as Colonel Pulleine, is mentioned several times in Timothy's diaries inspecting the North York

174 NYCRO ZAW 229 Letters Patent appointing Thomas Pullen [*sic*] Master of the Stud 1689.

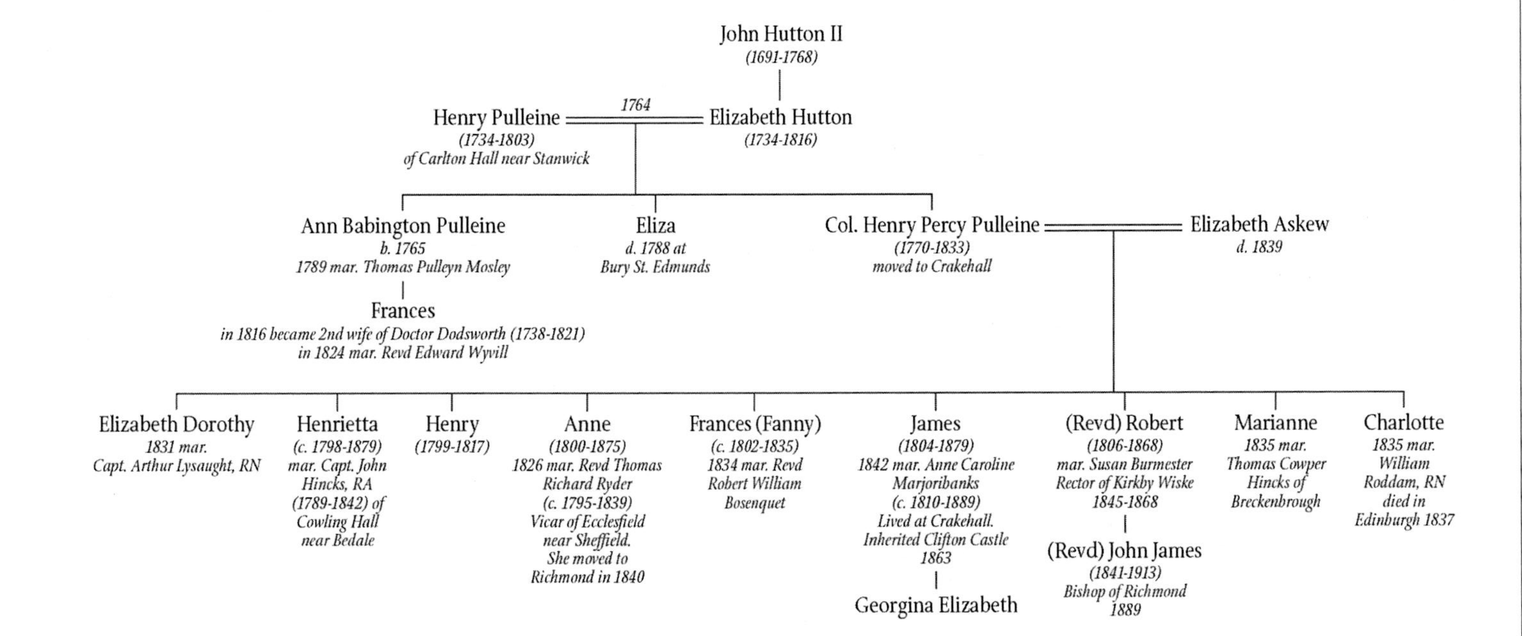
The Pulleine family of Crakehall
John Hutton II
(1691-1768)
Henry Pulleine
(1734-1803)
of Carlton Hall near Stanwick
1764
Elizabeth Hutton
(1734-1816)
Ann Babington Pulleine
b. 1765
1789 mar. Thomas Pulleyn Mosley
Frances
in 1816 became 2nd wife of Doctor Dodsworth (1738-1821)
in 1824 mar. Revd Edward Wyvill
Eliza
d. 1788 at
Bury St. Edmunds
Col. Henry Percy Pulleine
(1770-1833)
moved to Crakehall
Elizabeth Askew
d. 1839
Elizabeth Dorothy
1831 mar.
Capt. Arthur Lysaught, RN
Henrietta
(c. 1798-1879)
mar. Capt. John
Hincks, RA
(1789-1842) of
Cowling Hall
near Bedale
Henry
(1799-1817)
Anne
(1800-1875)
1826 mar. Revd Thomas
Richard Ryder
(c. 1795-1839)
Vicar of Ecclesfield
near Sheffield.
She moved to
Richmond in 1840
Frances (Fanny)
(c. 1802-1835)
1834 mar. Revd
Robert William
Bosenquet
James
(1804-1879)
1842 mar. Anne Caroline
Marjoribanks
(c. 1810-1889)
Lived at Crakehall.
Inherited Clifton Castle
1863
Georgina Elizabeth
(Revd) Robert
(1806-1868)
mar. Susan Burmester
Rector of Kirkby Wiske
1845-1868
(Revd) John James
(1841-1913)
Bishop of Richmond
1889
Marianne
1835 mar.
Thomas Cowper
Hincks of
Breckenbrough
Charlotte
1835 mar.
William
Roddam, RN
died in
Edinburgh 1837
marriage with date if known
m. = married
b. = born
d. = died

Militia musters at Richmond. Pulleine acquired the Crown appointment of Receiver of Taxes for the North Riding, and Timothy was involved with helping raise the vast sums required as security for this.[175]

The many Pulleine offspring – three sons and eight daughters – were Timothy's cousins-once-removed. The eldest son, 'poor Henry Pulleine', died young on Christmas Day 1817, and 'was buried at Bedale, in the churchyard under the East Window.' The second son, James Pulleine (1804-79), had a distinguished career. After Trinity College, Cambridge, he joined the Middle Temple in 1827 and was called to the Bar in 1832. He became Chairman of the North Riding Sessions, and Timothy records on Tuesday 30 June 1857 'To Northallerton ....we dined with the Magistrates & others who after dinner presented Mr. Pulleine with a piece of plate in testimony of their gratitude for his services to the Riding.' James Pulleine, who succeeded to the Crakehall property, also inherited Clifton Castle estate on Timothy's death in 1863. He would later serve as High Sheriff of Yorkshire in 1870.

The third son, Robert Pulleine (1806-68), after Emmanuel College, Cambridge, entered the Church. From 1830 to 1845 he served as stipendiary curate of Spennithorne, where the Chaytor family lived, and from 1845 until his death was rector of Kirby Wiske near Northallerton.[176] Robert Pulleine served as Timothy Hutton's chaplain during his year as High Sheriff of Yorkshire in 1844. Robert Pulleine's third son, Revd John James Pulleine (1841-1913), became Bishop of Richmond in 1889, and his son Robert was also a clergyman.

Not all Henry Percy and Elizabeth Pulleine's daughters married, but several feature in the diaries as brides. It is a sad reflection on the period that in several cases one or other partner was to die a short time after their marriage. They did not of course necessarily marry in their birth order. The sister who married first seems to have been the second eldest, Henrietta (*c*1798-1879). Her wedding is not mentioned, which may have been because she was a particular favourite of Timothy Hutton's mother Anne. However, the death of her husband, Captain John Hincks of the Royal Artillery, is noted much later, by which time Timothy's distress over his mother's Will had presumably subsided; Friday 14 October 1842: 'Received an account of Capt. Hincks's death.' The couple had lived at Cowling Hall near Bedale,

175 Timothy's diaries show £45,000 being handed over on 11 September 1817, and £26,000 on 1 February 1823.

176 McCall, H.B., *Richmondshire Churches*, (1910), p.77. The patron of this living was Eleanor, dowager Duchess of Northumberland, who resided at Stanwick Hall, and had thus known the Pulleine family from their time at Carlton.

which belonged to the Dodsworth family. Seven days later Timothy went to Cowling and then on to Bedale Church where John Hincks was buried, aged fifty-three. He was the son of a Cheshire banker, she was probably his second wife.

The first marriage noted by Timothy was of the third daughter, Anne, on Monday 25 January 1826: 'Went to Crakehall in the morning to attend the wedding of Mr. Ryder & Miss Ann Pulleine. Dr. Scott married the couple.' The officiant, Revd Alexander John Scott, the vicar of Catterick, is of some interest, as he had been Admiral Lord Nelson's great friend and chaplain. The reason for Scott's involvement was that his wife, the former Mary Frances Ryder, was elder sister to the bridegroom. Revd Thomas Richard Ryder had, only the previous year, become vicar of Ecclesfield near Sheffield. Sadly, Timothy was to note on Thursday 1 August 1839: 'Heard today from Mrs. Chaytor that Mr. Thos. Ryder was dead. He married Anne Pulleine. He was taken ill on Sunday and died on Monday last at the Rectory House at Ecclesfield.' He was only forty-four.

In their short marriage, Thomas and Anne Ryder had two sons and four daughters. In 1840 the widowed Anne brought her young family to live in Richmond, presumably to be near her brother in Catterick, as well as to take advantage of the genteel social activities still taking place in Richmond. The eldest Ryder daughter, Mary, married Revd Charles Thomas Hales, who established Aysgarth School, and there is a window in the school chapel commemorating her. The two younger daughters, Elizabeth and Henrietta, remained single, and continued to live in Frenchgate House until they both died in 1913. Among the good deeds they accomplished in Richmond was the teaching of young orphan girls to knit. As a result of this, they went on to publish some very early printed knitting patterns. A son, Herbert Croft Ryder, had a military career, and lived in Minden House in Frenchgate while serving as army paymaster.

The eldest Pulleine daughter, Elizabeth Dorothy, got married while Timothy was staying at Boston Farm during the grouse-shooting season. On Monday 22 August 1831, he 'Set off for Crakehall to attend Miss Pulleine's wedding to Capt. [Arthur] Lysaught of the Navy.' This was followed on Tuesday 25 February 1834 by 'Went to Spennithorne.... to attend at Fanny Pulleine's wedding. She was married this day to Mr. Robt. William Bosanquet and after the ceremony they set off for Rock in Northumberland to spend the honeymoon. Robert Pulleine married them and James Pulleine gave his sister away.' Henry Percy Pulleine had died in 1833, hence her older brother James giving Frances away. Her brother Robert was the incumbent of Spennithorne. Revd Bosanquet had been Revd Thomas Ryder's curate at Ecclesfield 1827-1834, and would later become rector of Bolingbroke in Lincolnshire.

The Bosenquets' marriage was extremely short, for just under a year later, on Monday 12 January 1835, Timothy recorded: 'A note from Robert Pulleine to say his sister Fanny (Mrs. Bosanquet) died last night at 10 o'clock.' She was only thirty-two, and had died giving birth to a son, Charles, who lived. Five days later, Timothy 'Went to Crakehall to attend the funeral of poor Mrs. Bosanquet. She was buried in the churchyard at Bedale.'

Later that year there was the excitement of a double wedding. Perhaps such an unusual event was the reason for Elizabeth attending these Pulleine nuptuals. Or did she always go, and Timothy does not mention it? Thursday 17 September 1835: 'Mrs. Hutton & I went to Crakehall to attend the weddings of Mr. Hincks & Marrianne Pulleine and Mr. Roddam and Charlotte Pulleine. The Hincks's set off to Redcar, the Roddams for Chester-le-Street.'

Marrianne was marrying Thomas Cowper Hincks, the son, by an earlier marriage, of John Hincks who had married her older sister Henrietta. Thomas Cowper Hincks had made his home at Breckenbrough near Thirsk. Two of their daughters would later marry later generations of Pulleines. The marriage of Charlotte, the youngest of Henry Percy and Elizabeth Pulleine's daughters, was again to be very short, for Timothy recorded on Thursday 6 July 1837: 'Mrs. Roddam died at Edinburgh on Tuesday the 4th.' She had given birth to a daughter. Charlotte's husband, William Roddam, born in 1793, was a naval officer, and he was descended from another and earlier branch of the Pulleine family.

PART SIX: SIGNIFICANT PLACES

Richmond

Masham

Bedale

Walburn

Marske

RICHMOND

Timothy Hutton's links with Richmond through his schooling, playgoing, musters of the North York Militia, membership of the Freemasons' Lodge and the Guild of Mercers, Grocers and Haberdashers, and friendships with John Foss and the Bradley family, have already been described. His visits to the town were, however, for a variety of other reasons mentioned in his diaries. For example on Friday 29 November 1811 he went specially to hear the organ, only recently installed in St Mary's parish church in 1809.

Timothy counted amongst his wide circle of Richmond friends many members of the corporation which, during the early years of the diaries, was constituted under the town's second charter of Charles II of 1684, and consisted of two 'houses' – the 'upper house' of twelve aldermen, and the twenty-four-strong 'common council'. Only those 'free' of a Richmond trade guild were eligible either to serve on the corporation, or vote for the candidates. The aldermen were drawn from the common councillors, and one of the aldermen became mayor of the borough for a year, although some took office more than once.

Timothy was not a freeman of Richmond, and seems to have had no wish to become one in order to serve on the corporation, but he took a close interest in its affairs. He often attended formal dinners hosted by the mayor of the day, but was also on familiar enough terms with some of the aldermen to take tea in their private houses. There were two William Thompsons, father and son, on the corporation. Timothy was particularly friendly with William Thompson senior, who lived in a large house at the bottom of Cornforth Hill. Timothy often stayed the night with him there after attending civic functions, or took tea, as on Thursday 23 September 1813: 'After dinner went to Richmond, took tea at Mr. Thompson's, Cornforth Hill'.

At some of these events, Timothy's eldest brother John was there also, as on Monday 29 November 1813: 'Left Marske after breakfast & went to Richmond where I dined with Mr. Smith, it being his birthday. Met at dinner two Mr. Thompsons, Mr. Tate, Mr. Ellis, Mr. Rich'd. Anderson, Mr. O. Tomlin, Mr. Cuitt, Mr. Wright, Mr. Bradley, Mr. G. Smurthwaite & my brother.' This convivial group consisted not only of members and appointees of the corporation, but also other old friends such as James Tate and the elder George Cuit.

Another dinner party was fully described on Thursday 21 October 1819, when William Thompson senior was serving his third term as mayor:

> 'A cover of snow in the morning, the day extremely cold. Mr. Foss & me rode to Richmond to dine with Mr. Thompson, the Mayor of Richmond. Twenty of us dined at the Mayor's – Mr. Dundas, Sir Rob't. Dundas, Mr. Ald'n. Terry, Mr. Goodwill jun'r., Mr. Kay, Mr. Ald'n. Macfarlan, Mr. Ald'n. Smurthwaite, Mr. Ald'n. Foss, Mr. Ald'n. W. Thompson [junior], Mr. E. Macfarlan, Mr. Alderman Smith, Mr. Ald'n. Gill, Mr. Alderson, Mr. Bradley, Self, Mr. Tate, Mr. Readshaw, Mr. Thos. Thompson, Mr. Pratt, Mr. Mayor. Slept at Mr. Wm. Thompsons.'

Later, on Monday 27 April 1829, when the younger William Thompson was serving his second term as mayor: 'Left Clifton at one o'clock & went to Richmond to dine with the Worshipful the Mayor Wm. Thompson. Got home at eleven o'clock.' Subsequently Timothy noted, on Sunday 28 August 1831: 'Death of my friend William Thompson of Richmond.' But the invitations to the formal mayoral dinners continued: Tuesday 4 December 1832, 'Rode to Richmond & dined with the worshipful the Mayor (Mr. Smurthwaite) 78 dined.'

Following the Municipal Corporations Act of 1835, Richmond corporation became a much smaller body, consisting of a mayor, four aldermen and twelve councillors, elected by all the then ratepayers. This 'new' corporation soon became very proud of its record of achieving many modern improvements to the infrastructure of the town. Timothy continued to fraternise with this body, such as on Wednesday 24 October 1849, 'Went to Richmond & dined with Mr. I. Fisher the Mayor about 98 sat down to an excellent dinner & all well arranged.' It was rare for a dinner to receive such an accolade. That year's mayor, Isaac Fisher, was a director of the Hutton and Other bank as well as an old friend of Timothy's.

Sometimes the dinners were connected with Richmond's civic officers rather than the mayor, such as that of Recorder, the important civic legal post granted to the corporation under Queen Elizabeth I's charter of 1577 which had been held by Timothy's father-in-law William Chaytor. Timothy's diary records for Monday 14 January 1833: 'My brother, Mr. Smith & self dined at Richmond. Mr. Elsley gave a dinner on being appointed Recorder of Richmond to the Corporation & some of his friends. I went on horseback and by way of Feldom (from Marske).'

Timothy had already met the new recorder in Richmond on Wednesday 5 December 1832: 'Dined at Mr. Bradleys. Mr. Elsley the new Recorder dined there.' Charles Heneage Elsley (1792-1865) combined his Richmond appointment with the same post for the City of York, where he was involved in building St Leonard's Place in 1834, the handsome sweeping Regency terrace opposite the Theatre Royal. He himself occupied the last house, No. 9. There is a portrait of him in the National Portrait Gallery in London.

Charles Heneage Elsley was buried in the parish church of the family's manorial seat, Patrick Brompton. Timothy knew the Elsley family as the squires there, and had earlier recorded the death of Charles Heneage's father, Colonel Elsley, while out hunting near Ripon on Wednesday 23 January 1828. When some of Elsley's property at Ulshaw Bridge was sold on Wednesday 18 October 1837, Timothy had attended the sale.

The diaries show that Timothy kept abreast of news of other civic officials. For example, on Monday 28 February 1842 he 'Got a letter from Mr. C. Bradley to acquaint me of the death of Mr. Tomlin which took place yesterday morning about one o'clock.' Ottiwell Tomlin had become the Town Clerk of Richmond from 1820 to 1836. Sadly his son of the same name, a young attorney, was to die less than three years later, on 22 December 1845, at the age of only twenty-seven. Both have tombstones in Richmond churchyard.

Many Richmond corporation members that Timothy knew were also tradespeople with whom he dealt, such as William Terry, the clockmaker who got Clifton Castle's second-hand stable clock going, and George Smurthwaite the wine merchant. Some of the visits to Richmond were therefore to settle outstanding accounts, such as on Saturday 15 December 1810 when Timothy rode from Clifton to Richmond and paid his bills with Messrs. Porters, Bowmans, Whitlocks & Goodburnes. Later in his life, the task of paying bills was delegated to Thomas Carter, who with his wife Ann had long been on the staff of the Hutton family.[177] Carter was a well-respected, if somewhat cantankerous, middle-aged man, who could be trusted with the substantial sums involved, and was one of the valued retainers bequeathed £100 in Timothy's Will.

Timothy seems to have liked to settle the Richmond bills on or about 6 January, which he referred to in one diary entry as Old Christmas Day,

177 The couple are shown as living at Marske Hall on the 1841 census.

there having been eleven days 'lost' when the country changed from the Julian to the Gregorian calendar in 1752. On 6 January 1853 he noted, 'Gave Thos. Carter a cheque for £448 7s. to settle the Richmond bills', and on 7 January 1857, when Timothy was at Clifton Castle, 'Thos. Carter came from Marske & brought the Richmond &c Bills, gave him a Draft cheque for the amount of £346 3s 0d.'

Many of the references to Richmond events later in Timothy's diaries concern his attendance at meetings as a trustee of various charities. The Hutchinson Charity, which had links with St Mary's parish church, met on the last Saturday of October each year. During his visit for this in 1850, Timothy met the new rector, Revd Lawrence Ottley, incumbent at Richmond 1850-61, and younger brother of the Ottleys who had been Timothy's fellow-pupils at Richmond School.

Timothy similarly attended meetings of the Hutchinson Charity in 1851, and 1853, when it was held in the office of James Robinson Tomlin, second son of the former Town Clerk, who like his father was a solicitor. The same office was used for the annual trustees' meeting of the Gilling Charity, which also met each October, though the day varied, and Timothy attended in 1852, 1856 and 1857. Timothy rarely recorded how much he donated to a good cause, but on Thursday 8 October 1857 he again travelled to a meeting in Richmond, where he 'gave a subscription to the Indian relief fund for Mrs. Hutton & self £30.'

Throughout the diaries, Timothy recorded news of families in the Richmond area. His note on the death of John Yorke on Friday 29 January 1813 has already been mentioned. On Thursday 27 June 1818 he similarly recorded that Sir John Lawson had died at Brough Hall, and on Friday 16 June 1820 that Lord Dundas had died at Aske the previous Wednesday. The sad death of Marmaduke Theakston of St Martin's while out hunting in 1823 has also already been noted. As with Elsley, Theakston's death was followed by Timothy acquiring some of his property, and again it obviously took some years for the deceased's affairs to be settled. On Monday 12 November 1832, Timothy 'Rode to ..... Richmond to attend the sale of Mr. Theakston's property. I bought two houses and half an acre of land £180.'

Later in his life Timothy had dealings with the Swire family who were linked with the Melsonby area. On Tuesday 12 June 1855, 'The Revd. John Swire came to Clifton & brought me some plans for me to see for a School House &c. at Manfield.' Some two years later, Timothy 'Went to Melsonby to attend the funeral of my old friend Mrs Swire who died at her house at Barningham on 15 May.' This was Bessy, the mother of Revd John Swire, who had died at the age of eighty-four.[178] Then, on Friday 20 January 1860, 'Revd. John Swire died at Manfield age 63', followed six days later by 'Left home early for Melsonby to attend the funeral of my late excellent friend the Revd. John Swire.'

178 National Burial Index.

MASHAM

Clifton Castle lies only a couple of miles from the small market town of Masham, the hinterland of which was often called Mashamshire. Masham was the nearest settlement to Clifton Castle with any commercial activity, so the household must have made frequent visits there for various domestic reasons. For example on a May Saturday in 1842, Timothy walked into Masham to get his hair cut!

Masham is, and was, a very attractive little town, and two of Timothy and Elizabeth's closest friends, the elder Julius Caesar Ibbetson, and the younger George Cuitt, were drawn to settle there, largely through the patronage of William Danby of Swinton Castle. When William Danby died, in 1833, he left behind his second and much younger wife, Anne, who clearly enjoyed playing the role of 'merry widow' in Masham. Just before Christmas 1835, she threw such a splendid ball at the King's Head Inn there that a report of this Masham event was carried by the *Yorkshire Gazette* newspaper.[179] Timothy Hutton had arranged the event for Anne, and he acted as steward for what sounds to have been quite an exhausting evening.

Upwards of a hundred and twenty of the local gentry attended, their forty or so carriages arriving in Masham to find the townspeople had brightly illuminated their shops and homes specially to greet the visitors. Even the parish church bellringers toiled merrily to add to the party atmosphere. The dancing began at 10p.m., and continued for seven hours through the night. Presumably many of those carriages set off to get their occupants home in time for breakfast, but those revellers who lived too far away were put up at Swinton Castle and Clifton Castle.

John Lightfoot, the licencee of the King's Head, brewed his own ale, and fed some of the resulting mash to his prize pigs. The brewing tradition, if not the breeding of oversized porkers, has of course famously continued in Masham. Formerly, however, the town was also a centre of textile manufacture, with a cottage industry based on wool and flax. A watermill, to spin flax into linen yarn for handloom weaving, was developed by the Prest family just across the river Ure from Masham in the township of Low Burton. The site of its proposed weir, to channel river water onto

179 I am very grateful to Valerie Slater of Northallerton for sharing this snippet from her researches.

the waterwheel, had been inspected by John Foss early in January 1820, at the request of William Danby, to see if it would impact on neighbouring landowners. Foss had reported back that it would not affect Clifton, but was likely to lower the summer level of Swinton's water.

These early spinning mills, often termed manufactories, were notorious for catching fire, as dust from the fibres accumulated on the machinery. The Masham establishment did, indeed, dramatically suffer a disastrous fire. Timothy recorded in his diary on Friday 15 December 1820 '.... saw Masham Mill[180] on fire. Rode there. When I arrived the whole was nearly burnt down except the walls which remain standing. Thank God no lives lost. ..... A great part of the front wall fell after I left. What are standing are so much damaged they must be taken down.'

The following day, the benevolent Timothy Hutton walked into Masham to start a fund 'for the relief of those that are thrown out of employment occasioned by the manufactory being destroyed by fire at Masham.' A few weeks later the mill owner, Mr Prest, and another Masham business man, Mr Durham, set up a subscription to purchase a fire engine for Masham. This was acquired and Timothy went to see it on 24 July 1821.

The poor mill owner never recovered from his financial, and presumably also emotional, loss which the mill fire engendered. Despite soldiering on for some years, the sad news came on Saturday 3 November 1842 that 'Buckle returned to Marske and brought the melancholy account of Mr. Prest having thrown himself into the Mill Dam.' Timothy Hutton was not merely a concerned neighbour, but he owned the house where the Prest family had lived. This was the ancient manorial base of Burton-on-Ure, which had extensive later pleasure grounds including a grotto. After the tragedy, Timothy converted the old house into a farmhouse in which he installed his farm bailiff, Christopher Mudd.[181]

Like Low Burton, Clifton Castle is located on the opposite side of the wide river Ure to Masham, but journeys between the two had been facilitated by the building in 1754 of Masham's four-arched stone bridge. This elegant structure was designed by Robert Carr, father of the great York architect and bridge-master John Carr. A distant vista of this bridge was one of the features which the landscaping of Clifton Castle was designed to include. In May 1815 John Foss supervised the taking down of some trees to open up the view. A prominent feature still visible when looking in that direction is the tall spire of Masham's fine medieval parish church, in which Timothy Hutton, as a local landowner, had a pew.

180 This textile mill should not be confused with Masham corn watermill.

181 Whellan, *op.cit.*, p.368.

Masham was the base of the Loyal Masham Volunteers, the militia group with which Timothy Hutton was first connected as an officer. It was from Masham that a group of militiamen set out on Saturday 16 March 1805 to what was thought to be news of a Napoleonic invasion, transmitted by the lighting of beacons. Fortunately it turned out to be a false alarm.

Sometimes Timothy recorded in his diaries an item of local Masham news which interested him. For example, on Saturday 8 June 1822, he noted that Miss Mary Spence of Masham 'had her house broken open & a quantity of money & plate taken away.' Perhaps this was one of the events which led Timothy later becoming involved with the establishment of a police presence in Masham.

A news item unrelated to any other Masham topic was recorded on Tuesday 28 September 1841: 'Mr. Wharton went to Masham to attend a meeting there being appointed revising Barrister for the North Riding.' Timothy was, of course, always generous in extending Clifton Castle hospitality for those going about official business, even if he seems to have had no connection with them. Another somewhat puzzling diary entry was written on Wednesday 14 March 1860: 'Miss Wrather died this morning at Masham.' She was a gentlewoman who had outlived her brothers Samuel and Thomas, but neither she nor her demise would appear to have any connection with Timothy.

As well as its weekly market, Masham had annual fairs for the sale of animals. Timothy, a connoisseur of well-bred animals, clearly enjoyed attending these. Masham Sheep Fair was held each 17 September, and was followed the next day by Masham Cattle Fair. The diaries sometimes comment on the minutiae of organising such events, as in 1842, when the Cattle Fair had to be postponed until Monday 19 September because the 18th fell on a Sunday.

Towards the end of his life, Timothy was involved with a local good cause close to his heart, the provision of a Mechanics Institute, paid for by a public subscription which was raised in memory of the much loved vicar of Masham, Revd Thomas Riddell, who had died in 1855.[182] The foundation stone was laid by Admiral and Mrs Harcourt on Saturday 15 March 1856, and when completed the facility provided a great asset to Masham, with a library containing about 2,500 books, and the reading room taking all leading newspapers and periodicals.[183]

182 Clergy of the Church of England database.

183 Bulmer, *op.cit.*,p.501.

A major aspect of Timothy's life seemingly not offered by Masham was that of legal services. These were instead provided by Middleham, another small market town, also on the river Ure, about seven miles north-west of Masham. Middleham was the home of the Topham family, several of whom acted as lawyers for Timothy. They occur somewhat confusingly in his diaries as three generations of them were called Christopher.

Many of the diary entries refer to Timothy making, and re-making, his Will. On Wednesday 22 October 1828, shortly after Timothy's mother had died, and infuriated him by virtually leaving him out of her Will, he noted: 'After breakfast set off for Middleham. Went to Mr. Topham's to execute my will which was witnessed by Mr. Topham, Mrs. Topham & their son Christopher.'

The father was also called Christopher, and he had another son, Thomas, both of whom witnessed some of Timothy's Wills. Timothy noted the death of Christopher Topham senior on Thursday 31 May 1832: 'Went to Middleham to attend the funeral of my late friend Topham. He was buried in Coverham churchyard near to Mr. Breare.' The family were all buried in Coverham churchyard. Thomas Topham also had a son called Christopher, who sadly died young. Timothy reported on Monday 22 December 1862: 'Christopher Topham died this morning at Middleham aged 25.' Three days later, immediately after Christmas, Timothy was 'At Middleham to attend the funeral of Chris'r. Topham which took place at Coverdale.'

Sometimes the making of a new Will was prompted by an important event in Timothy's family, as that which followed his mother's death. Soon after the death of his eldest brother John, Timothy noted on Saturday 4 December 1841: 'Executed my Will and Mr. Cuitt, Mr. Buckle and Mr. Thos. Topham witnessed it.' Again, just after his wife's death, on Wednesday 14 January 1859: 'Mr. Thos. Topham engaged all the day in making my will.' Thomas Topham also accompanied Timothy when he went to London later that year, and sold Elizabeth's diamonds there. Occasionally Thomas Topham accompanied Timothy on happier excursions, as on Monday 25 March 1844, when Timothy had been in York for the Assizes: 'Mr. T. Topham & I left York at 7 o'clock by the railway.' They were returning home via Northallerton.

On other occasions, there seems to have been no obvious reason for updating his Will, although perhaps some change in his financial circumstances, not commented on in Timothy's diaries, prompted him. A variety of witnesses are named, some of them his senior employees, such as

Christopher Mudd, and in December 1852: 'Went to Leyburn to meet Mr. Thomas Topham to execute my Will. Mr. Ralph Lodge & Mr. Grime at the Bank witnessed.'

BEDALE

Bedale is a market town about four miles north-east of Clifton Castle. In addition to its weekly market, Bedale had from 1837 fortnightly fairs for cattle and sheep[184] which Timothy sometimes attended. Bedale would become the nearest railway station to Clifton Castle available during Timothy's lifetime, after the Wensleydale line began gradually creeping west from Northallerton. A nearer station to Clifton would later be opened at Masham, linking the area to Ripon, but this was in 1875, after Timothy's death. The workhouse in Bedale served the Poor Law Union which included Clifton, and occasionally Timothy was involved in the need for poor relief amongst those with whom he had some connection.

Several of Timothy's close associates lived in Bedale, including Henry Glaister, a solicitor who oversaw the affairs of the Huttons' young orphaned cousin D'Arcy. It was with sadness that Timothy recorded on Friday 7 August 1846: 'My friend H. Glaister died this day at Bedale.' Bedale was also where John Buckle, Timothy's medical adviser for many years, lived. Not only did Buckle attend to Timothy, but also of course to other people in the area. For instance, on Sunday 25 July 1852, 'Mr. Wilson of Watlass died at Bedale, he had been there for some months to be near Mr. Buckle. If he had lived to the 20th of Nov'r. he would have been 79.' Timothy became increasingly interested in the age of people when they died.

At the north-west end of Bedale's wide main street-cum-marketplace is the large church of St Gregory, across the road from which is the equally large and imposing Bedale Hall, the two being juxtaposed in classic manorial tradition. The Peirse family had been lords of the manor from the reign of Charles I and, as owners of the hall, had enlarged and beautified it in early-Georgian style. The staircase, its rich Italianate plasterwork, and that of the large and impressive entrance hall-cum-ballroom, make this one of North Yorkshire's finest country houses, albeit set within the town.

Timothy knew the Peirse family well. On Saturday 22 May 1824 there was the funeral of Henry Peirse: 'he would have been 70 this day.' A few weeks later, on Friday 25 June 1824, Timothy rode to Bedale to attend the sale of Henry's famous stud of horses. In the parish church is a fine

---

184 Bulmer, *op.cit.*, p.360.

The Peirse family of Bedale

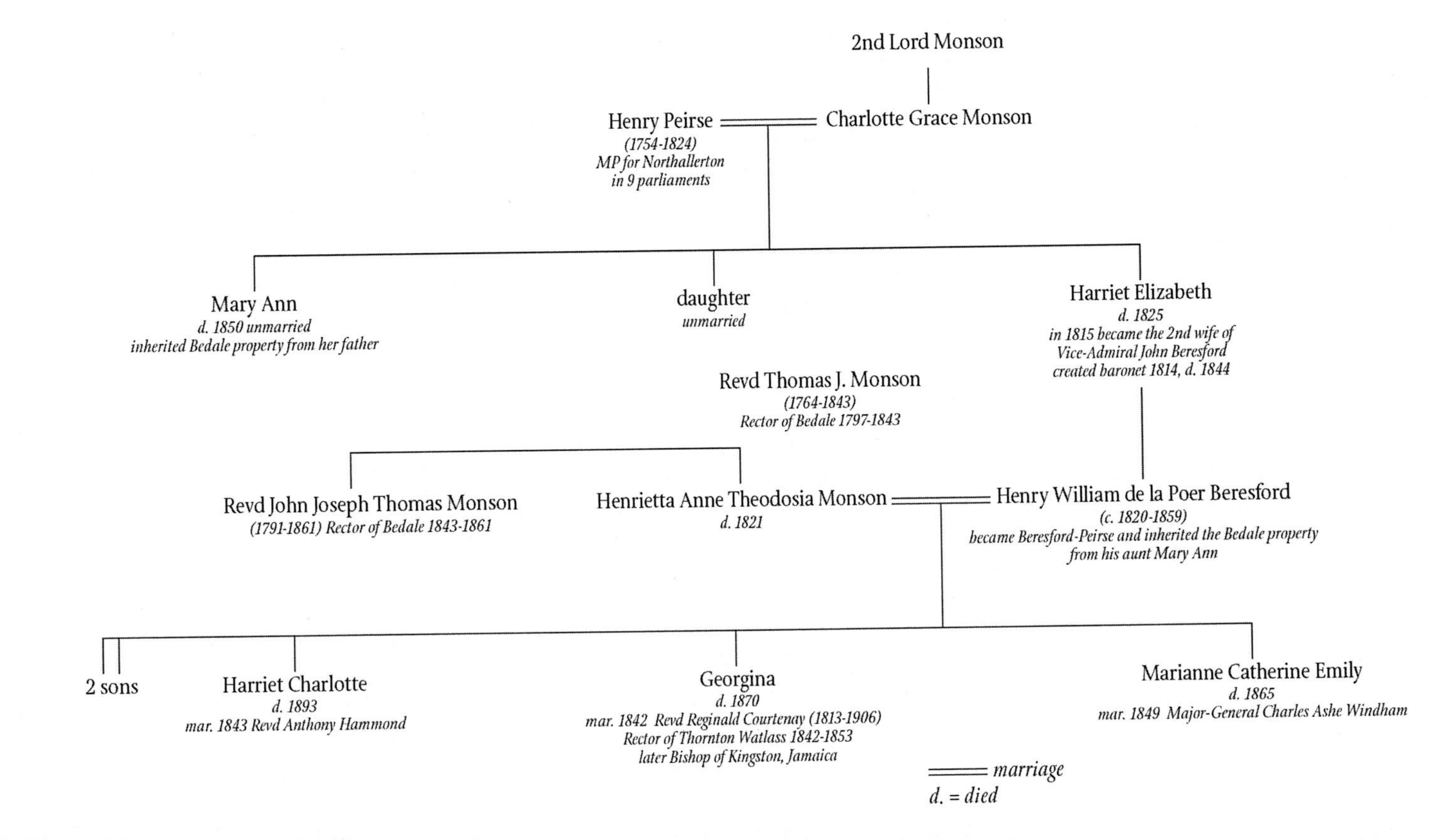

Grecian-style monument by Sir Richard Westmacott to Henry Peirse. He had been MP for Northallerton since 1775, but died without a son, and was succeeded at Bedale Hall by his unmarried eldest daughter Mary Ann.

Henry Peirse's youngest daughter, Harriet Elizabeth, is also commemorated on his Westmacott monument, as she died not long afterwards, in 1825. She had become the second wife of Vice-Admiral John de la Poer Beresford, created baronet 1814, and thus referred to by Timothy as Sir John Beresford. Sir John died in 1844, and the baronetcy descended to his son by his first marriage. The son of his second marriage, Henry William, later took the additional name Peirse in order to inherit the Bedale property from his unmarried aunt Mary Ann, and so became Henry William de la Poer Beresford-Peirse. Timothy attended his funeral too, on Saturday 30 July 1859; he had died at the early age of thirty-eight.

Henry had married Henrietta Anne Theodosia, only daughter of Revd Thomas J Monson,[185] the long-serving rector of Bedale between 1797 and 1843, and a member of a noble family which was already related by marriage to the Peirses. Timothy had noted in his diary on Monday 3 April 1843: 'The Hon. Thos. Monson died this afternoon at his house the Grange, Bedale.' Monson's son, Revd John Joseph Thomas Monson, succeeded him as rector of Bedale. The Monsons are one of many examples in Timothy Hutton's time of members of gentry families entering the Church of England and holding livings which were in the gift of their own or a related or inter-married gentry family.

Henry and Henrietta Beresford-Peirse had five children, and Timothy kept abreast of their doings, particular the marriages of the three daughters. On Tuesday 26 July 1842 he and Elizabeth went over to Bedale: 'we call'd on Sir John Beresford and Miss [Mary Ann] Peirse to congratulate them on Miss G. Beresford's marriage to Mr. Courtenay.' Georgina Beresford's new husband, Reginald Courtenay (1813-1906), had just been appointed rector of the parish which included Clifton Castle, Thornton Watlass. After serving there until 1853, he later became Bishop of Kingston, Jamaica, from 1856 until 1879.

Georgina's older sister, Harriet Charlotte, married the following summer. Her husband too was a clergyman, Revd Anthony Hammond, and she became his second wife. In 1849 the third Beresford daughter, Marianne Catherine Emily, married an army officer, Charles Ashe Windham of Felbrigg Hall in Norfolk. When Windham returned to England

185 *Ibid.*

as a hero of the Crimean in July 1856, he was warmly welcomed back and raised to the rank of major-general. Timothy thought Bedale should join in the celebrations, and before the month was out, went there to organise a committee to plan a grand reception. Very typically, Timothy combined business with pleasure that day, going on from the committee meeting to watch an archery competition taking place in the garden in front of Bedale Hall, the Beresford-Peirse family home. On Friday 8 August 1856, Timothy went to Bedale station to head the welcoming party, commenting: 'A large tent was fixed in the Market Place where a large company dined.' Windham would later additonally become a hero of the Indian Mutiny, and be knighted.

Timothy had also played a major part in the fortunes of a distant relative of the Bedale family of Peirse, Richard William Christopher Peirse of Hutton Bonville, and later of Littlethorpe near Ripon. Largely through Timothy's immense effort canvassing for him, he was elected in 1829 to the registrarship of the Deeds Registry for the North Riding of Yorkshire, based in Northallerton. He held this lucrative post until his death. Timothy's diary entry for Friday 20 December 1844 reads: 'Richd. Peirse died yesterday near Ripon he was Registrar for the North Riding.'

A Bedale institution particularly close to Timothy Hutton's heart was the Savings Bank set up in 1818, with Revd Thomas Monson as its Hon Secretary. This was a good cause spawned by the intriguingly-named Bedale Book Society. The Savings Bank prospered under Monson's leadership, and largely through his generosity a building was erected in 1840 which included not only a bookshop, and a room serving as the bank, but also a large first-floor room to be used for assemblies and as meeting space for the Poor Law Union and local magistrates. It was rebuilt in 1862, and included an institute with library for young men, and reading rooms, including a separate one for women.[186]

Bedale's hinterland includes the village of Crakehall, with which Timothy had several links, starting in his youth as it was the home of Christopher Pickering, one of the trustees of his future inheritance. Timothy's relatives the Pulleine family also made their home there. Another Crakehall resident was James Robson, related to Thomas Robson of Holtby, and one of Timothy's close gentlemen friends. James Robson was a frequent and welcome dinner guest at Clifton Castle, for instance dining there with members of the Tate family on Tuesday 26 July 1842.

186 *Ibid.*

On Saturday 22 February 1851 Timothy noted, sadly, 'Received an account this morning of the death of my good friend James Robson of Crakehall.' It was followed on Friday 28th by 'To Crakehall to attend the funeral of my much esteemed friend James Robson. We left Crakehall at half past 11 for Kirkby Fleetham where the interment took place on the south side of the chancel.' Timothy, and John Hutton of Sowber, who had married Thomas Robson's daughter Caroline, were the two trustees James Robson had appointed by his Will. And so on Tuesday 5 April 1851: 'Went to Bedale to meet Mr. Robson, Mr. Js. Robson [junior], Mr. R. Anderson & Mr. Hutton of Sowber to prove the Will of the late Mr. Js. Robson of Crakehall.'

Another nearby village is Theakston, not far south-east of Bedale, where the Carter family were squires. Edward John Carter had married Caroline Chaytor, Elizabeth Hutton's sister, and Carter's sister Anne had married Elizabeth's brother Clervaux. Timothy rallied some of his friends in the legal profession to support Edward John Carter over a transaction for the spiralling growth of railways in the late-1840s. On Thursday 3 February 1848, 'Mr. Thos. Topham & Mr. Henry Robinson came to examine some deeds relating to Mr. Carter's property at Theakston having sold part to the railway company.'

Edward John Carter's children were Elizabeth Hutton's nieces and nephews, and Timothy was typically generous to them. On Tuesday 3 January 1843, Timothy 'Rode to Bedale and met Carter and his son Charles at the Bank where I made arrangement to advance £500 for Charles's outfit to India.' Charles Carter, safely returned from India, was waved off from Richmond station by his father and aunt on Wednesday 19 September 1855: 'Mrs. Hutton & Mr. Carter went to Richmond & took Mr. C. Carter for the railway station who was going to Northallerton.' Charles was back in time to go shooting grouse on Skelton Moor on the 'Glorious Twelfth' of August in 1856.

Other Carter offspring also appear in the diaries. The eldest daughter was given away by Timothy when she married 'Mr. Harvey' on Wednesday 22 May 1850, and the sad news of a son's death was recorded on Tueday 5 July 1853: 'Mr. C. Bradley ..... came from Theakston & brought an account of the death of Augustus Carter at Mauritius on the 26th of April.'

WALBURN

As well as Clifton-upon-Ure, on his majority in 1800 Timothy Hutton also inherited the small estate of Walburn, purchased by the second John Hutton from the Beckwith family of Aldburgh near Masham in 1755. Walburn, about four-and-a-half miles south-west of Richmond, now mainly belongs to the Ministry of Defence. The humps and bumps of a deserted medieval village surround its surviving fortified manor house, Walburn Hall, which in 1718 had been described as 'an ancient pile, but somewhat ruinous. It is encompassed with a very strong wall, embattled on the top, and in the Civil War time was garrisoned against the king.'[187] Further out is the hamlet of Stainton, plus Boston Farm, the former farm of Wathgill (now a small army camp), and large upland tracts of moorland.

The early diaries contain few references to Walburn, as Timothy Hutton's attention was then focussed on building Clifton Castle, although on Wednesday 10 October 1810 Timothy records, 'Paid Mr. Gale 5/- for putting up boundary stones at Walburn.' Timothy's tenant at Walburn Hall was then Ralph Wilkinson, a breeder of prize-winning cattle and a man held in high regard by Timothy. Timothy bought a fine cow from him which he named 'Wilkinson'. Timothy's diary noted on Thursday 10 August 1820: 'My tenant Ralph Wilkinson died at Walburn Hall.' He was buried in Downholme Church on the 13th, at the age of fifty-five, and Timothy was the executor of his Will.[188]

Ralph Wilkinson's son, also Ralph, was buried there a few months later on 10 April 1821, at the age of only nineteen. Dorothy, wife and mother to the two Ralph Wilkinsons respectively, was to live as a widow until she died on 2 March 1856. The next tenant farmer at Walburn Hall was John Armitage, who lived there with his wife Mary, and children John, Elizabeth and Robert,[189] the latter succeeding his father as tenant after John senior died in 1872 at the age of eighty-five. At some time Timothy carried out a major restoration of Walburn Hall, although strangely this does not feature in the diaries.

187 "Journal in 1718-19 of John Warburton, FRS, FSA, Somerset Herald", *Yorkshire Archaeological Journal*, vol.15, (1900), pp.65-66.

188 NYCRO ZAW 189/2, Microfilm 1780.

189 Tombstone in Downholme churchyard.

Near where the road from Walburn joins the Richmond to Lancaster turnpike road, there is a farm still called Halfpenny House, from the price of the toll into Richmond. This farmhouse also served as an inn for travellers using the turnpike road. A well of good spring water on the opposite side of the road from the farmhouse was used for brewing the beer, and Timothy erected a handsome brewhouse beside it, which is still there. On Thursday 1 November 1832 he noted: 'Went in the gig to Halfpenny House to see the new Brew House erecting for Mason.' This was Charles Mason, noted as the victualler there in a trades directory of 1840.[190] Halfpenny House became the place where Timothy collected the rents from his Walburn estates, and being licensed it was a suitable location for the ensuing hospitality provided on such occasions. Timothy recorded on Thursday 27 June 1839: 'My rent day, the receipt at Halfpenny House.' It was also used as a location for cattle shows.

Timothy Hutton's diaries make mention of some members of the distinguished Ellerton family, who lived near Downholme. Richard Ellerton and his wife Catherine had three sons, Edward, Richard and Christopher. Edward Ellerton (1771-1851) attended Richmond Grammar School when Anthony Temple was headmaster, and the Hutton brothers were scholars there. Edward went up to University College, Oxford, became a senior fellow of Magdalen College, Oxford, and a distinguished theologian, becoming Doctor of Divinity in 1815. He, with his two brothers, founded a school at Downholme in 1814,[191] and in 1848 established a scholarship for Richmond schoolboys to attend the then newly-established University of Durham.[192]

Timothy Hutton observed on Sunday 5 May 1839: 'Christopher Ellerton died at Downholm', and a few days later he paid a commiserative visit to his brother Edward, 'Rode to Downholm to call on Dr. Ellerton.' The compliment was returned on Sunday 2 June 1839: 'At Marske. Dr. Ellerton took the whole of the morning service.' Later, on Tuesday 10 October 1843, Timothy recorded 'Rode to Ellerton Lodge to call upon Dr. Ellerton.' Ellerton Lodge, named after the family, lies a mile north of Downholme.

The outlying farms of his Walburn estate also occur in Timothy's diaries. That at Wathgill was mentioned on 30 September 1831: 'Called at Wathgill.... to enquire after Frank Lodge, he had died..... he was the oldest tenant I had.' Francis Lodge's age was recorded as sixty-eight in the

190 White, *op.cit.*, p. 617.

191 *Ibid.* p. 615.

192 Wenham, *History of Richmond School*, p.92.

Downholme burial register, so perhaps Timothy meant that Lodge was the tenant who had been in residence longest.

The tenant of Boston Farm was Anthony Croft, the death of whose son William, as the result of an accident with a gun in 1827, has been referred to previously in the chapter on Sporting Activities. Anthony Croft suffered further misfortune when part of one of his haystacks suffered an arson attack in April 1839. As the new crop of hay would not be ready until high summer, this was a serious loss of very precious animal feed.

When Timothy took up grouse shooting on the moors of the Walburn estate, he converted the Boston farmhouse into a shooting lodge. He noted the alterations to the house as ongoing on Friday 31 October 1834: 'Went..... to Boston to meet James Raw who is making alteration in [the] house by laying the Stable to it for a Servants Hall.' Poor James Raw was not to last much longer. On Wednesday 1 July 1835 Timothy was at Boston for 'the funeral of my old mason, James Raw.'

By then the building conversion had been completed, and for several years the Hutton household decamped to Boston each summer. The servants went on ahead to get the house ready, as on Wednesday 9 August 1837: 'Sent the carts and two women servants &c. to Boston.' The next day, 'Mrs. Hutton set off for Boston.' Timothy then followed, so as to be in residence the day before the grouse shooting started on 12 August.

The family had a scare shortly before the shooting season one year. The diary entry gives a brief insight into the quality of the house at the time. Thursday 7 July 1836: 'The house at Boston was struck with lightning and damaged one of the chimneys and the window in the room through the Dining Room, and shivered two bedposts in the room we sleep in.'

While staying at Boston each August, Timothy could enjoy outings in that part of the country. On Sunday 14 August 1836 (no shooting taking place on the Sabbath), he rode from Boston 'to see the new road', this being the Richmond to Reeth turnpike road then under construction.

The following year, on 23 August, his friend James Robson of Crakehall and he 'walk'd towards Hartleap Well.' This well-head, located alongside the Richmond to Lancaster turnpike road on the top of the moor at Barden Fell, is now hard to find, but was a popular spot in Georgian romanticism. It was the subject of a poem by William Wordsworth, *Hart-Leap Well,* published in 1800, which told the story of a splendidly fine hart pursued by the hounds in an extraordinarily long chase, until only one huntsman remained, and the poor animal, worn out by its exertion, dropped down dead beside the well.

Anthony Croft and his wife Margaret continued to live at Boston, keeping on eye on the shooting lodge as well as farming, until he died on Sunday 22 December 1850, aged eighty. Margaret Croft was still there when the 1851 census was taken; described as an 'annuitant', she was clearly in receipt of a pension from Timothy. She was assisted by two servants, Solomon Coats aged twenty-six, and Susanna Spence, sixteen. The tenant farmer was now Aaron March, who was still there in 1861, and he received £100 in the codicil Timothy added to his Will in 1864.

Walburn lies within the parish of Downholme, and as squire Timothy was patron of the ancient parish church of St Michael and All Angels at Downholme. Thus he appointed incumbents and saw to repairs, several references to both of which occur in the diaries. On Thursday 20 May 1841, Timothy 'left Marske after breakfast, met Anty. Croft at Downholm Church and took a look at the building to see the repairs that it wanted, being ordered to be repaired by the Venerable Archdeacon Headlam.' Timothy acted promptly to make sure the repairs were quickly carried out, and by the end of that July was back at the church to receive estimates for the work.

The following month, August 1841, Timothy's eldest brother John died, and Timothy had to turn his attention to many extra duties necessitated by this sad event. Repairs to Downholme church were undoubtedly carried out, but they drop out of the records that Timothy made in his diary. It was, however, at Downholme church that Elizabeth, in 1859, and then Timothy, in 1863, chose to be buried.

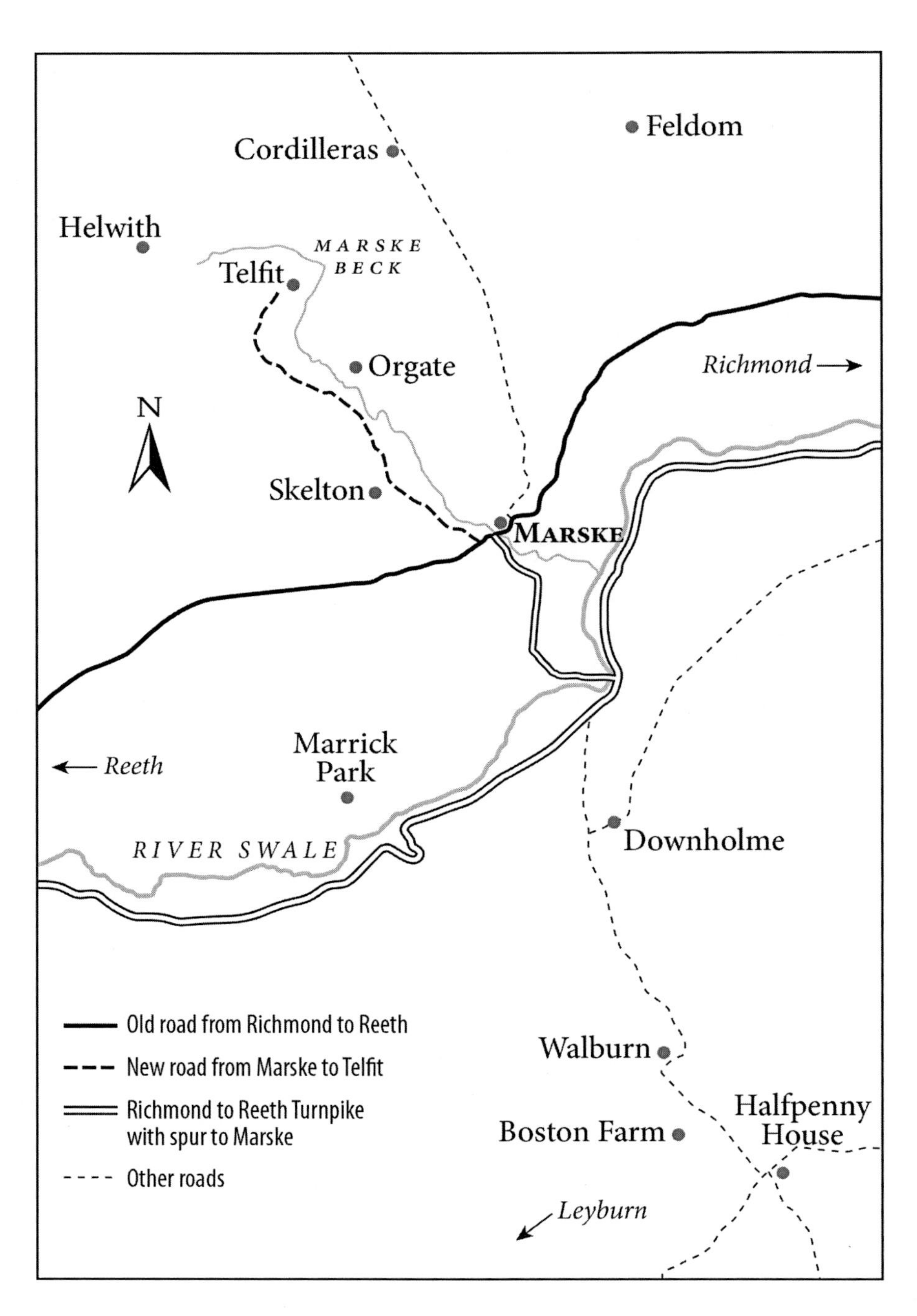

Places near Marske in Swaledale

MARSKE

Timothy Hutton's links with the Marske estate fall into three chronological periods. First, it was his family home, where he had been born, his base while growing up and to which he returned during school and university vacations, until he set up his own establishment at Clifton. Second, it was the seat of his eldest brother John and, after the unforeseeable deaths of their two intermediate brothers, they as the remaining sons became very close, with Timothy frequently spending time with the bachelor John at Marske. Third, after John's death in 1841, Timothy became responsible for Marske in addition to Clifton, and the diary entries show how he carried on the improvements to the estate and its property initiated by John.

From Timothy's regular visits to Marske he would be well aware of John's style as squire, and what was going on there, although the diaries provide few references. The entry for Sunday 14 January 1827, 'Johnson the gardener at Marske died', must reflect the great blow that this dealt to the work being put in to improve the grounds of Marske Hall. Later, on Tuesday 19 January 1836, Timothy 'Rode to Feldom to see Mrs. Wilkinson who will be 91 tomorrow.' That must have been a great age at the time. Feldom lies high up on the moors to the north of the Marske estate and the land is now a wild area used for military training.

On Wednesday 10 June 1840, Timothy noted that 'Mr. Topham told me that my brother had purchased Mr. Errington's property at Clints.' Clints, the neighbouring estate less than half a mile west of Marske, had always been in separate ownership. There was a manor house here, since demolished, and a walled garden and stable block which survive. In the early-seventeenth century Clints had belonged to the Willance family, from whom it passed by marriage to the Bathursts in the middle of that century. By the mid-eighteenth century it was held by the Turners of Kirkleatham, followed by the Erringtons. Since James Tate, writing to John Hutton as early as 15 November 1832, had commented that the last Errington had died, it would seem that John had toyed with the idea of acquiring Clints for some time. Or perhaps it had taken several years for him to raise sufficient capital to make a bid for it.

Whatever the reason, the Clints purchase had not been completed by the time John Hutton died in 1841, and it was Timothy who finally paid

£12,250 for it on 13 May 1842.[193] On Monday 16 May 1842, Timothy noted in his diary, 'Went to Richmond and gave Mr. Gilbert Stapleton [the banker at the Richmond 'Old' Bank] a cheque for £29,500 for the Clints and Skelton property.'

The Skelton estate, which lies across Marske Beck from Clints, belonged to the Stapleton family, and the price Timothy paid included £17,250 for Skelton.[194] Skelton appears on the ground now to be worth less than Clints, being on the north-facing side of the tributary stream, but its hinterland included lead mines.

There were other financial matters to settle in the aftermath of John Hutton's death. And so on Friday 3 June 1842 Timothy 'Rode to Leyburn, met John Topham there and made arrangement at the Bank for the payment to him when call'd for the money to pay the Legacy Duty which will amount to upwards of £3,500 having to pay the full duty of 10 pr. ct. on the personal property of my late brother.'

Some of the financial matters that Timothy had now to resolve related to the fact that, as John had got older, much of the running of the estate had been left in the hands of his steward, Thomas Carter. A somewhat crusty individual, Carter seems to have got a bit above himself as he assumed more responsibility. As early as 1823, James Tate had implored John Hutton to attend his parish church more often, because Carter was ruling the roost there. In 1825 Tate actually wrote to John to complain that Carter had treated himself and his wife Margaret uncivilly in not having prepared to receive them at Marske Hall with hospitality after a Sunday morning service, despite John having left instructions for this to be provided in his absence. However, these are incidental comments made over sixteen years before Timothy became responsible for the Marske estate.

Although after John's death in 1841 Timothy and Elizabeth spent more time at Marske, nevertheless the Hall there was mostly left in the charge of domestic staff. Both the 1851 and 1861 censuses show four of them in occupation, each time a housekeeper, housemaid, dairy maid and a male servant. The housekeeper in 1861, forty-year old widow Mary McLean, received a legacy of £100 from Timothy.

There are few references to Timothy and Elizabeth's domestic arrangements at Marske Hall, although there is one somewhat alarming diary entry, on Friday 22 December 1843: 'The bed in our room at Marske burnt.' It is likely that they were at Clifton at the time, as they usually spent

193 Raine, *Marske*, pp.78-9.

194 *Ibid.* p.81.

Christmas there, in which case they would not have been put in any danger. Although then the question arises, how did the bed catch fire?

Off the first-floor long gallery of Marske Hall are two handsomely-fitted bed-chamber suites, dating from the early-Georgian improvements made by John Hutton I about 1730. It was presumably in one of these suites that Timothy and Elizabeth's bed came to grief. Each bed-chamber has a recess for a tester bed, with flanking closets, and there is high-quality walnut woodwork, and in one of them, vestiges of red silk wall panels. From a letter James Tate wrote to John Hutton on 2 September 1822 concerning the hospitality arrangements for the Bishop of Chester's forthcoming Visitation to Marske Church, we learn that the other one was known as the Green Room.

In general terms Timothy seems to have kept Marske Hall much as his brother had left it, but he certainly made at least one significant change early on in his ownership. He created a billiard room which utilized a large Elizabethan fireplace cavity as a space in which to store the cues. A graffito on the plaster recorded 'John Coates, Mason, Filled this recess Jan'y. 29th 1844 for T. Hutton Esq.'

Timothy's diaries tell us much more about his activities to continue the improving work his brother had carried out on the Marske estate. Timothy significantly developed the local infrastructure, and invested in upgrading many of the farmhouses on the estate which are still occupied more than sixty years after the Huttons' Marske estate was sold off. Timothy also improved the agricultural fields, and added to the tree planting around Marske Hall which John had begun.

Timothy seems to have been particularly pleased with the new road, and its associated bridges, designed by Thomas Bradley, which were constructed on the Skelton side of the Marske Beck. This road still gives access to the isolated housesteads at Orgate and Telfit. On Wednesday 5 July 1848: 'Mr. C. Bradley walked with me up the new road towards Telfit', and on Thursday 7 September 1848 he 'Went with Buckle [the family doctor] to let him see the road I have made to Skelton, Orgate and Clints.'

On Marske land high up on the hillside below Deer Park Wood, John Hutton had earlier built an unusually large barn for the wintering of cattle, and the storage of the hay for their winter feed. Built in the Gothick style, it also served – and still serves – as an 'eye-catcher' in the landscape. By 1850 Timothy was replanning the use of the fields at Marske, with a view to making the land more productive and suitable for breeding better animals. On Monday 8 April 1850 he wrote: 'Went to Marske. Christ'r. Mudd went with me to see the cattle there and arrange the land for pasture and meadow.' Some of the fields near the village were then used for arable, for on Wednesday 31 August 1853 Timothy noted 'Began to cut the wheat at Marske', although such areas are not considered suitable for corn growing today.

In 1852 Timothy decided to improve the land around the remote Telfit farm. Monday 2 February 1852: 'Went to Marske, ...Mr. C. Bradley ..... brought Smith the tile maker to look at the clay in Greathead's farm at Marske which he much approves of for draining tiles.' Later that month, when at Marske, 'I went with March [of Boston Farm] & Carter [Thomas Carter, the estate steward] to see the ground where the draining tiles are to be made.' By the end of 1852 kilns for baking the clay into drainage tiles had been built: Wednesday 1 December 1852, 'Went with Aaron March to the Tile Kilns at Marske.'

A few weeks later Timothy showed them off again on Monday 10 January 1853: 'Left Mr. Bradley at Marske to receive the cottage rents. We walked to the Tile Kilns.' Sadly the improvements to the Telfit land brought no solace to the tenant, for on Saturday 3 January 1857 'Buckle called on his way [from Bedale] to Marske to hold an inquest upon Peter Greathead of Telfit who has destroyed himself.' On Wednesday 11 February, Timothy 'Walked [from Marske] to Telfit to the sale of the late Peter Greathead's cattle &c. &c.'

John Hutton had put significant investment into the dwellings in and around Marske itself, and Timothy clearly continued this policy, spending large sums on the outlying farmhouses over a period of many years. Wednesday 8 July 1846: 'Went to Marske, call'd at Park Top, the masons have laid in the foundation of the Farm House there', and Monday 25 July 1853, 'I went to Applegarth to the House now building'. Finally, on Thursday 23 August 1855, 'Walk'd [from Marske] to the new building at Bushy Park.'

Other details relating to the Marske estate occur throughout the later diaries. For example, on Wednesday 9 November 1859, '.....A fire at Cordilleras in the Haybarn, not much damage to me but the loss of a great quantity of hay to the tenant Simon Harker.' Cordilleras was the name John Hutton gave to the impressive model farm he created on an extremely inhospitable part of the estate, about 350 metres above sea level. About 800 acres of land had been allotted to him following the enclosure of Marske Moor by an Act of Parliament of 1809.[195] The name John Hutton gave

195 Chapman, Vera, "North Country Farms of the Moorland Fringe, Won from the Moor", *Beamish One – First Journal of the North of England Open Air Museum*, (1978), pp.40-59.

the farm came from the Spanish word 'cordillera' (an extensive chain of mountains), and Spanish names were also given to the individual fields of productive farmland he astonishingly created at this altitude. This choice of names seems to have been inspired by the independence from Spanish and Portuguese colonists being achieved by South American countries in the early-nineteenth century.

Situated two miles north of Marske up a steep and narrow road, the land was laboriously walled, ploughed, and drained. Still surviving in the Marske area are many of the limekilns which produced the lime with which the acidic soil was sweetened. The aim was to produce crops – mainly oats – to help feed the English nation at the height of the Napoleonic wars, and also turnips to sustain the shorthorn cattle John was breeding.

Timothy's habitual concern for his Clifton tenants was clearly extended to those at Marske, as on Tuesday 20 February 1855: 'James Hutchinson of Helwith died this morning.' Helwith was another remote farm on the estate, north-west of Marske. Again, on Monday 8 October 1849: 'Buckle ......went to Marske to hold an inquest upon a child of my keeper's that was burnt to death', and on Thursday 6 June 1850, 'Buckle ..... came to Marske to hold an inquest on the poor boy that was drowned yesterday in the beck below the Clints gardens. Joseph Plews, the son of Rich'd. Plewes, one of my carters.'

The planting of some of the fine trees which still stand near Marske Hall is recorded in Timothy's diaries. On Tuesday 21 October 1851: 'Got some laurels planted near the house to hide the road from the gates to the pond. Planted 3 cedars and 3 pines below the island north side of the beck'. Then on Tuesday 15 November 1852, 'Got 6 Deodar Cedars & 6 pines planted on the Conywarren bank at Marske.' The diary entry for Wednesday 17 October 1860 records 'Mr. Fitch planted some pines &c. &c. that arrived this day from Mr. Warterer, Bagshot.' This diary entry does not state where the pines were planted, but some fine American redwoods remain at Marske, and they were a speciality of Michael Waterer who had taken a famous nursery at Bagshot.

PART SEVEN:
FINALE

The Story Concludes

THE STORY CONCLUDES

Timothy Hutton's diaries contain an enormous amount of valuable information about his life and times. But what do they tell us about him as a person? We have seen how he was an astute businessman, an improver of his estates, and a benevolent person acting kindly towards his tenants and his various relatives. How did he see himself?

Timothy's family background was a strange mixture of eminent churchmen and unconventional relationships. His eldest brother John, ostensibly the life-long bachelor, who rejected James Tate's imploring him to marry and thus by implication ensure the continuation of the family lineage at Marske, did apparently father an illegitimate child. The Richmond parish registers record the baptism, on 22 February 1800, of Mary Ann, the 'bastard' daughter of Jemima Hurworth, '& of John Hutton Esq're of Marske'. As the term 'reputed father' is not used, it would seem that there was no dispute. What happened to Mary Ann is not known, she does not occur again in the Richmond registers. Her mother Jemima had another daughter, baptised Elizabeth, also out of wedlock, three years after Mary Ann, although the father this time is not named. Elizabeth only lived a few days.

Timothy, recently returned from Cambridge University, seems not yet to have started keeping diaries, so we have no record of his comment on John's indiscretion, which he presumably knew all about. Similarly we have no account of Timothy's thoughts on his childhood, growing up with a widowed mother who was not of the same social background as his father, his own legitimacy, or the illegitimacy of his brothers. Neither do the later diaries contain any hints of regret that he did not have a direct heir, nor indeed how he envisaged the future history of his estates. What follows is an attempt to bring together what we can interpret about his view of himself, and in particular his self-awareness of his membership of the historic Hutton family.

Timothy was very aware of his lineage and his relationship to the various families into which the Huttons had married in the past. At some unidentified time, apparently before the main series of surviving of diaries begins in 1810, he gathered together in a notebook a lot of genealogical information about his family. What prompted this is unclear. Possibly there was already some outside legal challenge to his brother's inheritance of the Marske estate, or maybe his mother was unhappy with her financial and social lot in widowhood.

There is only one mention in the diaries referring to a generation further back than that of his parents: on Tuesday 24 April 1821, 'The picture of my grandfather arrived.' There is no indication of how he came to acquire what was, presumably, a portrait of the second John Hutton rather than of Richard Ling. John Hutton II would be of particular interest to Timothy because this was the ancestor who had purchased the old Clifton Castle in 1735, and to whom Timothy presumably felt some gratitude for ultimately providing him with a source of such satisfaction in his life. The following day, Timothy 'Wrote to Mrs. Thornton of London to thank her for the picture of my grandfather which she made me a present of.' There seems to be no other reference to Mrs Thornton, so where she fitted into this story is a mystery.

What is very clear from his diaries and other sources is that Timothy greatly mourned the loss of the two older brothers between him and his eldest brother John. James, the second son, was the first to die. In his genealogical notebook, Timothy wrote 'James Hutton my 2nd brother died at Marske Jan'y. 24th (his birthday) buried at Marske Jan'y. 27th 1803.' James Tate noted that James Hutton had died at 1a.m. on 24th March at the age of only 27.[196] The loss of James continued to reverberate with Timothy, as shown by his diary entry for Thursday 24 January 1811: 'Eight years this day since my brother James died.'

James Hutton had made a Will[197] on 5 March 1801, describing himself 'now a Captain in the Second West York Regiment of Militia.' This regiment, sometimes known just as the York Regiment, became the 3rd Battalion of the Prince of Wales's Own West Yorkshire Regiment. In the Will, James made his brother 'Captain Matthew Hutton' his residiary legatee, and left his 'dear Mother Ann Hutton of Marske' a yearly annuity of £100 to be paid each half year on 5 January and 5 July.

In a codicil dated 22 January 1803, by which time James describes himself as 'late a captain' in the same regiment, now living at Marske, and by implication of the wording being seriously ill – it was, after all, only two days before he died – he additionally makes thirteen bequests. These range from one to ten guineas to named individuals at Marske, seemingly all connected with the hall and presumably responsible for nursing him

196 Wenham, *James Tate*, p.428.

197 National Archives PRO PROB 11/1388/234.

there, and he also repaid £50 which had been lent by 'William Mason of Clifton-upon-Yore' to his brother Matthew.

At the end of 1813 the family suffered another grievous loss, that of the third son. Matthew, who seems to have already retired from his army career, had settled in Macclesfield and established a home there. Having heard that Matthew was seriously ill, Timothy and Elizabeth, taking his mother Anne with them, had travelled over to Macclesfield for a few days in mid-November. Timothy would later note in his diary that Matthew had died 'a few minutes before 12 in the night', on 12 December, just a few days short of his thirty-sixth birthday.

The letter bearing the sad, if not unexpected, news of Matthew's death reached Clifton Castle on 14 December 1813. Timothy and Elizabeth reacted immediately the letter arrived: 'My wife & I set off for Macclesfield at half past 11am & got to Halifax about 8 in the evening.' The following day, 'Mrs. Hutton & I left Halifax at half past 7 in the morning. Got to Macclesfield before three where we found my brother John who had arriv'd in the morning from London.'

By the following weekend, it would seem that John, Timothy and Elizabeth Hutton had all returned to Yorkshire, but it took longer in pre-railway times for Matthew's body to be brought home. That Sunday, the day after Christmas Day, Timothy's diary notes the then custom of not attending Morning Service while awaiting a family funeral: 'My brother not being buried I did not go to church in consequence.'

The funeral took place two days later, on the morning of Tuesday 28 December, the service being taken by James Tate, in his capacity as rector of Marske as well as a close family friend. Tate entered the details in his own hand in the burial register of Marske church[198] as follows: 'Matthew Hutton, 3rd son of the late John Hutton Esq'r. of Marske, aged 36 [*sic*], of Macclesfield in Cheshire where he died on Saturday night, 11 December.'

There is nothing untoward about this register entry, apart possibly its length. However, it was no ordinary interment. After the funeral service taken by Tate in St Edmund's Church at Marske, Matthew was not buried, as might have been expected with his ancestors in the family chapel there. Instead, a mournful procession behind Matthew's coffin wound its long hilly way to the summit of the Deer Park, the highest point on the Hutton estate. The sixty-foot high obelisk that marks the spot is a landmark for miles around. Its architectural style inspired by ancient Egypt had become

198 NYCRO PR/MAK/1/1, microfilm 2561.

very fashionable following Lord Nelson's defeat of Napoleon at the Battle of the Nile in 1798.

There are no references in Timothy's diaries to the building of Matthew's obelisk, so perhaps John Hutton arranged for it to be put up. A plaque inscribed in Latin describes it as Matthew's burial place, and says he died in Macclesfield at the age of thirty-five. Strangely, there is a mistake on the inscription. It states that he died on 12 December 1814. There is no doubt that the actual year was 1813. Did no-one check the inscription panel before it was put in place, or visit the completed obelisk? Such a structure must have taken some time to commission, so perhaps the precise details had faded from memory by then.

The site high up in the Deer Park was obviously an unusual choice for a burial, it not being consecrated ground. It is said that this was the place where Matthew had requested burial, as it had been his favourite spot as a boy, providing such wonderful views of the surrounding countryside and Hutton estate. That this was indeed Matthew's burial place, as stated by the Latin initials H.S.E. [*Hic Sepulchris est*], and that the obelisk is not merely a memorial, is confirmed by Timothy's diary for Friday 7 January 1814: 'Mr. Smith & I .... went to the Park to the place where poor Mat. was buried.'

Subsequent annual diaries for 12 December often refer to Matthew, for example in 1815, '.....two years this day since my brother Mat. died.' Timothy speaks of his brothers James and Matthew by name, often using the familiar 'Mat' for Matthew. Significantly, Timothy never uses the name John for his eldest brother, who is always just 'my brother'. This contemporary phraseology matches the manner of referring to, say, an eldest sister, as, for example, 'Miss Chaytor', rather than by her Christian name, Mary.

It is likely that Matthew had retired from the army due to ill health, possibly as a result of service during the Napoleonic campaigns,[199] for when he made his Will[200] on 5 November 1813, just a few weeks before he died, he does not refer to being a captain, and his witnesses were a surgeon and an attorney. Matthew owned a house in the Market Place at Macclesfield, where there also resided Mr Benjamin Swann and his wife Ellen, and the Will shows he was at pains to provide well for them. Matthew's executors were his brother John, and his exact contemporary Sheldon Cradock of Hartforth near Gilling West.[201] Matthew left his silver watch to Mr Robert

199 One account says he was in the 24th Regiment of Foot, which suffered severe losses.

200 National Archives, PRO PROB 11/1550/416.

201 History of Parliament.

Trapps of Nidd Hall near Ripley in Yorkshire and, like his brother James, some income for his 'dear mother Ann Hutton' – the interest on his dividends and government security stock for her life.

However, it would seem that this bequest did not satisfy his mother. Matthew had stipulated that the rest of his estate should be sold and the proceeds used to set up a charity for the relief of the poor in the Marske area either by money payments, the purchase of provisions and 'cloathes', education or instruction, or the distribution of religious books. After Matthew's Will had been proved, Anne sought Counsel's Opinion[202] as to whether she should have been left Matthew's estate. The lawyer commented, 'Mrs. Hutton, the Testator's mother, is living, & under the impression that the ultimate devise is void.' He went on, that she could only dispose of the property herself with a Grant from the Crown, and it was unlikely that this would be made.

The dispute continued, and delayed the implementation of the charity.[203] It was only on 17 January 1835, more than six years after Anne Hutton died in 1828, and over twenty years since Matthew had died, that the Hutton Charity was formally set up as a trust. John Hutton was chairman, Matthew's executor Sheldon Cradock of Hartforth and Revd William Kendall, the rector of Marske, became trustees, and Richmond banker Thomas Smurthwaite was appointed clerk to the trustees on a salary of £20 per annum. Timothy Hutton would join the panel of trustees on 1 July 1837, thus adding to his portfolio of obligations to worthy causes, this time with a strong family tie.

Soon after the charity was at last set up, later in 1835, and in keeping with the original intention, the trustees endowed William Gill, the schoolmaster at Hudswell, with £15 a year to teach ten extra scholars, and Joseph Walton at Marske £20 to teach another fifteen scholars. In the first year, six boys and four girls were so educated at Hudswell, and nine boys and six girls at Marske.

The manner in which Matthew Hutton's wishes were fulfilled was mainly as a medical charity. At a meeting held in Richmond on 5 September 1835 it established dispensaries in Richmond, Reeth and Leyburn. These were to open on two days per week at each place, the charity providing for each of these places a qualified 'surgeon' to give expert medical advice.

Richard Atkinson was appointed for Richmond at a salary of £40, John Richard McCollah at Reeth and John Terry at Leyburn, the latter two at

202 A paper copy of this report is deposited in NYCRO ZAW 93.

203 White, *op.cit.*, p.635.

£30 each. The medical men were already established in each location, and continued to practise as before rather than erecting new dispensary buildings, for example Richard Atkinson was living at Frenchgate in Richmond. The stipends, which reflected the relative size of population covered in each location, meant that the doctors were to treat the poor without charge, but were expected to account for such. The charity also subscribed donations of £25 per year to York County Hospital, Leeds General Infirmary, Newcastle-upon-Tyne Infirmary and the York Lunatic Asylum in order to be able to send difficult cases on for more specialist treatment. By the end of January 1836, the Richmond dispensary had seen 122 patients, one of whom had been sent to the Leeds Infirmary, Leyburn had dealt with thirty-three and Reeth with fifty-eight.

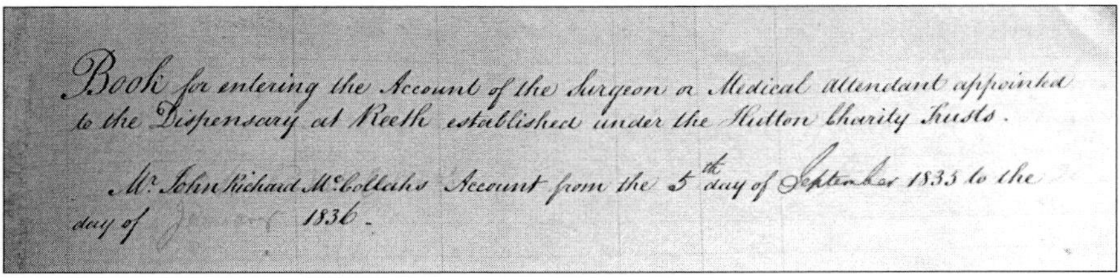
Book for entering the Account of the Surgeon or Medical Attendant appointed to the Dispensary at Reeth established under the Hutton Charity Trusts.

Mr. John Richard McColloh's Account from the 5th day of September 1835 to the day of January 1836.

Heading on opening page of account book of Reeth Dispensary. Courtesy of Richmondshire Museum. Photo: Guy Carpenter.

The account book survives for the Reeth dispensary.[204] Its opening heading is 'Book for entering the Account of the Surgeon or Medical Attendant appointed to the Dispensary at Reeth established under the Hutton Charity Trusts. Mr. John Richard McColloh's Account from the 5th day of September 1835 to the 27th day of January 1836.' That first accounting period shows that of the fifty-eight patients treated, thirty-three had been 'discharged cured', three were 'discharged relieved', one was 'incurable', and twenty-one 'are still patients'. The following two half-years saw seventy-five and sixty-one patients respectively.

By 1903, when the numbers stopped being kept sequentially, 9,291 patients had been seen. The numbers gradually declined to about five per half year, and the account book ends in 1948 with the advent of the National Health Service. Each set of accounts was signed off by the chairman of the time, starting with John Hutton, followed by Timothy Hutton, whose diaries record his attendance at the twice-yearly meetings, and finally the

204 Now in the Richmondshire Museum.

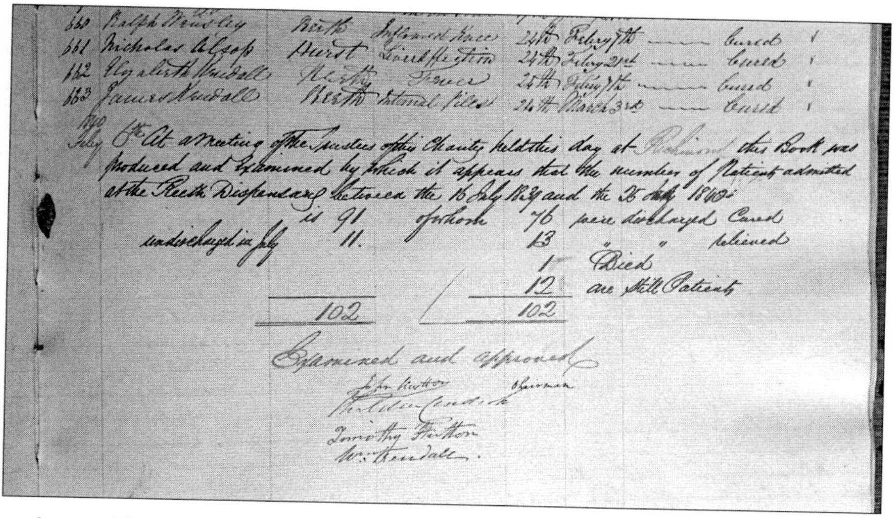

663 James Kendall Reeth Internal piles 24th March 3rd — Cured 1

1840 July 6th At a meeting of the Trustees of this Charity held this day at Richmond this Book was produced and examined by which it appears that the number of Patients admitted at the Reeth Dispensary between the 16 July 1839 and the 25 July 1840 is 91 of whom 76 were discharged Cured

undischarged in July 11. 13 " " relieved

1 Died

12 are still Patients

102 102

Examined and approved

John Hutton Chairman

Timothy Hutton

Account book of Reeth Dispensary, end of year 1839-1840, signatures of John Hutton as chairman, and Timothy Hutton.
Courtesy of Richmondshire Museum. Photo: Guy Carpenter.

succession of John Timothy D'Arcy Huttons. All this remarkably successful Hutton venture was only due to the sad early demise of Matthew.

Clearly both the two Hutton brothers who were to die young, before their mother, had felt they should make some provision for her in their Wills, which implies they had been providing financial support for her during their lifetimes. Knowing their benign characters, it is likely that John and Timothy also contributed to her finances, although Timothy does not mention any payments to her in his diaries. As she considered Matthew's post-mortem provision inadequate, she may have thought the same of that of James. There are hints that her dissatisfaction with her lot worsened her relationship with her surviving sons.

Timothy makes several diary entries referring to his mother, but none do so with any hint of affection. Sometimes he paid her a visit, as on Saturday 15 October 1814: 'Rode to Richmond, dined with my mother'. On other occasions he stayed with her after attending an event in the town, as on Thursday 27 December 1821: '.....Dined at the Free Masons' Lodge...... Slept at my mother's in Frenchgate.'

By the later 1820s it would seem Timothy was becoming anxious about his mother's future, perhaps both financially and regarding her health. On Wednesday 21 November 1827, when in Richmond, he noted, 'Called upon my mother & persuaded her to purchase the house she is in for £1200.' It may have been the case that Timothy was proposing to supply her with that capital sum. It seems that she had by now moved across Frenchgate to a large house near the top of Church Wynd, for among her papers are deeds by which the trustees under the Will of John Foss conveyed a house to her for £1200 in May 1828.[205] This was, of course, the same John Foss who had designed Clifton Castle for Timothy Hutton.

Only a few months later, on Tuesday 23 September 1828, Timothy records: 'Got a letter at half past 12 o'clock to inform me of the death of my mother. She died at nine o'clock. Set off for Richmond & arrived there at a quarter before five. Went to Marske afterwards.' Presumably he went there to discuss the news with John, who must also have been informed of it.

His mother's death triggered an uncharacteristically petulent entry in Timothy's diary on Monday 29 September 1828:

> 'My mother was buried this morning in Easby churchyard. ....I declined attending my mother's remains to the grave in consequence of her having shown so much disrespect to me in her will & not leaving the slightest remembrance to my brother or me but recorded in the Will three painted tables (which I gave to her) were to be sent or returned to Clifton. The whole of my mother's property is left to James & Robert Pulleine, Mr. Pulleine being appointed executor.'

Anne Hutton's Will[206] must indeed have been rather a shock. It is dated 9 July 1828, so less than three months before her death, less than eight months after Timothy was persuading her to buy her house, and only a few weeks after the house became hers. The main beneficiaries were Timothy's cousins-once-removed. James, the elder son, hence the reference to him as Mr Pulleine, was a distinguished lawyer, so an appropriate executor.

The Will starts by Anne 'bequeathing', but actually returning, furniture which had been given her to help set up her home. The first mentioned is the eldest Pulleine sister, Henrietta, who had provided 'A Chest of Drawers lined with Cedar in my Lodging Room' and 'a Tea Chest.' Next, Anne specified that her son John was to get back 'A Double Chest of Drawers, a Bureau, an Arm Chair and a Chamber Clock.' Then the bequest which so offended Timothy: 'three painted Tables which belong to him.'

James and Robert Pulleine were left Anne's residiary estate, and 'as tenants in Common and not as joint tenants' her 'messuage or dwelling house situate in Richmond aforesaid wherein I now reside.' If Timothy had

205 NYCRO ZAW 93.

206 West Yorkshire Archive Service, RD/AP1/175/94.

substantially helped her buy the house, it is understandable that he felt he had been kicked in the teeth.

Anne's witnesses to her Will were Octavius Leefe, an attorney who lived at the corner of Frenchgate and Ryders Wynd, Christopher Bowes, a doctor, and Thomas Wilson. Probate was granted to James Pulleine. The stamp office forms record Anne as having £331 in cash in the house, and total personal effects worth £1,150 0s 2d. It would seem that the Pulleine brothers held on to the house for a while, for their father, Henry Percy Pulleine 'of Crakehall', is listed as a resident of Richmond in the 1830s.[207] James Pulleine eventually left his share of the house to his clergyman brother Robert.

Despite Timothy's annoyance, someone, be it James or Robert Pulleine, or John or Timothy Hutton, or even James Tate, had a small plaque, of white marble mounted on black, below a shallow pediment, erected inside the east wall of the chancel of Easby Church, inscribed *IN MEMORY OF ANNE, RELICT OF IOHN HUTTON ESQUIRE OF MARSKE, WHO DIED AT RICHMOND, 23 SEPTEMBER 1828, AGED 74.* Easby Church was attended by many Richmond inhabitants, particularly if they did not own a prestigious pew in St Mary's parish church, and it would seem Anne had been part of that Easby congregation.

Wall monument to Anne Hutton in Easby Church.
Photo: Guy Carpenter.

207 Pigot and Co., *London and Provincial New Commercial Directory,* (1822), p.893.

On 9 October 1828, almost immediately after his mother's death, Timothy instructed his solicitor Thomas Topham to draw up a new Will. The implication is that his mother would have been a beneficiary in his existing Will. By 22 October it was ready for signing:

> 'After breakfast set off for Middleham. Went to Mr. Topham's to execute my Will which was witnessed by Mr. Topham, Mrs. Topham & their son Christopher Topham. Two wills I executed, one of which I brought home & lodged in one of the drawers where I keep my deeds. The former Will I destroyed when I got home...... I never made a Will that was more to my satisfaction than the one I executed this day. My wife & my brother are the only persons named in the Will.'

Somewhat ironically, in view of his 1828 reaction, and several Wills later, the Pulleine brothers would feature prominently in Timothy's own final Will, thirty-six mellowing years later in 1864.

It would appear that Timothy had known from childhood two of his maternal aunts. His records of their deaths in his diaries show that both had married men from the Marske area. As his mother Anne was the eldest Ling sister, perhaps the other two had followed her over from Westmorland. The next sister in age was Jane, who as Jane Whaley aged sixty-four was buried at Marrick on 24 June 1823. Timothy noted on Sunday 22 June 1823: 'Got a letter from Marrick to acquaint me that Mrs. Whaley (my mother's sister) was dead.' William Whaley, presumably her husband, had been buried at Marrick on 9 November 1821, at the age of seventy-three.

Timothy's younger aunt was Sarah Ridley, who was buried at Marske on 2 April 1832 aged seventy. He wrote in his diary on Thursday 29 March 1832: 'Sarah Ridley (my mother's sister) died at Skelton near Marske.' Subsequently, Timothy noted on Friday 3 January 1834, 'Mrs. Ridley died at Marske', the burial register for 6 January noting her as Mary Ridley aged eighty-four. The connection, if any, between the two Mrs Ridleys is not explained, though there was also a Francis aged eighty-three buried there on 3 February 1836.

This second Mrs Ridley was, however, clearly important to the family, for Timothy went to Marske on Monday 6th to attend her funeral, 'Mr. Smith, Mr. Fryer and self attended Mrs. Ridley's funeral.' Mary Ridley had been left the not inconsiderable sum of ten guineas in James Hutton's Will, so she had obviously meant a great deal to the family. Could she have been the boys' nursemaid?

The 'Mr. Fryer' accompanying Timothy Hutton to Mary Ridley's funeral was Michael Fryer, employed as librarian to John Hutton, who had one of the finest libraries in Yorkshire. Acting also as a kind of personal secretary, Fryer was a central figure in John's life, and lived with him in his household at Marske Hall. Despite being of relatively little significance to Timothy, who seems not to have shared John's passion for collecting books and manuscripts, Fryer merits some attention here in his own right.

John Hutton's book plate, with Hutton family coat of arms.
In a private collection. Photo: Guy Carpenter

Michael Fryer (1774-1844) was well-known in the Richmond area as a close associate of the Hutton brothers, but he was also quite a famous mathematician of his day and would be considered sufficiently distinguished to be afforded an obituary in *The Gentleman's Magazine.*[208] Apparently the son of John Fryer (1745-1825), a Newcastle mathematician, Michael had probably been educated at Sedbergh School, for he dedicated one of his books to John Dawson of Sedbergh, who had presumably been his teacher.

208 Wallis, Peter, *Newcastle Mathematical Libraries*, Literary and Philosophical Society of Newcastle-upon-Tyne, 1972; *The Gentleman's Magazine* 1844 p.434.

Michael Fryer published several books for university students on algebra, Euclidian geometry and trigonometry. He spent some years in Bristol as secretary and lecturer to the Literary and Philosophical Society there, before moving to Marske Hall about 1814. Here James Tate got to know him, and clearly held him in high regard. Writing to Timothy Hutton on 6 September 1837, Tate enquired: 'Of poor Michael Fryer I get no intelligence. Pray, when next you see him, remember me to him very kindly. His early life was a scene of most praiseworthy exertion; and his attainments have been – always – of a very singular kind and extent.'

When one of Tate's 'Invincibles', George Peacock,[209] in 1830 published *A Treatise on Algebra* which he dedicated to his old headmaster, Tate, writing to thank Peacock for the compliment, noted: 'Mr. Hutton and Michael Fryer who live very much of their time in Mathematics at Marske, will be delighted as well as myself with a work which promises in so pleasing a manner to reflect credit back from Cambridge to Richmond.'[210]

It was Tate's view, as a close friend of John Hutton, who appreciated how much his librarian meant to him, that Hutton should show his regard for Fryer by leaving him a bequest. In 1837, writing to John from his canon's residence in London, Tate even had the temerity to suggest this: '.....what your affectionate heart must approve ...... some provision for Michael Fryer, who in your hospitable house with bed, board, wardrobe, and what not, must be left .... if ever he lose your protection ...... in a state of want and of inability to work, far worse now, than when you took him to the Hall as Literary Agent and Librarian.'[211] Two years later, when John made his last Will,[212] the advice had been followed, for John left to 'Michael Fryer now residing with me a pension of one guinea a week for life.'

The 1841 census, taken shortly before John Hutton died, shows Michael Fryer 'of Independent means' residing in Marske Hall. Four weeks after John Hutton's death, Fryer departed from Marske, having lost his status, his patron, close friend and fellow intellectual. Despite his small pension it would seem from Tate's observation that he was likely to find it difficult to make a new life for himself. Timothy Hutton was clearly aware of the sadness associated with this departure, recording on Sunday 12 September 1841 that,

209 Revd. George Peacock (1791-1858), from 1814 a Fellow of his alma mater, Trinity College, Cambridge, noted as a mathematician specialising in algebra and calculus, Lowdean Professor of Astronomy and Geometry at Cambridge University from 1837 and Dean of Ely from 1838.

210 Wenham, *Letters of James Tate*, p.101.

211 Wenham, *Letters of James Tate*, p.81.

212 National Archives, PRO PROB 11/1956/196.

after attending morning service at Marske church, and the customary lunch at Marske Hall that followed it, 'Mr. Fryer left Marske. I sent him in the Gig to Richmond.' From Richmond, Michael Fryer travelled back to Newcastle-upon-Tyne, where he died in 1844. Some of his own collection of books are now in the library of the Newcastle Literary and Philosophical Society.

The extent of John Hutton's interest in mathematics is not recorded, although we know he became president of the Richmond Scientific Society and was keenly interested in technological developments assisting agricultural improvement. It can be assumed that John Hutton inherited a reasonable library among the family possessions in Marske Hall, but he himself pursued a very specialised interest in collecting valuable manuscripts, particularly Arabic and Persian works, as well as some splendid medieval chronicles. John is frequently mentioned by Timothy as having just returned from London, so perhaps he spent a lot of time there searching out such purchases. Timothy would in 1842 present many of these treasured possessions of John to his alma mater, Christ's College, Cambridge.[213] Sadly the College does not have a record of this as a separate bequest, as they were incorporated into their main collection rather than being kept as an entity.[214]

John and Timothy, as the only survivng Hutton brothers, became increasingly closer as they got older, and spent a lot of time in each other's company. John was as convivial as Timothy, if not more so, and hosted elaborate parties on his birthday, a day which Timothy usually spent at Marske. For example, on Tuesday 24 September 1833: 'My brother's birthday. Rode to Marske, 44 dined.' The following year, 'My brother's birthday...... 39 sat down to dinner', while in 1835 the number was forty-five, and thirty-six in 1836. Timothy was aware of how much he and his brother depended on their manservants, recording on Saturday 1 September 1832, 'Blyth my brother's servant died at Marske.'

Timothy's diaries give no hint that John's health was causing concern, but James Tate's letters to him tell a different story, indicating that he suffered many years of poor health, and also implying that John eschewed seeking, or perhaps following, medical advice. Writing to Timothy from Amen Corner on 6 September 1837, Tate asks 'How is your brother's

213 Venn *Alumni*, states that Timothy bequeathed them to Christ's, but college records show that they were given in his lifetime. They are not mentioned in his Will.

214 Letter of 19 September 1989 to L P Wenham from Dr C P Courtney, Christ's College Librarian. However, the donation had been considered suffiently important for the Arabic and Persian scholar Edward Granville Browne (1862-1926) of Pembroke College to catalogue them – ed. H. Rackham, *Christ's College in former Days*, CUP, (1939), p.285.

health? From Mr. Bowes[215] now some months ago in London we heard that he had experienced an attack of illness which made even him think of medical advice. But from Mr. B. I was glad to hear that he was decisively better again.' On New Year's Day 1838 Tate again wrote to Timothy, saying '....as to your brother, Pray, tell me (for he never writes, he has not done it lately) in what state of health he is.' In August 1839 Tate wrote to John saying he had been delighted to hear from Timothy that John had improved sufficiently to get as far as Wensley.[216]

Still without commenting on John's health in his diary, Timothy records travelling to Marske as usual for John's birthday on 24 September 1840. But this would prove to be his last birthday visit. A possible hint that John had become incapacitated is provided by Timothy's diary entry for Monday 2 August 1841: 'Col. Cradock and Mr. Kendall were at my brothers when I arrived, waiting for me to sign the books for the Hutton Charity.' Timothy's diaries show that he visited Marske more often than usual in the early part of that August.

A few months earlier, when the 1841 census was taken for Marske Hall, Timothy's wife Elizabeth is staying there, and it would seem from a later reference that she moved there for about a year. One might infer from this that she was there to help nurse John, although there is no specific documentary evidence for this. However, as John left her a legacy of £1,000, and as she would not have been in needy circumstances, presumably he had a particular reason to be grateful for her. John's Will recognised two female servants, Isabella Greenhow and Elizabeth Plews, who received £50 each, perhaps having nursed him, and the steward, Thomas Carter, was left £100, having increasingly managed the estate.

Elizabeth seems to have been assisted in nursing John by her elder sister Mary Chaytor. Timothy had left them at Marske Hall while he took up residence at Boston for the annual grouse shooting as usual, and was on his own there when the sad news arrived that would change Timothy's life. It was brokered by Anthony Croft, the Boston farmer. The diary entry for Saturday 14 August 1841 reads: 'Ant'y. Croft came into my bedroom in the morning about 7 o'clock to inform me my brother was dead. Set off from Boston to Marske about ½ past 8.' The news was conveyed to James Tate in London, who noted that on that date, 'About *vi* or *vii* a.m. poor John Hutton died.'[217]

215 John Bowes, son of Richmond surgeon Christopher Bowes.

216 Wenham, *Letter of James Tate*, p.84.

217 Wenham, *James Tate*, p.449.

Timothy stayed on at Marske, recording on Monday 23 August 'Mrs. Hutton & me attended the funeral of my poor brother. A melancholy day at Marske.' Timothy continued to stay on at Marske, although he, with Thomas Bradley, travelled briefly into Richmond on Saturday 28th, returning to Marske. On the Sunday morning a number of those closest to Timothy accompanied him to Marske church: Elizabeth Hutton and Mary Chaytor, Frank and Charlotte Morley and Michael Fryer.

On Monday 30th, Timothy left Marske after breakfast to return to Clifton Castle. Another group of old friends visited to offer condolences: landowner William John Anderson of Swinithwaite, Anne Harcourt of Swinton Park and banker Christopher Other. His old friend George Cuitt came over from Masham and stayed the night.

The following morning, Timothy was at the Bedale office of the family bank where three of the directors made an informal request that he would now become a director of the bank. This was ratified on Friday 3 September at the Leyburn branch, where he was additionally invited to become 'a trustee in the place of my late brother.' In the days in between these banking meetings, Timothy returned to Marske and met up with Robert Pulleine and his wife Susan, and with Elizabeth Hutton they went through some of John's business papers.

On 27 November Timothy went to London and, as executor, 'Proved my late brother's Will and afterwards was sworn to it by Mr. James Tate.' Tate was, of course, a canon residentiary of St Paul's Cathedral, and carried out this sad duty as a dear friend of both John and Timothy. Probate was granted the following 1 January at the Prerogative Court of Canterbury, in the records of which the Will is copied.[218] It was not for four months after John's death that Elizabeth felt able to leave Marske and the task of sorting through John's things. At least she was back at Clifton Castle with Timothy in time for their first Christmas without John. Timothy noted in his diary on Wednesday 15 December 1841: 'Mrs. Hutton came from Marske, having been upwards of twelve months from Clifton.'

John had left the Marske estate to Timothy, the inheritance of which necessitated Timothy paying a large sum in tax. On Friday 3 June 1842 he 'Rode to Leyburn, met John Topham there and made arrangement at the Bank for the payment to him when call'd for the money to pay the Legacy Duty which will amount to upwards of £3,500, having to pay the full duty of 10 pr.ct. on the personal property of my late brother.'

218 National Archives PRO PROB 11/1956/196.

Another important task was occupying Timothy's mind. Traditionally the Hutton family had not marked their interments in Marske church with wall monuments within it, although the hilltop obelisk had been put up to Matthew. Timothy decided to put up a suitable memorial to John on the north chancel wall, above the family pew which had recently been installed in the church, along with pitch pine box pews for the congregation, when John had refurbished the church in 1830. In February 1843 the London sculptor Thomas Smith was commissioned to make the large and impressive monument, which consists of a plaque surmounted by a portrait bust of John. Timothy Hutton had asked James Tate to compose the inscription, and its tone betrays the closeness of his friendship with John Hutton:

> *The generous patron of societies for agriculture, literature and science. The liberal landlord, and kind encourager of all practical improvements. The steady supporter on every occasion of political reform, and the hospitable gentleman in the hall of his ancestors, honored [sic] and beloved by all who entered it as guests and friends.*

Timothy would run both the Marske and Clifton Castle estates for the twenty-plus years he outlived John. When this major change began, Timothy was over sixty, but nevertheless he got on with his busy life. As soon as 1844 he took up his long-arranged term of office as High Sheriff of Yorkshire, perhaps very conscious that he was following in the footsteps of his brother who had held that position in 1825.

There were now more Hutton institutions to administer, including the school in Marske which John had founded about 1820, and at which he paid for the education of the children of his tenants and staff. The bank now took up a great deal of Timothy's time, and also the Hutton Charity, which was based at the bank's Richmond branch. After Timothy became its chairman, he always attended the twice-yearly meetings at which the accounts were agreed. Timothy's diaries record the gradual changes in the trustees from the original ones, Col Cradock of Hartforth, and Revd William Kendall, the rector of Marske. By August 1845 they were Revd John Swire, Timothy's old friend who was rector of Melsonby and lived at Manfield, and George Gilpin of Sedbury. By 1859 it was a younger Mr Cradock, and Revd J Wharton of Gilling, who attended.

As the years wore on, though in good health for their ages, both Timothy and Elizabeth inevitably suffered medical problems. Timothy, as we have seen, had a cataract operation in 1848. He makes no reference to

Elizabeth's health in his diaries, even obliquely, until he starts referring to her birthdays: on Thursday 17 April 1851 'Mrs. Hutton 72 this day' and the following year 'Mrs. Hutton 73 this day.' Then, with no further explanation, on Sunday 21 June 1857: 'Mrs. Hutton came down stairs to dinner the first time for 3 months.'

There is no further mention of her until Tuesday 4 January 1859: 'Mrs. Hutton became gradually worse all the day & died at 7 o'clock at night. Buckle was by at the time which was some consolation to me.' A week later, 'Mr. J. Hutton & Mr. Buckle came to breakfast. At nine o'clock all was ready to start with the remains of Mrs. Hutton to Downholm, we arrived at the church at ½ past 12. We got back to Clifton at 4 o'clock. All went off quietly and to my satisfaction.' In addition to the loyal family doctor who accompanied Timothy in this sad task, he was supported by John Timothy D'Arcy Hutton of Aldburgh, whom he would appoint to succeed him at the Marske estate.

Elizabeth, like Timothy in due course, had chosen to be buried in the ancient parish church of St Michael and All Angels at Downholme, in which parish his Walburn estate lay, rather than in Thornton Watlass church, near Clifton Castle. Timothy had, as the local squire and patron of Downholme church, been responsible for appointing incumbents and repairing the church in the early 1840s. Later, a Hutton family pew was installed: Monday 16 October 1854, '75 this day...... Walked.... To Downholm church..... to measure a part of the chancel where I want to place a pew.' The pew, which would only be used by Timothy and Elizabeth for a few years, has since been moved to the back of the church. Near its original location in the chancel, painted glass was installed in the east window in 1855.

As was his habit whenever his circumstances changed, Timothy made a new Will. Thus within a few weeks of Elizabeth's death, on Thursday 20 January 1859, he 'Executed my will in the presence of Edwd. John Carter [his brother-in-law] & John Hudson my tenant.' Shortly afterwards, on Thursday 10 February, he went to the Bank in Bedale to add a codicil. He would change his Will yet again before he died.

Timothy must have begun to dispose of things which had belonged to Elizabeth, as there was no obvious female relative to whom to give them. The only item he mentions are her diamonds. In October 1859, shortly after his 80th birthday, Timothy went down to London with his friend Thomas Topham, the Middleham solicitor: 'Took the late Mrs. Hutton's diamonds to Hunts & Roskell's for sale, I left them there.'

After a few days sight-seeing, including two trips to Windsor to see Prince Albert's model farm and its fine Devon, Hereford and shorthorn cattle, and just before they caught the evening train from London back to York, Timothy 'Call'd at Hunts & Roskell's respecting the diamonds & Mr. Hunt said the value he put upon them was £600 which I readily accepted. I believe they cost £850.'

As if running both the Clifton and Marske estates from 1841 was not enough, Timothy continued to add to his property portfolio and to improve his existing properties. He built a house 'for Davison' in Crakehall in 1843, and purchased Low Burton from Marmaduke Wyvill for £5,250 in 1847. A year later six cottages there were converted into three, to make better accommodation. In 1861, twenty-seven acres of land near Mill House were bought for £1,500, and in 1862 Timothy was inspecting new buildings at Oscar Farm, Burrill, nearer Bedale than Masham.

Timothy's thoughts now had to turn to what would happen to his properties when he died. He was a childless widower, none of his brothers had left heirs, and having lived into old age, he had outlived his cousins. So it was the next generation of cousins-once-removed that became his heirs. He seems to have decided that he could bequeath the Clifton Castle estate as he chose, but that the Marske estate, though not entailed, should pass to a family member called Hutton.

There is no hint in his diaries for 1862 that Timothy was coming to the end of his life, as the entries follow his normal pattern throughout the year. Even early into the following New Year, he seems to have been getting out and about as usual, for example on Wednesday 7 January 1863, 'The morning concert at Bedale, a very good meeting.' The final entry in the diaries he had kept for so many years, is unusually brief: Saturday 10 January, 'At home.' Perhaps he was starting to be unwell, but he lived on, without further record, until 18 November 1863, when he died at Clifton Castle.

The Downholme parish register records his burial on 25 November 1863, but without him as our informant we have no details of the occasion. Presumably it was a quiet affair, as when Elizabeth had died. The hatchment from his funeral remains inside Downholme Church, and a large red marble ledger stone in the churchyard, on the north side of the church near the east end, marks the burial place of Timothy and Elizabeth.

On the inside of the south chancel wall of Marske Church is a white marble monument commemorating them both: *In Memoriam / Timothy Hutton Esq. / of Marske and Clifton Castle / Nat. Oct. 16th 1779 / Obiit. Nov.*

18th 1863 / Also of / Elizabeth his wife / Nat. Apr. 17th 1779 / Obiit Jan. 4th 1859. Although they had chosen to be buried at Downholme, James Pulleine, who inherited Clifton Castle, had stained glass inserted into the three-light east window of Thornton Watlass church as a memorial to Timothy Hutton.[219]

219 Bulmer, *op.cit.*, p.610.

PART EIGHT: POSTSCRIPTS

TIMOTHY HUTTON'S WILL

Throughout his life Timothy had made many Wills, and he inevitably changed his testamentary intentions yet again after Elizabeth's death. We rarely have any hint of how much alteration he made each time and, as always with such documents, we only actually know of the last one proved in the York Probate Registry after his death. His last Will was made on 19 May 1862, and a codicil was added the following day. A second codicil was added on 9 November 1863, a few days before his death.

He began his last Will by outlining how he was the last surviving son of his father, whose Will had set out in such detail for the descent of his property through his sons and their children, and that there were none. He bequeathed all his farm stock from both estates, and monies other than his shares in the Swaledale and Wensleydale Banking Company, to his executors, James Pulleine of Crakehall, William Burrill late of Bedale but now of Liverpool, and Thomas Topham of Middleham, to pay his funeral expences etc and discharge his legacies, which totalled £16,500. James Pulleine and Thomas Topham have already appeared in this account of Timothy's life, but William Burrill, now to play a part in the aftermath of his death, is a mystery.

The Marske estate, and the heirloom contents of the Hall, were left to John Timothy D'Arcy Hutton (son of James Henry D'Arcy Hutton) and then to his son of the same name, or in default to John Timothy D'Arcy Hutton's brother, another James Henry D'Arcy Hutton, and his issue. The Clifton Castle estate and the contents of Clifton Castle, along with Timothy's shares in the family bank, and the residue of his estate, were left to James Pulleine. The younger Pulleine brother Robert was bequeathed £3,000.

The Pulleine sisters Eliza (Elizabeth) Dorothy Lysaught, Henrietta Hincks, Anne Ryder, Mary Ann (Marrianne) Hincks and the unmarried Sarah Pulleine were each left £1,000. Various younger members of the family were left £500 each, and other friends and distant relatives were left sums of either £1,000, £500 or £100. The Morley family of Marrick also received some rather involved property bequests.

The first codicil to the Will left £100 each to his long-serving staff at Walburn and Marske, Aaron March of Boston Farm, Thomas Carter the Marske steward and Mrs McLean the Marske housekeeper, and likewise

£100 each to Joseph Simpson, Christopher Mudd, Thomas Robinson, Mrs Cordukes and Edward Gaun of Clifton Castle. All other servants who had been in his employment for at least a year were to have a year's wages.

Joseph Simpson had been in Timothy's employment a long time, and been his butler for many years. Christopher Mudd had also been with Timothy a long time, having arrived as a coachman in 1827, and later becoming his farm bailiff and being installed in some style at Burton House near Masham. Anne Cordukes, once Elizabeth's lady's maid, had been kept on as Timothy's housekeeper, and Edward Gaun was the gardener. The codicil also asked that the sum of £100 be given to John Robinson, son of his Clifton Castle servant Thomas Robinson, who Timothy had 'in part educated', in order that his education was not neglected.

Timothy had been adding to his property portfolio right up until the time of his death, and the second codicil had to account for his recent purchases of Gebdikes, near Thornton Watlass, from the Marquess of Ailesbury, some arable land called Burton Field near Masham, and at Thorpe Understone near Hudswell. The first two were added to James Pulleine's Clifton inheritance, and the last to his trustees as part of the residue of the estate.

The D'Arcy Hutton line which inherited the Marske estate was descended from Timothy's uncle James Hutton (1737-98), the youngest sibling of his father, and his wife Mary.[220] Their home, Aldburgh Hall, lies about two miles south-east of Masham. Timothy inconsistently spells the place-name both Aldborough and Aldbrough, but it is spelled Aldburgh on modern Ordnance Survey maps. The house had been built about 1625 by the Beckwith family on the site of a monastic grange belonging to Fountains Abbey. It contained the portrait of James D'Arcy, created Baron D'Arcy of Navan in Ireland, who died in 1731,[221] and from whom Timothy's relations inherited the D'Arcy of their name.

Timothy had noted, in a collection of genealogical information about the family, that 'James Hutton my father's brother died at his house at Aldborough near Masham 2 March 1798, and was buried 9 March 1798 underneath his pew in the chancel of Masham Church.' James and his wife Mary, who died in 1803, had an only son, James Henry D'Arcy Hutton, born on 24 March 1796, when his father was in his late-fifties.

This child was just under two years old when his father died, and only seven when his mother died. It would seem that Timothy, as the boy's

220 Daughter of John Hoyle of Ashgill near Middleham.

221 Whellan *op.cit.*, p.368.

much older first cousin, and presumably Elizabeth also, kept a pseudo-parental eye on the boy. Much of the day-to-day running of his affairs seems, however, to have been left to Timothy's friend the Bedale solicitor Henry Glaister.

Timothy always refers to his young cousin as D'Arcy. He was the heir to the Sedbury estate near Scotch Corner, which had belonged to his grandmother, Elizabeth daughter of Lord D'Arcy of Navan, and it was a family requirement for owners of Sedbury to be named D'Arcy. When Sir Robert D'Arcy Hildyard died at Sedbury Hall on 6 November 1814, young D'Arcy Hutton was still in his teens. When he came of age on Monday 24 March 1817, Timothy and Elizabeth went to stay at Sedbury for the party that evening. Sedbury would be sold by D'Arcy Hutton early in January 1825 to Revd John Gilpin, cousin of the artist and landscape designer William Sawrey Gilpin.

D'Arcy had married Harriet Aggas of Bungay in Suffolk on Saturday 9 June 1821 in London. The couple moved in to Aldburgh Hall, and soon started a family. So, on Thursday 10 October 1822, Timothy noted: 'We dined at Aldbrough. The little boy was christened. Mrs. Hutton was godmother, Major Gamble & Col. Pulleine the god fathers.' This child would eventually inherit the Marske estate as the first John Timothy D'Arcy Hutton.

D'Arcy and Harriet had a second son, James Henry D'Arcy Hutton, born 2 November 1823, who received £3,000 in Timothy's Will. Following that bequest he would, in middle age in April 1868, marry Amy Robson, the daughter of the rector of Marske.[222] James Henry had a sister, Harriet Emma, whose son Richard Cattley was to receive £1,000 from Timothy when he reached his majority.

Regrettably, Harriet Hutton did not live to see her children grow up, for she died on 16 October 1837 at the age of forty-one. James Tate, writing to Timothy on New Year's Day 1837 concluded by saying '.... Poor D'Arcy is left alone: how are the young ones of that family?.....' The armorial hatchment from Harriet's funeral still hangs above the north nave arcade in Marsham church. Harriet's husband did not long outlive his wife. Timothy recorded on Saturday 30 December 1843: 'Henry Glaister came in the afternoon (to Clifton) from Aldborough to inform me of the death of D'Arcy. He died betwixt one and two this afternoon.' Timothy was one of the trustees for his affairs.

222 *Darlington and Stockton Times* of 20 April 2018, quoting from the 18 April 1868 edition of the newspaper. The groom was described as Mr J H D'Arcy Hutton of Bushy Park, London.

John Timothy D'Arcy Hutton, the eldest son of D'Arcy and Harriet, married on Tuesday 26 November 1844, Timothy noting: 'John Hutton of Aldborough & Miss Lamb were married this day at Spennithorne.' 'Miss Lamb' was Emily, the daughter of Thomas M. Lamb Esq. of Middleham.[223] This was followed by more news on Tuesday 13 January 1846: 'Mr. Carter, Mrs. Hutton & self went to dinner at Aldbrough, being the christening of John Hutton's daughter'. Then on Tuesday 12 October 1847, 'To Aldbro...... the boy was christened John Timothy D'Arcy.' This second John Timothy D'Arcy Hutton would in due course also inherit Marske Hall, as would his son, a third of the same name.

223 Raine, *Marske*, pedigree.

THE MARSKE ESTATE AFTER TIMOTHY HUTTON'S DEATH

The first John Timothy D'Arcy Hutton, to whom Timothy bequeathed Marske Hall, its contents, the estates – and its responsibilities – continued to live at Aldburgh Hall. Indeed he refronted that old mansion in 1870, presumably using some of his inheritance to do so. He visited Marske Hall occasionally, for example in order to attend important meetings in Richmond such as those of the Hutton Charity.

When he died in 1874, he too was buried as squire of Walburn in the churchyard at Downholme, where his grave is marked by a large tombstone of red marble, near that of Timothy and Elizabeth Hutton. On it he is described as John Timothy D'Arcy Hutton of Marske and Aldburgh Hall, 1822-1874. The hatchment from his funeral still hangs in Downholme Church. He had in 1844 married Emily Lamb, and their only son became the second John Timothy D'Arcy Hutton (1847-1931). Their two daughters, Emily Harriet and Elizabeth Jane, were mentioned in Timothy's Will. The younger daughter was buried in Downholme churchyard, and has a tombstone near her father's, naming her as Elizabeth Jane Gothorp, who died 14 January 1931 aged eighty-one.

The second John Timothy D'Arcy Hutton married Edith Constance Phipson. They and their five children moved to Marske Hall, keeping up the family tradition of signing off the Hutton Charity accounts as J.T. D'Arcy Hutton.[224] Eventually they moved into Rose Cottage at Marske, and let the mansion to tenants who fancied life in a large country estate with shooting rights, but did not have the means to purchase such. In 1890 the Hall was 'at present' the residence of Richard Forster Matthews, and there was a resident caretaker-cum-gamekeeper William Batey.[225] The estate was looked after by the long-serving estate bailiff, Thomas Genger, who lived in his own house in the village.

A small notebook survives,[226] entitled 'Inventory of Furniture, Fixtures, Fittings and Effects now in or upon the Mansion House called Marske Hall

224 Hutton Charity account book.

225 Bulmer, *op.cit.*, p.493.

226 In the author's possession.

The three generations of squires of Marske called Timothy D'Arcy Hutton

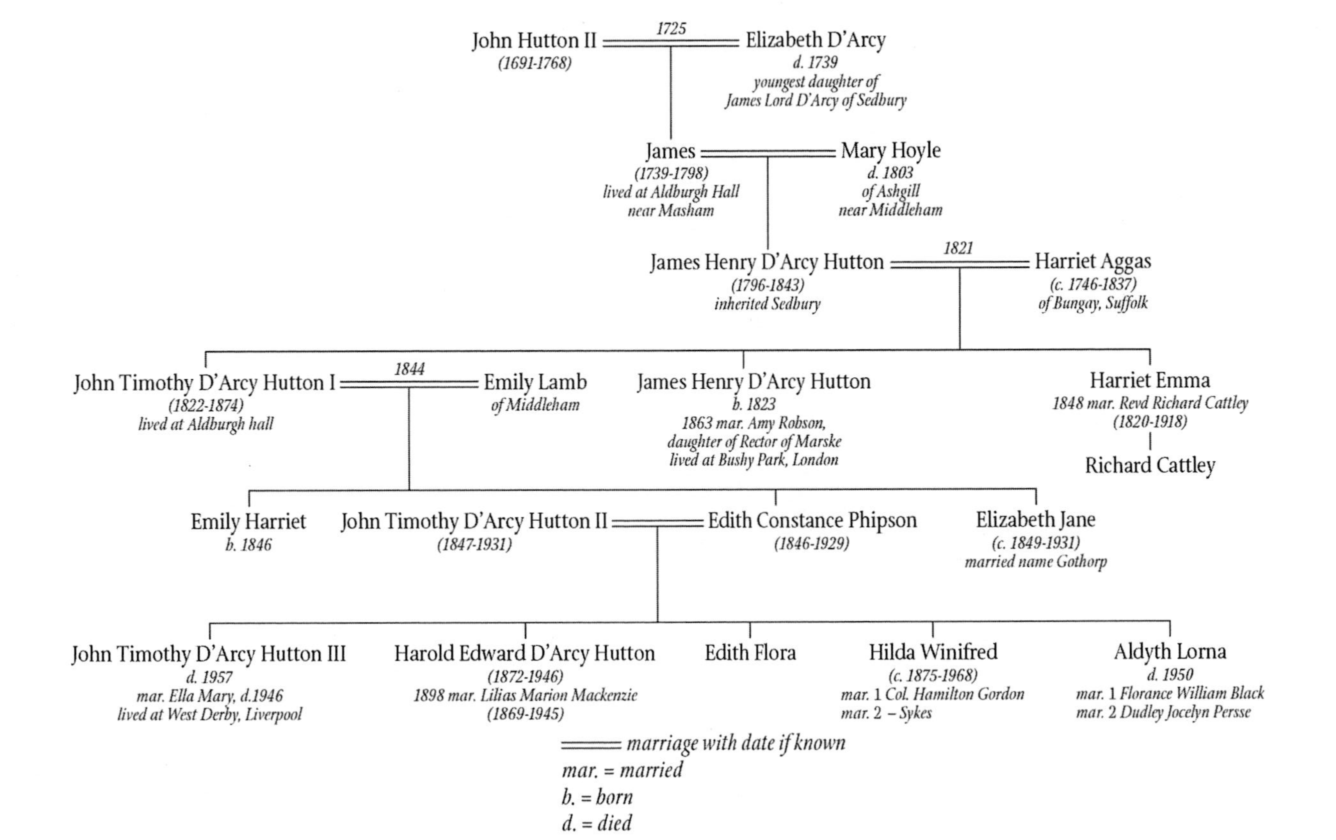

and Premises referred to in the Indenture of Lease dated [blank] day of [blank] 1890 Between John Timothy D'Arcy Hutton Esq. and [blank].' The room by room list begins with Linen Room, goes through twelve bedrooms (one of which is subtitled Schoolroom), then continues through Dressing Room, Night Nursery, Small Night Nursery, Day Nursery, Yellow Bedroom, Brown Room, Green Room, some smaller bedrooms and closets.

The first floor Long Gallery is described as Picture Gallery, and details several Hutton family portraits plus several others. One of these is of particular interest, being entitled *Mulatto on Panel*. The term 'mulatto' was often used to describe a male who was of mixed race, rather than being only negro in origin. Many such 'black' individuals were actually the result of a liaison between a white man and a black female slave on his plantation. Could this portrait be of John York, the black servant who was held in such high regard by the Hutton family? And if so, might it be that the two men Elizabeth Campbell brought with her to Yorke House in Richmond were actually her half-brothers? Sadly we may never know.

The Entrance Hall of Marske Hall included more family portraits, plus stags heads and a buffalo skin, and many stuffed birds in cases. The Smoke Room was seemingly nearby, and the Dining Room contained twenty-four chairs. The Library's books are not listed, though there was a set of library steps. Two Drawing Rooms had comfortable furniture, silk hangings, and needlework-covered ottomans. Timothy Hutton's Billiard Room and servants' work spaces took the number of itemised rooms up to forty-nine. Plants in the greenhouses are listed in great detail, including a large number of orchids and ferns.

The list of gardening tools, even down to the step ladder and two trowels, is followed by the signatures of J.T. D'Arcy Hutton and Captain Frederick Mosenthal, a career soldier who, with Mrs Mosenthal, is listed as resident at Marske Hall in 1891.[227] Sadly, however, he exceeded himself financially, for *The Times* included a notice on 18 August 1891 concerning his insolvency: 'F. Mosenthal of Marske Hall, captain in the Princess of Wales's Own Regiment, accounts have been filed which disclose gross liabilities £10,699, of which £7,562 are unsecured, and assets £3,315.'

The next, and more satisfactory, tenant of Marske Hall after the unfortunate Mosenthal, was Colonel John William Cameron, who was there by 1894, and also took over control of the sporting rights of the Marske estate.[228] He became part of the community and, after he died aged

227 Spencer's *Richmond Almanack etc.* 1891, p.22.

228 Spencer's *Richmond Almanack* etc. 1894, p.15.

fifty-five on 28 December 1896, his family donated stained glass for the east window of Marske Church in his memory, with a brass plaque on the south chancel wall explaining the subjects depicted in each of the three lights.

By 1892 instead of a bailiff the estate was employing an agent, E T Umpleby, who lived in quite grand style at Marske Lodge, and who later also acted for the Manfield and Aldbrough estates and became chairman of Marske Parish Meeting.[229] By the early-twentieth century the tenant of Marske Hall was Frank Stobart JP,[230] a member of a County Durham family of some standing.

The second John Timothy D'Arcy Hutton lived on until 1931. There is a memorial plaque on the south wall of the nave of Marske Church to him and his wife, which reads *John Timothy D'Arcy Hutton Esq. / of Marske / Born 5 June 1847 / Died 4 January 1931 / and of Edith Constance / his wife / Born 14 January 1848 / Died 11 April 1929.*

The couple's eldest child became the third John Timothy D'Arcy Hutton. They also had another son, Harold Edward D'Arcy Hutton (1872-1946), and three daughters, Edith Flora D'Arcy Hutton, Hilda Winifred D'Arcy Hutton and Aldyth Lorna D'Arcy Hutton. The last John Timothy D'Arcy Hutton gave his address as Marske Hall in 1932,[231] but spent little time there as he and his wife Ella made their home in West Derby near Liverpool. His wife died first, her death notice in *The Times* stating 'On January 29, 1946, at 1 Haymans Green, West Derby, Liverpool, Ella Mary D'Arcy Hutton, beloved wife of J.T. D'Arcy Hutton of Marske, Richmond, Yorkshire.' He died at the same address on 10 April 1957.

The youngest daughter, Aldyth Lorna, married twice. After the death of her first husband, Florance William Black,[232] of Kailyie, Perthshire, she in 1938 married Dudley Jocelyn Persse of Roxborough, County Galway. By this time both her parents had died, she being described in her engagement notice in *The Times* on 22 November 1938 as daughter of the late Mr and Mrs D'Arcy Hutton of Marske Hall. Her second husband was a novelist, known as Jocelyn Persse, a friend and ardent correspondent of Henry James.[233] She had no children by either of her marriages, and died in 1950. Her older sister, Hilda Winifred, became by her second husband Mrs D'Arcy Sykes,

229 Spencer's *Richmond Almanack* etc. 1892 p.36; 1896, p.14.

230 Cookes, C.E. and Son, *Richmondshire, An Account of its History & Antiquities, Characters & Customs, Legendary Lore & Natural History*, (1910), p.80.

231 Austin, G.E., *Directory of Richmond & Rural District Area and Almanack*, (1932), p.25.

232 The Peerage website.

233 The Peerage website.

and continued to keep up her connections with Marske, being buried there at the age of ninety-three on 27 July 1968. Some Georgian silver candlesticks were given to Marske Church in her memory.[234]

On the outbreak of World War II in 1939 the Hall was unoccupied, and likely to be requisitioned by the army. The War Department had already taken over the moorland parts of the estate in 1932,[235] and Catterick Garrison still has training facilities at Feldom and Cordilleras. The Hall itself took on new life when it was leased by Scarborough College, an independent boys' school, in September 1940.

The many rooms of Marske Hall now came into their own, although the whole house was very cold in winter. Rooms on the top floor became classrooms, and the first-floor long gallery housed school assemblies. The ground-floor library at the south-west corner was used for showing films on Sundays, and the largest ground-floor room became the senior dormitory. A gymnasium was improvised in the stable block, where a large upstairs room was used for speech days and the school's drama productions, a piano being carried up the steep staircase for that purpose.

It was not possible to equip any science laboratories, so the boys travelled down to Richmond Grammar School for science lessons. Many masters had been called up for military service, so the remaining staff had to deliver lessons outside of their normal subjects. For example, the headmaster, a geography graduate, had also to cover mathematics, Latin, mechanics and religious knowledge. A positive outcome was that the boys greatly increased the numbers, and musical provision, at Marske church on Sundays.[236]

Peacetime did not bring the D'Arcy Hutton family back to Marske Hall, as they remained at West Derby. Most of the house's contents were sold in 1950. The Richmond auctioneer C.W. Tindill held a two-day sale in the hall on Wednesday and Thursday 20 and 21 September. The catalogue of furniture, pottery, bedding, copper pans, carpets, curtains and Bechstein grand piano concluded with lot 487, 'sundry worn carpets.' Two longcase clocks had been made in Askrigg in Wensleydale, famous for its Georgian clockmakers: 'Lot 107, Antique Mahogany Long case clock with Brass and Silver Dial by J.Wilson, Askrigg', and 'Lot 260 Grandfather Clock by Metcalfe, Askrigg, out of order.'

234 Geograph Britain and Ireland website.

235 Deeds of Marske Lodge seen by the author.

236 Bailey, Patrick, "Wartime Schooldays at Marske Hall", *The Dalesman Magazine*, September 1990, pp.496-500.

The best items, including gold and silver plate, were auctioned at Christie's in London on 5 October 1950. Three pieces were valuable early-eighteenth century silver-gilt racing cups, and there were several silver candlesticks, along with other items of table silver. The sale made John Timothy D'Arcy Hutton £9,701.

There must also have been a sale of the many paintings known to have graced Marske Hall including, it is said, a portrait of every member of the family[237]. At least one precious item is known to have been kept back, for after his death, his executor sold, again at Christie's, the silver-gilt cup given by Queen Elizabeth I to her goddaughter Elizabeth Bowes, hallmarked 1589. A private collector paid £8,000 for it.[238] It was a well-known piece, having been the subject of an article by silver expert Charles Oman in *Burlington Magazine* in October 1931. It weighed over 34oz.

Marske Hall, meanwhile, had also been put up for sale soon after World War II. Many such mansions were surplus to requirements, their families having lost their sons and heirs to the war. If they were demolished, their fabric could be salvaged as buildings materials, which were then scarce and subject to strict licences. Indeed, it was a Richmond builder, George Shaw, who bought Marske Hall in 1950 with just that in mind. However, his son George William Shaw persuaded his father that the mansion would produce a similar financial return if converted into housing units. This did, of course, also save a precious country house. Thus Marske Hall itself, excluding the stable block and other outbuildings, was turned into ten rented apartments, and continued so to be used into the early-twenty-first century, when it was put up for sale by George William Shaw's daughter Elizabeth.

237 Raine's "Marske in Swaledale" gives a list of the most notable portraits he saw in Marske Hall, where their names could be assigned. Among them is a portrait in the Morning Room of John Hutton I, "A good-looking man, in brown coloured coat and wig"; also in the Morning Room, John Hutton II, "A tall person, in brown coat and wig, and full face"; in the Dining Room, Timothy's father, John Hutton III, "in brown coat and wig, the face beams with kindness and animation", [this "fine brilliant portrait" was by the noted artist Thomas Hudson]; in the Dining Room, Timothy's brother, John Hutton IV, "a small picture, a very intelligent face"; plus portraits of Timothy's other brothers "Captain James Hutton" and Matthew.

238 Letter from Christie's dated 1 October 1970.

THE CLIFTON CASTLE AFTER TIMOTHY HUTTON'S DEATH

James Pulleine, who became only the second owner of Clifton Castle in its sixty years' history when Timothy Hutton died in 1863, moved into the house, and rented out Crakehall Hall, where he had been living. Despite belonging to a generation younger than Timothy, James did not share his precursor's longevity, and enjoyed his inheritance for only a few years. He was buried at Thornton Watlass church on 29 March 1879 at the age of seventy-four. A Maltese cross on the west wall of the south chapel of Thornton Watlass church remembers him as 'James Pulleine of Clifton Castle and Crakehall, born Carlton Hall in the parish of Stanwick on 31 October 1804, died at Clifton Castle 23 March 1879.'

James Pulleine had married Anne Caroline Marjoribanks, who lived on at Clifton Castle until she too was buried at Thornton Watlass exactly ten years later on 30 March 1889. They had an only child, a daughter, Georgina Elizabeth Pulleine, to whom both the Clifton and Crakehall estates descended. Clifton Castle now entered a period when it was lived in by owners who had connections with much higher echelons of society than Timothy Hutton and James Pulleine had had.

Georgina Pulleine had in 1868 married Sir John Clayton Cowell[239] and thus was Lady Georgina when her mother died. John Clayton Cowell (1832-94) was a British army officer who was 'head-hunted' by Prince Albert to provide some manly tutorage for two of the younger royal children,[240] Prince Alfred and Prince Leopold. When they grew up, Cowell was appointed Master of the Queen's Household and made a Knight Commander of the Order of the Bath. He retired from the army in 1879 with the honorary rank of major-general, and in 1892 was appointed lieutenant-governor of Windsor Castle.[241] The clock in the tower of Thornton Watlass church was given in his memory by his wife in 1896, and electric power was added to it by a later generation of the family.[242]

---

239 Family information taken from a pedigree handwritten by Lady Alice Curzon-Howe in 1945 for L P Wenham, and now in the possession of the author.

240 Information given verbally to the author by Monny Curzon-Howe-Herrick.

241 Wikipedia.

242 Brass plaque next to the tower door in the church.

THE DESCENDANTS OF JAMES PULLEINE

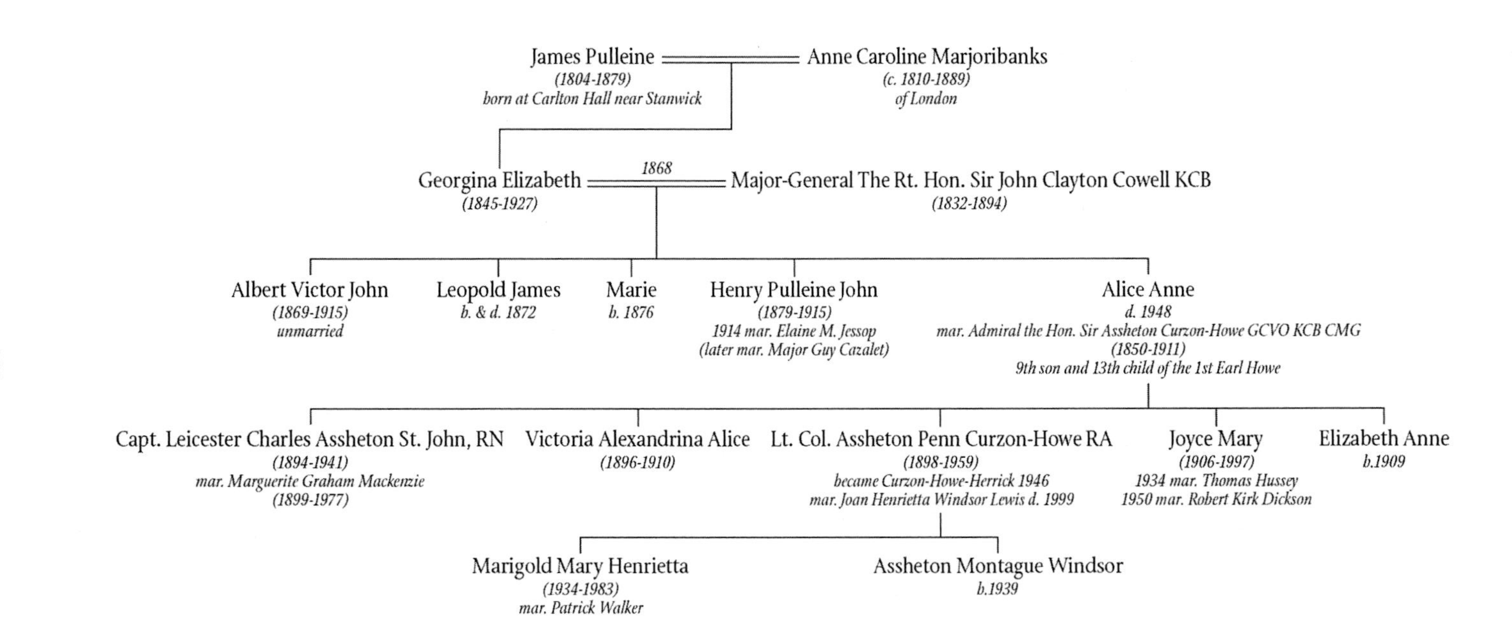

After Sir John's death in 1894, Lady Georgina continued to live at Clifton Castle. We know that much of Timothy and Elizabeth Hutton's original furniture was still in place there, but Lady Georgina must have decided to upgrade the finest piece in the house, the fine canopied bed in the best bedroom, for the estate joiner, H. Simpson, signed his name on its woodwork when the original fabric hangings were replaced in 1896.

Sir John and Lady Georgina had five children, three sons and two daughters. The two elder sons were named after members of the royal family. The first-born, Albert Victor John Cowell (1869-1915), inherited Clifton Castle from his father in 1894, but as an unmarried army officer had no opportunity to take up residence in the house, and when he died at the age of forty-five, he left no heirs. The second son, Leopold James, had died aged eight months in 1872. The third son and youngest child, Henry Pulleine John Cowell, born in 1879, died of wounds received at Suvla Bay on the Aegean coast of Gallipoli in 1915, at the age of thirty-six. He had married Elaine Jessop, but they had no children, and after several years of widowhood she later married Major Guy Cazalet.

Lady Georgina, perhaps typically of that generation so badly affected by World War I, outlived four of her offspring. Clifton Castle therefore passed to her daughter, Alice Anne Cowell, who had been brought up at the court of Queen Victoria.[243] She had, many years earlier, married an older man, Admiral the Hon Sir Assheton Gore Curzon-Howe (1850-1911), KCB, CVO, CMG, youngest child and ninth son of the thirteen children of the first Earl Howe, and by him had five children.

Lady Alice Curzon-Howe, who had long been a widow, moved into Clifton Castle when her mother died in 1927. She was still there during World War II when Clifton Castle's woodlands were taken over by the Royal Army Ordnance Corps as an Ammunition Storage Depot, abbreviated in military parlance to ASD. Thus it was Lady Alice who in 1944/5 generously gave L P Wenham, then a lieutenant in the RAOC, who was billeted at Clifton Castle, permission to study Timothy Hutton's diaries, which were housed in the library there.

Lady Alice Curzon-Howe continued to live at Clifton Castle until 1946, then for the last two years of her life moved to live with her daughter Joyce Hussey in Hampshire. As her elder son, naval captain Leicester Charles Assheton St John Curzon-Howe, had died in 1941, her property passed to her second son. Lt Col Assheton Penn Curzon-Howe (1898-1959) of the

243 Information given verbally to the author by Monny Curzon-Howe-Herrick.

Royal Artillery was only able to return to Clifton Castle during periods of leave during World War II.

In 1946 he legally changed his surname to Curzon-Howe-Herrick to inherit property in Leicestershire.[244] In 1947, after his return from war service in Burma, he moved into Clifton Castle with his wife, young daughter and son, whose names had also been changed to Curzon-Howe-Herrick. His widow, Joan Henrietta, moved to The Hermitage, Thornton Watlass after the family sold the Clifton Castle estate in 1963.

Thus it was only in 1963 that Clifton Castle passed out of the family through whom it had descended, albeit somewhat convolutedly and sometimes through the female line, from its creator Timothy Hutton. The purchaser was Robin Hill, later the eighth Marquess of Downshire (1929-2003), whose family seat, Hillsborough Castle,[245] had become the residence of the Governor of Northern Ireland in 1924. He chose Clifton Castle to be a suitably gracious setting for the family's fine furniture and portraits.[246] Clifton Castle is now the cherished home of his son Nicholas, the ninth Lord Downshire.

244 The Peerage website.

245 Obituary in *The Darlington and Stockton Times* January 16, 2004.

246 Worsley, *op.cit.*

PART NINE: INDICES

ACKNOWLEDGEMENTS

My greatest debt is to Timothy Hutton for creating diaries providing such a treasure-trove of material recording his life and times. Here lie, jumbled together amongst family joys and sorrows and business meetings, national events such as the celebrations for a king's succession, and the pomp of the Duke of Northumberland's London funeral.

My second debt is to Peter Wenham, who patiently transcribed Timothy Hutton's diaries while a young army officer billeted for part of his military service in Clifton Castle, Timothy Hutton's former home, having been given permission to work in the Library there. One of Peter Wenham's notebooks has written on the front '1944-5 from the original diaries in the possession of Lady Curzon-Howe at Clifton Castle.' Peter Wenham brought his wartime notebooks, some rather scrappy due to paper shortages, to Richmond some thirty or so years later. If he had not bequeathed me his research papers, I would have remained unaware of Timothy Hutton as such an invaluable source of material for the study of a large area of North Yorkshire.

My third debt is to Bob Woodings, who has been alongside me while I have written the book. A late convert to the Huttons, and to Timothy in particular, he has done much to encourage this book's publication. From his former publishing experience, he greatly helped to re-organise the presentation of the story, suggested the elaboration of certain details and the elimination of others, and made useful contributions to the finding of contexts for understanding some aspects of Timothy's material. Above all, he put on hold his own writing projects in order painstakingly to edit my text before it went to York Publishing Services.

I am further indebted to many people who have generously shared with me their knowledge of individual details of Timothy's story, and to those I have forgotten to include I apologise. Clifton Castle is now the cherished home of Nicholas, the ninth Lord Downshire, who has willingly offered much assistance over the years, and kindly given permission for many photographs to be taken to illustrate this book. Monny Curzon-Howe-Herrick, descendant of the family which inherited Clifton Castle from Timothy Hutton, provided much helpful and pertinent comment and memories of living there as a small boy. Peter Boughton, Keeper of Art at the Grosvenor Museum in Chester, generously shared his study of the works and correspondence of George Cuitt, and my friend Richard Green, formerly Curator of the City of York Art Gallery, helped identify some of the artists mentioned. Dr Peter Trewby of Richmond helped interpret details of Timothy Hutton's eye operation, and local history researcher Val Slater of Northallerton shared snippets from her findings. The staff of the North Yorkshire County Record Office in Northallerton have, as always, been extremely kind and helpful. Zoë Johnson of Richmondshire Museum has given me willing help with illustrations. Some interesting details about Marske Hall were told to the author by the then owner, George W Shaw of Richmond, on a visit on 29 June 1991.

For the final production of the book I am grateful to Cathi Poole of York Publishing Services and her colleague Clare Brayshaw, the Design Manager, who has taken great pains with the book's layout, and also prepared the cover design. Andy Thursfield, graphic designer of Richmond, has produced the many pedigrees, maps etc. Guy Carpenter, photographer of Richmond, has patiently taken the colour illustrations.

SOURCES

The Clifton Castle archive at the North Yorkshire County Record Office, NYCRO ZAW, includes material not only from Timothy Hutton's time but also from Clifton Castle's later owners Pulleine and Cowell. The diaries, and other material which Peter Wenham transcribed, are not deposited with this archive. Most, but not all, of what he saw was loaned briefly for microfilming in 2010 [NYCRO microfilms nos 4599-4608]. The number of microfilms indicates the quantity of material, and it is hoped that this book may stimulate others to explore its wealth of information. There is of course also a large archive of the Hutton family of Marske, NYCRO ZAZ.

The material which Peter Wenham copied out came from the main run of diaries, starting 1 January 1810, and continuing almost up to Timothy Hutton's death in 1863, except for gaps from 19 May to 2 June 1812, when he was based in Richmond with the Militia, and from March 1818 to April 1819. There were also part diaries for 1803 and 1805, and some notes Timothy had kept of events going back earlier.

The author has also made use of Wills, not only that of Timothy, but also of a number of family members. The importance of the Hutton family meant that other published material was available, notably by both father and son James Raine. Timothy's many links with Richmond meant that much other complementary material lay within the studies of Peter Wenham, who confusingly published under several variations of his name, as will be seen in the bibliography below.

BIBLIOGRAPHY

Major Works

Baker, Christopher, *J.M.W. Turner, The Vaughan Bequest,* National Galleries of Scotland, (2018).

Cannadine, David, *Victorious Century, The United Kingdom, 1800-1906,* Allen Lane, (2017).

Clarkson, Christopher, *The History & Antiquities of Richmond in the County of York,* (1821); also Arrowsmith, James, his annotated copy of Clarkson's History, now in York Minster Library.

Cliffe, J.T., *The Yorkshire Gentry from the Reformation to the Civil War,* University of London Historical Studies, Athlone Press, (1969).

Evans, Eric J., *The Forging of the Modern State, Early Industrial Britain 1783-1870,* Longman, (1983).

Gunnis, Rupert, *Dictionary of British Sculptors 1660-1851,* Odhams, (1953).

Hatcher, Jane, *Richmondshire Architecture,* (1990).

Hendra, Leslie Anne (ed.), *A Voice from Richmond Yorkshire, The Letters of Henry Wood 1825-1832,* (2012).

McCall, H.B., *Richmondshire Churches,* (1910).

Pattison, Ian R., and Murray, Hugh, *Monuments in York Minster,* Friends of York Minster, (2000).

Park, G.R., *Parliamentary Representation of Yorkshire,* (1886).

Raine, Revd James, (ed.), *The Correspondence of Dr. Matthew Hutton, Archbishop of York etc.,* Surtees Society Publications, (1843).

Raine, Revd James, *Marske, A Small Contribution towards Yorkshire Topography,* Newcastle-upon-Tyne, (1860).

Rosenfeld, Sybil, *The Georgian Theatre of Richmond, Yorkshire, and its circuit,* The Society for Theatre Research, London, York, (1984).

Royal Commission on Historical Monuments, *An Inventory of the Historical Monuments in the City of York, vol.ii, The Defences,* (1972).

Waggett, Ralph, *A History of the Company of Mercers, Grocers and Haberdashers of Richmond*, PBK Publishing Ltd., (2002); also his typescript 'A Transcript of the Company of Mercers, Grocers and Haberdashers of Richmond, Yorkshire 1580-1980'.

Wenham, L. Peter, *Gray's Court, York,* St John's College, York, (*c.*1963).

Wenham, Leslie P., *James Tate, Master of Richmond School, Yorkshire and Canon of St Paul's Cathedral, London,* North Yorkshire County Record Office Publications No. 46, (1991).

Wenham, L.P., *Letters of James Tate,* Yorkshire Archaeological Society Record Series, (1966).

Wenham, L.P. (ed.), *Richmond Burgage Houses, North Yorkshire,* North Yorkshire County Record Office Publications No. 16, (1978).

Wenham, Leslie P. (ed.), *Richmond, Yorkshire in the 1830s,* (1977).

Wenham, Leslie P., *The History of Richmond School, Yorkshire,* Herald Press, Arbroath, (1958).

Directories

Austin, G.E., *Directory of Richmond & Rural District Area and Almanack,* (1932).

Baines, Edward, *History, Directory & Gazetteer of Yorkshire, East and North Ridings,* (1823).

Bulmer, T. *History, Topography and Directory of North Yorkshire,* (1890).

Cookes, C.E. and Son, *Richmondshire, An Account of its History & Antiquities, Characters & Customs, Legendary Lore & Natural History,* (1910).

Pigot and Co., *London and Provincial New Commercial Directory,* (1822).

Spencer, Thomas, *Richmond Almanack, Diary and Directory and Swaledale &Wensleydale Book of Reference,* various dates.

Whellan & Co., *History and Topography of the City of York and the North Riding of Yorkshire,* (1859).

White, William, *History, Gazetteer and Directory of the East and North Ridings of Yorkshire,* (1840).

Articles etc.

Bailey, Patrick, "Wartime Schooldays at Marske Hall", *The Dalesman Magazine*, September 1990, pp.496-500.

Cartwright, J.J., "List of Persons in Yorkshire who Paid the Tax on Male Servants in 1780", *Yorkshire Archaeological Journal*, vol.14, (1898), pp.65-88.

Chapman, Vera, "North Country Farms of the Moorland Fringe, Won from the Moor", *Beamish One – First Journal of the North of England Open Air Museum*, (1978).

Gilbert, C., "Furniture at Temple Newsam & Lotherton Hall", vol.1, (1975).

Horne, Peter D., "Aerial Archaeology in Yorkshire, Recent Work by RCHME", *Yorkshire Archaeological Journal*, vol.66, (1994), pp. 242-4.

Raine, Revd Canon James, "Marske in Swaledale", *Yorkshire Archaeological Journal*, vol.6, (1881).

Wallis, Peter, *Newcastle Mathematical Libraries*, Literary and Philosophical Society of Newcastle-upon-Tyne, (1972).

Wenham, Peter, "John Foss of Richmond", *York Georgian Society Annual Report for 1976.*

Wenham, Peter & Hatcher, Jane, "The Buildings of John Foss", *York Georgian Society Annual Report for 1977.*

Worsley, Giles, "Clifton Castle, Yorkshire", *Country Life*, September 22, 1988.

Websites etc.

Burke's History of the Landed Gentry – ancestry.co.uk

Clergy of the Church of England – clergydatabase.org.uk

History of Parliament – historyofparliamentonline.org

National Burial Index for England and Wales – Federation of Family History Societies [on C.D.]

Oxford Dictionary of National Biography – oxforddnb.com

The National Archives – nationalarchives.gov.uk

The Peerage – thepeerage.com

Venn, *A Cambridge Alumni Database 1200-1900* – venn.lib.cam.ac.uk

Wikipedia – en.Wikipedia.org

CAST OF CHARACTERS

A large number of people flit through the pages of Timothy Hutton's diaries. Some of them he knew throughout his, or their, life, or at least until their death was sadly noted. Others were important to him for a period of his life or, perhaps, for a short but critical time, such as his eye surgeon. Some had a dual role, such as an aunt intrinsically important through the blood relationship, but also as the wife of someone influential in Timothy's life, for example Elizabeth and Henry Pulleine. The married women in Timothy's diaries may occur under their maiden name when single, and later under their married name. A few people confusingly shared exactly the same name, without having any connection, such as Timothy's friend John Hutton of Sowber. The author offers this, albeit idiosyncratic, Cast of Characters in the hope of resolving such confusion, as well as demonstrating the wide range of people featuring to a greater or lesser extent in Timothy Hutton's diaries. The format of the entries has been standardised where possible.

ALEXANDER, Henry (d.1859), leading London surgeon and oculist to Queen Victoria, who operated on Timothy Hutton in 1848. Alexander's son Charles was also an eye specialist.

ARMITAGE, John (*c.*1791-1850), tenant farmer at Walburn Hall.

BAINES, [Revd] John (*c.*1726-1820), of West Tanfield, friend of Timothy Hutton. His son, also John (*c.*1760-1821), was a surgeon in Masham.

BRADLEY, Thomas (*c.*1781-1870), Richmond land surveyor responsible for the Richmond to Reeth Turnpike Road in the 1830s. Appointed Timothy Hutton's land agent for Clifton in 1817, to collect his rents and advise on his acquisition of additional property. Bradley's eldest son, Christopher Lonsdale Bradley, later acted in a similar capacity for the Marske estate.

BUCKLE, John (*c.*1792-1857), of Bedale, medical practitioner to Timothy and Elizabeth Hutton from the late-1830s.

CAMPBELL, Archibald (*c.*1775-1837), of Bedale, medical practitioner to Timothy and Elizabeth Hutton from the late-1820s until 1837.

CARTER, Anne, of Theakston – see CHAYTOR, Anne.

CARTER, Charles, friend of Timothy Hutton, who served with the East India Company. He had a son, also called Charles, who also went out to India.

CARTER, Edward John, the squire of Theakston near Burneston, married Elizabeth Hutton's sister Caroline Chaytor.

CARTER, Thomas, steward to John Hutton, and later to Timothy, at Marske Hall. His wife Ann also worked at Marske Hall.

CHAYTOR, Anne (d.1856), as Anne Carter of Theakston married Elizabeth Hutton's brother John Clervaux Chaytor in 1810. The couple lived in Clifton Lodge. After Clervaux's death in 1834, Anne and their children moved into Clifton Castle.

CHAYTOR, Clervaux – see CHAYTOR, John Clervaux.

CHAYTOR, Elizabeth (1779-1859), daughter of William and Jane Chaytor of Spennithorne, married Timothy Hutton in 1804.

CHAYTOR, Jane (d.1825), née Lee of Appleby, wife of William Chaytor of Spennithorne, and Timothy Hutton's mother-in-law.

CHAYTOR, John Clervaux (d.1834), Elizabeth Hutton's youngest brother, known as Clervaux, married Anne Carter of Theakston in 1810. Lived at Clifton.

CHAYTOR, Mary (1771-1854), eldest daughter of William and Jane Chaytor of Spennithorne. Unmarried, she spent a lot of time with Elizabeth Hutton.

CHAYTOR, Matthew William (d.1825), son of William and Jane Chaytor of Spennithorne, lived at Agglethorpe Hall near Coverham.

CHAYTOR, William (1733-1819), of Spennithorne, Recorder of Richmond 1792-1811. One of the trustees appointed by John Hutton III to look after Timothy Hutton and his brothers. Later became Timothy Hutton's father-in-law.

CHAYTOR, [Colonel, Sir] William (1771-1847), eldest son of William and Jane Chaytor of Spennithorne. Married Isabella Carter of Tunstall near Richmond. Colonel in North York Militia. Created Baronet 1831. Built the Victorian Gothic Clervaux Castle at Croft 1839/44.

CLARKE, Christopher, né Mudd, took the name Clarke by Royal Licence in November 1850 to inherit from the Will of an older Christopher Clarke. Lived at The Hermitage, Thornton Watlass.

CLARKE, [Revd] George Foord (d.1823), rector of Thornton Watlass and perpetual curate of Hutton Bonville. Father of Louisa Clarke (d.1833) and Christopher Clarke (d.1850).

CLEVELAND, first Duke of, see VANE, William Henry.

CORDUKES, Anne, lady's maid to Elizabeth Hutton, later Timothy Hutton's housekeeper at Clifton Castle.

COWELL, [Lady] Alice (1873-1948), of Clifton Castle, married the Hon. Assheton Gore Curzon-Howe, later Curzon-Howe-Herrick.

COWELL, [Lady] Georgina Elizabeth (d.1927), daughter of James Pulleine, inherited Clifton Castle and lived there as a widow. Mother of Alice.

COWELL, John Clayton PC, KCB (1832-94), married Georgina Pulleine in 1868.

CROFT, Anthony (d.1850), the tenant farmer at Boston Farm near Walburn.

CUIT, George [the elder] (1743-1818), Richmond artist, close friend of Timothy and Elizabeth Hutton. George and his wife Jane Cuit were the parents of George Cuitt [*sic*] the younger.

CUITT, George [the younger] (1779-1854), son of George Cuit [*sic*] the elder, an artist. Lived in Chester and then in Masham. He and his wife Catherine were close friends of Timothy and Elizabeth Hutton.

CURZON-HOWE, [Lady] Alice (1873-1948), daughter of John and Georgina Cowell. As owner of Clifton Castle gave L P Wenham permission to study the diaries of Timothy Hutton 1944-5. Married the Hon. Assheton Gore Curzon-Howe, later Curzon-Howe-Herrick.

CURZON-HOWE, [Lt. Col.] the Hon. Assheton Gore (1898-1959), youngest son of the first Earl Howe, married Alice Cowell. The name was changed to Curzon-Howe-Herrick in 1946.

CURZON-HOWE-HERRICK, Assheton Penn, sold Clifton Castle to Robin Hill, Earl of Hillsbrough, in 1963. His wife, Joan Henrietta, later moved to The Hermitage at Thornton Watlass.

DANBY, William (1752-1833), owner of Swinton Park, one of the neighbouring estates to Clifton Castle, a close friend of Timothy Hutton.

DARLINGTON, third Earl of, see VANE, William Henry.

D'ARCY, Barbara (1600-95), married Matthew Hutton in 1617.

D'ARCY, Elizabeth (1706-39), married John Hutton II in 1727.

DIXON, [first name unknown] (d.1854), of York. Friend of Timothy Hutton.

DODSWORTH, [Dr] Frederick (1761-1821), of Thornton Watlass Hall, youngest child of Timothy Hutton's great-aunt Henrietta. Married twice, but had no children, and the family name eventually became Smith-Dodsworth.

DODSWORTH, Henrietta (1701-98), youngest child of John Hutton I, and thus Timothy Hutton's great-aunt. She married John Dodsworth of Thornton Watlass, their youngest child was Frederick.

DOWNSHIRE, eighth Marquess of, (1929-2003), as Robin Hill bought Clifton Castle in 1963.

DOWNSHIRE, ninth Marquess of, (b.1959), owner of Clifton Castle from 2003.

ELLERTON, Edward (1771-1851), of Downholme, scholar and theologian.

FISHER, Isaac (d.1854), eldest son of Revd John Fisher, rector of Marske. Became the director in charge of the Richmond branch of the Hutton and Other Bank.

FISHER, [Revd] John (1773-1808), rector of Marske from 1803.

FOSS, John (1745-1827), Richmond stonemason and architect. Among his many commissions was Clifton Castle.

FOSS, William (1772-1844), son of John. Acted as clerk of works for the construction of Clifton Castle. Continued the family business as a stonemason after his father's death.

FRYER, Michael (1774-1844), of Newcastle-upon-Tyne, a distinguished mathematician who served as the full-time librarian at Marske Hall from 1814 until John Hutton's death.

GLAISTER, Henry (d.1846), of Bedale, solicitor friend of Timothy Hutton. He oversaw the affairs of the orphaned D'Arcy Hutton.

GREATHEAD, Peter (d.1857), tenant farmer and cattle breeder at Telfit Farm near Marske.

GREENWELL, [Revd] William (1820-1918), angler, archaeologist, and later a minor canon of Durham Cathedral.

HARCOURT, [Admiral] Octavius (d.1863), married William Danby's widow Anne in 1838 and thus became the owner of Swinton Park.

HILL, Nicholas, see DOWNSHIRE, ninth Marquess of.

HILL, Robin, see DOWNSHIRE, eighth Marquess of.

HINCKS, [Capt] John (d.1842), of Cowling Hall, married Marrianne Pulleine in 1835.

HORNE, [Revd] Richard (d.1803), of Westmorland, rector of Marske from 1747. Planted fruit trees in garden of Marske rectory when it was built by John Hutton II. Close friend of John Hutton III and his wife Anne, and tutored their sons.

HUTTON, Ann (1731-81), eldest surviving daughter of John Hutton II. Married George Wanley Bowes of County Durham (buried Lincoln's Inn Chapel 1752). Died at Cheltenham.

HUTTON, Anne née Ling (*c*.1754-1828), of Westmorland, housekeeper to and then wife of John Hutton III. Mother of John Hutton IV, James, Matthew and Timothy Hutton. Later lived at Richmond. Buried at Easby.

HUTTON, Barbara née Conyers D'Arcy (1600-95), married Matthew Hutton in 1617.

HUTTON, D'Arcy – see HUTTON, James Henry D'Arcy.

HUTTON, Dorothy née Dyke (*c*.1662-1743), married John Hutton I.

HUTTON, [Lady] Elizabeth née Bowes (1570-1625), god-daughter of Queen Elizabeth I, married Sir Timothy Hutton of Marske and Richmond. Portrayed as an effigy on monument in St Mary's parish church in Richmond.

HUTTON, Elizabeth née D'Arcy (1706-39), daughter of James, Lord D'Arcy of Navan, of Sedbury near Scotch Corner. Became the second wife of John Hutton II, bringing the name D'Arcy into the Hutton family. Mother of John Hutton III.

HUTTON, Elizabeth (1734-1816), third daughter of John Hutton II, aunt to Timothy Hutton. Married Henry Pulleine of Carlton Hall near Aldbrough St John, later lived at Crakehall. Buried in the Duke of Northumberland's family vault at St John's Church, Stanwick. Grandmother of James and Robert Pulleine.

HUTTON, Elizabeth (1779-1859), daughter of William Chaytor of Spennithorne, wife of Timothy Hutton. Buried in Downholme churchyard.

HUTTON, Henrietta (1701-98), daughter of John Hutton I, married John Dodsworth of Thornton Watlass.

HUTTON, James (1739-98), youngest son of John Hutton II. Married Mary Hoyle of Ashgill near Middleham, lived at Aldburgh near Masham. Uncle of Timothy Hutton, father of James Henry D'Arcy Hutton.

HUTTON, James (1776-1803), second son of John Hutton III, and elder brother of Timothy Hutton. Buried in Marske church.

HUTTON, James Henry D'Arcy (1796-1843), known as D'Arcy. Son of James Hutton (1739-98), and thus first cousin to Timothy Hutton. Married Harriet Aggas (*c.*1796-1837), father of first John Timothy D'Arcy Hutton. Buried in Masham church.

HUTTON, John [I] (1659-1731), son of John Hutton (1625-64), as a small boy inherited the Marske estate from his grandfather. Married Frances Dyke. Improved Marske church 1683. Began *c.*1730 to remodel Marske Hall, wherein is carved on an overmantel his coat of arms impaling that of his wife. Buried in Marske church.

HUTTON, John [II] (1691-1768), eldest son of John Hutton I. Completed his father's remodelling of Marske Hall, and built the stable block behind it. Purchased Clifton-on-Ure in 1735. Squire of Marske at the time of the 1745 Jacobite Rebellion. Owned famous racehorses. By his second wife, Elizabeth D'Arcy, had children John Hutton III, Matthew, Anne (Wanley Bowes), Elizabeth (Pulleine) and James. Buried in Marske church.

HUTTON, John [III] (1730-82), eldest son of John Hutton II. Studied at Christ's College, Cambridge. Took into his household a black servant, John York, brought to England by Elizabeth Yorke of Richmond. By his housekeeper, Anne Ling, had children John Hutton IV, James, and Matthew and, after marrying her in 1779, Timothy. Buried in Marske church.

HUTTON, John [IV] (1774-1841), eldest son of John Hutton III, and elder brother of James, Matthew and Timothy. After Christ's College, Cambridge, joined the Inner Temple and then Gray's Inn. Became a banker, made major improvements to the Marske estate, and amassed an important library. Buried in Marske church, where a wall monument in the chancel extols his virtues.

HUTTON, John (1794-1857), of Sowber, unrelated to Timothy Hutton, who described him as his friend. Son of Robert Hutton and Margaret Squire. In 1824 built Sowber Hill near Newby Wiske, now Solberge Hall Hotel. Aged fifty married Caroline, daughter of Thomas Robson of Holtby Hall, and had two sons including John born 1847. Buried in North Otterington church on 2 January 1858.

HUTTON, John Timothy D'Arcy [I] (1822-74), of Aldburgh Hall near Masham. Elder son of James Henry D'Arcy Hutton. Married Emily Rebecca Lamb, father of John Timothy D'Arcy Hutton II. Continued to live at Aldburgh Hall after inheriting Marske Hall in 1863. Buried in Downholme churchyard.

HUTTON, John Timothy D'Arcy [II] (1847-1931), only son of John Timothy D'Arcy Hutton I. Married Edith Constance Phipson, father of John Timothy D'Arcy Hutton III. Lived at Marske Hall.

HUTTON, John Timothy D'Arcy [III] (*c.*1868-1957), of West Derby near Liverpool. Elder son of John Timothy D'Arcy Hutton II. Married Ella Mary. Disposed of Marske Hall and its contents in the 1950s.

HUTTON, [Revd] Matthew (*c.*1525-1606), Archbishop of York 1595-1606, Lord President of the Council in the North 1596-99. Bought property in Swaledale for his eldest son Timothy, and *c.*1599 built Marske Hall to a design probably by Robert Smythson. Buried in York Minster, where there is a monument to him and three of his children.

HUTTON, Matthew (1597-1666), son of Timothy (1569-1629), named after his grandfather Archbishop Matthew Hutton. Married Barbara Conyers

D'Arcy. Outliving all his sons, was succeeded by his young grandson John Hutton I.

HUTTON, [Revd] Matthew (1693-1758), second son of John Hutton I. Archbishop of York 1747-57, Archbishop of Canterbury 1757-8.

HUTTON, Matthew (1733-82), second son of John Hutton II. Died in Ripon and has a monument in the cathedral there.

HUTTON, Matthew (1777-1813), third son of John Hutton III, next eldest brother to Timothy Hutton. Is commemorated by an obelisk in the Park above Marske Hall.

HUTTON, [Sir] Timothy (1569-1629), eldest son of Archbishop Matthew Hutton (1529-1606). Married Elizabeth Bowes. Bought The Friary and other property in Richmond. Was knighted in 1605, and served as Alderman of Richmond in 1617 and 1629. Buried in St Mary's parish church in Richmond, where there is a large monument to him, his wife Elizabeth, and their many children. He is portrayed as an effigy on the monument.

HUTTON, Timothy, (1779-1863), youngest and only legitimate son of John Hutton III. Married Elizabeth Chaytor. Built Clifton Castle. Buried in Downholme churchyard.

HUTTON, [Sir] Thomas (1581-1621), a younger son of Archbishop Matthew Hutton (1529-1606). Established a branch of the Hutton family at Nether Poppleton near York.

IBBETSON, Julius Caesar (1759-1817), artist, moved to Masham in 1804, friend and neighbour of Timothy Hutton. Father of Julius Caesar Ibbetson (1783-1825) of Richmond.

JACKSON, [Revd] John (*c.*1596-1648/9), master of Richmond School 1618-20, and rector of Marske 1623-1648/9. Close friend of Sir Timothy Hutton (1569-1629), and composed the elaborate epitaphs on his monument in Richmond parish church.

KENDALL, [Revd] William (*c.*1783-1855). Curate of Marske church, then incumbent of both Marske and Downholme parishes from 1833. Married the sister of Revd John Fisher, his predecessor at Marske.

LEEDS, Dukes of, of Hornby Castle near Catterick. The sixth Duke died in 1838, and Timothy Hutton continued his friendship with his son, the seventh Duke.

LING, Anne – see HUTTON, Anne. See also her two younger sisters – WHALEY, Jane and RIDLEY, Sarah.

MARCH, Aaron, succeeded Anthony Croft as tenant farmer at Boston Farm near Walburn.

MASON, Charles, brewer and innkeeper at Halfpenny House near Walburn *c.*1830-40.

MEWBURN, Simon Thomas (*c.*1780-1846), Captain and Quartermaster in the North York Militia.

MILBANKE, Mark (1795-1881), owner of Thorp Perrow, one of the neighbouring estates to Clifton Castle. Married Lady Augusta Henrietta Vane.

MONSON, [Hon & Revd] Thomas, (1764-1843), the fifth son of the second Baron Monson, and rector of Bedale 1797-1843. He and his son, Revd John Joseph Thomas Monson, both married into the Wyvill family of Constable Burton.

MORLEY, Francis (1810-1844), known as Frank, inherited Marrick Park through his grandfather, a Richmond merchant who changed his name from Readsahw to Morley. Married Elizabeth Hutton's niece Charlotte, elder daughter of John Clervaux Chaytor, and they had a son, Frank Morley junior.

MUDD, Christopher, see CLARKE, Christopher.

MUDD, Christopher, coachman to Timothy Hutton, later farm bailiff.

OTHER, Thomas (*c.*1779-1834), of Elm House, Redmire in Wensleydale. Partner in the Hutton Bank, in which role he was succeeded by his eldest son Christopher.

OTTLEY brothers, Brooke and Warner, school friends of James Tate and Timothy Hutton at Richmond School.

PICKERING, William (d. 1803) of Crakehall, one of the trustees appointed by John Hutton III to look after Timothy Hutton and his brothers.

PULLEINE, Anne, second daughter of Henry and Elizabeth Pulleine. Married Revd Thomas Ryder, vicar of Ecclesfield near Sheffield. As a widow moved with her children to Frenchgate House in Richmond in 1840.

PULLEINE, Elizabeth (1734-1816), Timothy Hutton's aunt. Married Henry Pulleine of Carlton Hall near Aldbrough St John. Mother of Henry Percy Pulleine and grandmother of James and Robert Pulleine. Buried in the Duke of Northumberland's vault at St John's Church, Stanwick.

PULLEINE, Georgina Elizabeth (d.1927), daughter of James Pulleine. Married John Clayton Cowell PC, KCB (1832-94).

PULLEINE, Henry (*c*.1740-1803), of Carlton Hall near Aldbrough St John, married Timothy Hutton's aunt Elizabeth. Later lived at Crakehall near Bedale. Father of Henry Percy Pulleine and grandfather of James and Robert Pulleine.

PULLEINE, [Colonel] Henry Percy (1770-1833), of Crakehall. Timothy Hutton's first cousin. He and his wife Elizabeth Askew (*c*.1770-1839) had a large family, including James and Robert Pulleine.

PULLEINE, James (1804-79), of Crakehall, elder son of Henry Percy and Elizabeth Pulleine. A distinguished lawyer, and Timothy Hutton's executor. Inherited Clifton Castle in 1863. Married Anne Caroline Marjoribanks (*c*.1810-89). Father of Georgiana Elizabeth Cowell. Buried at Thornton Watlass.

PULLEINE, [Revd] Robert (1806-68), of Crakehall, younger son of Henry Percy and Elizabeth Pulleine. Vicar of Kirby Wiske 1845-68, and buried there. Served as chaplain to Timothy Hutton when High Sheriff of Yorkshire in 1844. Married Susan Burmester. Their third son Revd John James Pulleine (1841-1913) became Bishop of Richmond in 1889.

RAINE, [Revd] James (1791-1858), of Durham, noted scholar and antiquarian. Founded the Surtees Society, named after his friend Robert Surtees, author of the *History of Durham*. Raine's son James became Chancellor of York Minster, and published an important paper on the history of Marske and the Hutton family in 1860.

RIDLEY, Sarah née Ling (*c*.1762-1832), of Skelton near Marske, youngest sister of Timothy Hutton's mother.

ROBINSON, Thomas, Timothy Hutton's coachman at Clifton Castle, whose son John was educated at Timothy Hutton's expense.

ROBSON, James (d. 1851), of Crakehall, friend of Timothy Hutton who seems to have worked in the whisky trade.

ROBSON, John (d.1819), manager of the Hutton bank branch at Leyburn.

ROBSON, Thomas of Holtby Hall, an old friend of Timothy Hutton. Father of Caroline, wife of John Hutton of Sowber, and Revd Thomas William Robson.

ROBSON, [Revd] Thomas William, eldest son of Thomas Robson of Holtby. Became rector of Marske in 1855.

RUSSELL, Elizabeth (d.1861), of Newton House. The mistress, and from 1813 the second wife of, William Harry Vane, third Earl of Darlington and later first Duke of Cleveland. He converted Newton House into a hunting lodge, and as the dowager duchess she returned to live there. Daughter and sister of market gardeners both called Robert Russell at Newton House.

SIMPSON, Joseph, butler to Timothy Hutton at Clifton Castle.

SMITH, George (d.1828), friend of Timothy Hutton, who always referred to him as 'Mr. Smith'. An alderman of Richmond, he served as mayor in 1815 and 1827.

SMURTHWAITE, George (1785-1865), of Richmond, wine merchant. Mayor of Richmond in 1832, the year the Reform Bill was passed to much rejoicing in the town.

SMURTHWAITE, Thomas, clerk and later director of the Hutton and Other Bank.

SMYTHSON, Robert (*c.*1535-1614), of Derbyshire. Elizabethan architect linked with designs for Hutton projects.

STRAUBENZIE, Turner (*c.*1746-1823), of Spennithorne. An officer in the North York Militia.

TATE, [Revd] James (1771-1843), school friend of John and Timothy Hutton. Master of Richmond School 1796-1833, Canon of St Paul's Cathedral 1833-43.

TEMPLE, [Revd] Anthony (1724-95), Master of Richmond School 1750-95 and vicar of Easby 1770-95.

TOPHAM, Christopher (d.1832), of Middleham. Solicitor to Timothy Hutton. His sons Christopher and Thomas followed him in the practice.

TRAVERS, Benjamin (1783-1858), leading London eye surgeon, consulted by Timothy Hutton.

VANE, William Henry (1766-1842), third Earl of Darlington and later first Duke of Cleveland. His daughter Lady Augusta Henrietta married Mark Milbanke. Vane's second wife was Elizabeth Russell.

WARE, William (d.1842), manager of the Hutton bank branch at Leyburn.

WHALEY, Jane née Ling (*c.*1759-1823), of Marrick, younger sister of Timothy Hutton's mother.

WILKINSON, Ralph (*c.*1765-1820), tenant of Walburn Hall and noted breeder of cattle.

WYVILL, [Revd] Edward (*c.*1793-1869), of Constable Burton, rector of Finghall in Wensleydale. Married Frances Dodsworth (née Mosley) in 1824.

YARKER, Michael, licensee of the King's Head Hotel in Richmond *c.*1799-1823.

YORK, John (d.1820), brought from Jamaica as a boy by Elizabeth Campbell when she became the second wife of John Yorke of Richmond. Became a manservant at Marske Hall *c.*1772, and remained in the service of the Hutton family.

YORKE, John (1733-1813), of Yorke House on The Green in Richmond, where he hosted the 'Richmond Athenaeum'.

PLACES MENTIONED

ALDBURGH HALL The seat of Timothy's paternal uncle James, about two miles south-east of Masham.

BEDALE A market town about four miles from Clifton Castle. Here was a branch of the Hutton family bank, and the nearest railway station to Clifton.

BOSTON A farm on his Walburn estate which Timothy converted into a shooting lodge.

BURTON-UPON-URE A township of scattered habitations which included Clifton Castle.

CAMBRIDGE UNIVERSITY Where several generations of the Hutton family studied, including Timothy Hutton who went up to Christ's College in 1796.

CLIFTON CASTLE Timothy Hutton's mansion near Masham, set in landscaped grounds.

CLIFTON LODGE An older house on the Clifton estate, where Timothy Hutton lived before Clifton Castle was completed. For a time the home of Clervaux Chaytor and his family, and later converted into staff apartments.

CLINTS A neighbouring estate to Marske, added to the Marske estate in 1841.

CONSTABLE BURTON The seat of the Wyvill family.

CORDILLERAS The model farm built by John Hutton high up on the Marske estate.

COWLING HALL Near Bedale, owned by the Dodsworth family of Thornton Watlass.

CRAKEHALL A village near Bedale, home of the Pulleine family.

CROFT-ON-TEES The main seat of the Chaytor family.

DOWNHOLME The small Swaledale village of which Timothy Hutton was squire. He and his wife Elizabeth were buried there.

EASBY A small hamlet immediately east of Richmond. Timothy Hutton's mother was buried in Easby church.

FELDOM A remote farm high up on the moorland of the Marske estate.

HALFPENNY HOUSE Situated at an important road junction on the Richmond to Lancaster Turnpike Road, this farmhouse also served as an inn and brewed its own ale.

HELWITH A remote farm on the Marske estate.

HERMITAGE (The) A small gentry house on an eminence just outside the village of Thornton Watlass.

HORNBY CASTLE The seat of the Dukes of Leeds near Catterick. Much of the medieval, and Georgianised, building was demolished in 1930.

HUDSWELL A small village south-west of Richmond, where the school (since closed) was endowed by the Hutton Charity.

LEYBURN One of the larger market towns of Wensleydale, where the Hutton family bank had one of its main branches.

MARRICK PARK A small estate on the hillside above the village of Marrick, the home of Frank Morley and his wife Charlotte.

MARSKE The main seat of the Hutton family from Elizabethan times. Here was their home, Marske Hall, the extensive estate much improved by Timothy's elder brother John Hutton, and the parish church where many members of the Hutton family were buried.

MASHAM A small market town in Wensleydale, close to Clifton Castle.

MIDDLEHAM A small town in Wensleydale, a centre of racehorse training and the home of Timothy Hutton's lawyer, Thomas Topham.

NEWTON HOUSE near Londonderry. The home of the Russell family of market gardeners, later a hunting lodge of the first Duke of Cleveland. Demolished in 1956, the site is now part of RAF Leeming.

NORTHALLERTON The county town of the North Riding of Yorkshire. The opening of its railway station in 1841 facilitated Timothy's visits to York and London.

ORGATE A farm on the Marske estate high up in the valley of Marske Beck.

REETH A small market town in Swaledale, destination of the Richmond to Reeth Turnpike Road built in the 1830s to facilitate the transport of Swaledale lead.

RICHMOND The large market town of Swaledale, where the Hutton Bank was first established. Timothy Hutton attended the town's Grammar School, freemason's lodge, and guild of Mercers, Grocers and Haberdashers. His mother Anne lived in Frenchgate.

SKELTON A small dispersed settlement on the south side of Marske Beck, added to the Marske estate in 1841.

SPENNITHORNE The seat of the Wensleydale branch of the Chaytor family, into which Timothy Hutton married.

STRANDS A small hamlet in Swaledale between Gunnerside and Isles Bridge, where Timothy's lead mine agent lived.

SWINTON PARK A neighbouring estate to Clifton Castle, home of the Danby family.

TELFIT A remote farm on the Marske estate, high up the Marske Beck valley.

THEAKSTON A village near the Great North Road, home of the Carter family.

THIRN A hamlet on the Clifton Castle estate where several of its tenants lived.

THORNTON WATLASS The ecclesiastical parish in which Clifton Castle lies. The Dodsworth family lived in Thornton Watlass Hall.

THORP PERROW A neighbouring estate to Clifton Castle, home of the Milbanke family.

WALBURN An estate which Timothy Hutton inherited, encompassing a fortified manor house, some moorland farms and Halfpenny House.

WELL A village near West Tanfield.

YORK Yorkshire's capital city, where Timothy Hutton served on the Grand Jury of the Assizes, and spent much time during his year of office of High Sheriff of Yorkshire in 1844. London could be reached from the city's railway station from 1841.

CLASSIFIED INDEX
with the following headings

See also Pedigrees listed in Contents

The Hutton family

For obvious reasons this list does not include Timothy Hutton the subject of this book

Elizabeth Hutton's family

Timothy Hutton's extended family

Timothy Hutton's successors at Clifton Castle

Timothy Hutton's successors at Marske Hall

Timothy Hutton's staff and tenants

Employees of Timothy Hutton's relatives

Timothy Hutton's business associates

Timothy Hutton's friends

Timothy Hutton's clergy acquaintances

Artists, architects and sculptors

Lawyers

Medical practitioners

Public figures

Other figures

Animals

Banks

Communications

Educational

Entertainments

Mineral extraction

Sports

Places in Yorkshire

Places Outside Yorkshire

General subjects